Everybody Eats

COMMUNICATION FOR SOCIAL JUSTICE ACTIVISM

Series Editors

Patricia Parker, University of North Carolina at Chapel Hill

Lawrence R. Frey, University of Colorado Boulder

Everybody Eats

COMMUNICATION AND THE PATHS
TO FOOD JUSTICE

Marianne LeGreco
and Niesha Douglas

UNIVERSITY OF CALIFORNIA PRESS

The publisher and the University of California Press Foundation gratefully acknowledge the generous support of the Anne G. Lipow Endowment Fund in Social Justice and Human Rights.

University of California Press
Oakland, California

© 2021 by Marianne LeGreco and Niesha Douglas

Library of Congress Cataloging-in-Publication Data

Names: LeGreco, Marianne, author. | Douglas, Niesha Charisse, author.
Title: Everybody eats : communication and the paths to food justice / Marianne LeGreco and Niesha Douglas.
Other titles: Communication for social justice activism ; 3.
Description: Oakland, California : University of California Press, [2021] | Series: Communication for social justice activism ; 3 | Includes bibliographical references and index.
Identifiers: LCCN 2021006513 (print) | LCCN 2021006514 (ebook) | ISBN 9780520314238 (cloth) | ISBN 9780520314245 (paperback) | ISBN 9780520973978 (epub)
Subjects: LCSH: Food supply—Moral and ethical aspects—North Carolina—Greensboro. | Food security—Social aspects—North Carolina—Greensboro. | Communication—Social aspects—North Carolina—Greensboro.
Classification: LCC HD9008.G74 L44 2021 (print) | LCC HD9008.G74 (ebook) | DDC 363.8/830975662—dc23
LC record available at https://lccn.loc.gov/2021006513
LC ebook record available at https://lccn.loc.gov/2021006514

Contents

Illustrations

TABLES

Acknowledgments

When we decided to turn our experiences organizing around food in Greensboro, North Carolina, into *Everybody Eats*, we did so to recognize all of the intensely creative and sometimes heartbreaking work that went into community-based efforts to promote food justice. Before we acknowledge any other contributions, we must sincerely and humbly thank all of the people in Greensboro and Guilford County who have been a part of sustaining the conversations around food (in)security and food justice in our communities. Almost three thousand voices are somehow captured in the stories that we're sharing with our readers, and none of this work would have been possible without each one of them. All of us still have much work to do in communicating paths to food justice, and we hope that you will continue the conversation with us.

Within those three thousand voices, we are particularly indebted to Dr. Mark Smith, Mr. Otis Hairston, and Ms. Julie Lapham. Mark—in his quiet and unassuming style—brought a lot of people together when it came to organizing around food in Greensboro. Many of the conversations that led to the Warnersville Community Garden and the Mobile Oasis Farmers Market were made possible because he started drawing attention to disparities in food access well before the USDA started mapping food deserts. We are also forever grateful for Otis and Julie. Even though they are no longer with us and will not see this book come to fruition, they both played key roles in launching much of the work featured in this book. Otis connected city and county agencies to the Warnersville neighborhood, and he introduced the two of us—and we can never thank him enough for those two things. Julie networked so many people together around local food councils and food access before she made her exit, and both she and Otis encouraged many younger leaders to begin pushing the conversations along more meaningful paths.

Both the Warnersville neighborhood and Prince of Peace Lutheran Church played crucial roles in helping partners launch the Warnersville Community Garden and the Mobile Oasis Farmers Market. We want to recognize their contributions in bringing community voices, meeting and garden space, fundraising efforts and grant leadership, volunteer hours, and central organizing perspectives that help drive the conversations and stories featured in this book. We specifically thank members of the various community coalitions and leaders from the Warnersville neighborhood, as well as numerous Prince of Peace members for committing their time and talents to doing this work with us.

We also want to acknowledge the work of our students—especially students from UNC-Greensboro, NCA&T State University, Guilford College, and Greensboro College. Whether it was through a service-learning project, a research assistantship, or a variety of class projects, thousands of student hours went into work around food in Greensboro—and not just toward the chapters featured in this book. We have more students than we could ever mention here—and we have included several of them in our Cast of Voices featured in chapter 2. Thank you sincerely for every field note, interview, survey, and service-learning and internship hour at the garden or the mobile market. We would like to specifically thank Zithobile Nxumalo, Beth Archie, Jeanette German, Jenny Southard, Ranata Reader, Eddie Chia, and Nichole Patino for their assistance in data collection and organization that directly contributed to the completion of this book.

Several folks were instrumental in the technical production of this book, and we must heartily thank our co-contributors for adding their expert and community voices to many of the chapters. We also offer sincere thanks to Sarah Dempsey, Patricia Parker, and Larry Frey for their initial support of this manuscript at University of California Press, as well as Sarah, Lynn Harter, and Garrett Broad for their thoughtful and encouraging comments throughout the review process. And to Enrique Ochoa-Kaup, Lynn Uhl, and Kim Robinson, thank you for the support of UC Press in making this book a reality.

Marianne would like to specifically thank Mark Smith and Hunter Haith for being really solid mentors across so many of these conversations—I learned far more from you than you may know. I would also like to thank my immediate family—Susan and Chuck Soderstrom; Katie, Oliver, and Rylan LeGreco; Nathan LeGreco; and Alexis Soderstrom. And special thanks to my Grandma Mary Joy Ewers for sending me that "keep chaptering" while we were closing in on our first draft—it still makes me laugh. It's great to know that you all have my back. I also had a really great support network of friends and colleagues who deserve acknowledgment in far more ways than I can ever articulate here, and I'm especially grateful for Sara Manchester, Zithobile Nxumalo, Kathleen Edwards, and Gwen Frisbie-Fulton for how much time they shared in helping us attend to all of the details. And thanks to Kami, Ryan, and Tony; Omar, Mahal, Talia, Dania, Daria, and Nagat; Donna, Chris, Hab, Leena, Mike, Lavinia, Beth, Dawn, and Justin L.; George, Rhonda, and Jenn; Valerie, Lewvenia, and Anita; Justin H., Tanya, Cliff, and Ben; Christopher, Roy, and Spoma; Gus and Pru; and my entire family at Prince of Peace. Y'all are amazing folks, and I appreciate every random way that you helped make this book happen. And finally, if there is one thing for which I am most grateful when it comes to *Everybody Eats*, it's that this book introduced me to Niesha—you've been a great coauthor and friend, and I'm so blessed to have worked with you along the way.

Niesha would like to give special recognition to the Warnersville community and former Warnersville Recreation Center Supervisor Douglas Brown—I appreciate your willingness to be a part of the conversation of food insecurity by allowing access to the community recreation center. I also would like to thank my fellow alumni, Matthew King and Brandon Norman. These young men were such an inspiration and I appreciate their commitment. I also would like to thank Audrey and Nick Mangili, who were instrumental in keeping the Mobile Oasis project going after the initial launch—your passion about food sovereignty was refreshing. I would like to thank my Warnersville family: Janiya Brown, Shaneka Douglas, Robbie Douglas, Trina Wall, Nebraska Douglas, Jay and Adlois Shoffner, the Davis Family, and all of my community. Your love and support is greatly appreciated. I also would like to thank all of the partners in the community, including farmers George Smith, Vern Switzer, and Adrienne Wilson. Special shoutout to our "resident" chef N'Gai Dickerson, who provided us with meals and healthy recipes. Also, thanks to Dr. Tobias Lagrone, Bishop Todd Fulton, Lewvenia, Mr. James Griffin, Dr. Geleana Alston, Otis Hairston, the Mount Moriah Outreach family, Lisa, William, and Krystal, as well as a slew of others who supported me through the years. I am especially grateful to my "partner in crime" Marianne—I would not be where I am academically and professionally without your willingness to always include me in the conversation. I love and appreciate you, friend.

Overview

Between 2009 and 2019, Greensboro, North Carolina, experienced a dramatic rise and fall on the Food Research and Action Center's (FRAC) list of major US cities experiencing food hardship. FRAC is a leading non-profit organization that highlights data and policy opportunities around hunger and poverty—particularly through their semi-annual publications regarding *Food Hardship in America*. After first appearing on FRAC's list in 2010, with a rank of 17 and a food hardship rate of 28.4 percent, Greensboro and its neighbor High Point rose to the number 2 spot in 2013 before reaching number 1 in 2015, with a food hardship rate of 27.9 percent. Greensboro's response to the FRAC rankings—launched through a strategic set of partnerships across our food system—led to a collection of microlevel interventions to promote food security and food justice. Within one year of reaching the top of FRAC's list, Greensboro/High Point dropped from number 1 to number 9, and we reduced our food hardship rate to 22.2 percent. More recent rankings in 2018 place Greensboro at number 14, with a food hardship rate of 19.2 percent.

The story of facing food hardship in Greensboro illustrates both innovation and resilience as communities formed partnerships to promote food security and created paths to food justice. Organizers, activists, nonprofit groups, health and government agencies, researchers, and everyday community members focused not only on food hardship, but also on larger questions of building food systems that are vibrant, equitable, resilient, and secure. With efforts ranging from mobile farmers markets to shared-use kitchens to urban farms, the stories featured in this book center the importance of communication and community in food justice organizing. But Greensboro's response to the FRAC numbers is perhaps even more important, because it's an everyday story—one about regular people working together to ensure that everybody eats.

Everybody Eats: Communication and the Paths to Food Justice features a series of scholarly, community-based case studies that illustrate how communication interventions and social justice activism can mobilize community partners to confront inequities in local food systems. Both Marianne LeGreco and Niesha Douglas have played key stakeholder roles in many of the interventions launched across Greensboro during this time period, so we are positioned to offer a first-person perspective on communicating across communities to create paths to food justice.

Everybody Eats is grounded in the language of food justice, critical organizational and health communication, and communication activism research to center the importance of communication—especially first-person accounts of communication interventions—in working toward equity across food systems. As such, our contribution focuses on building vibrant, equitable, and resilient food systems as those systems relate to topics like food (in)security, food access, paradoxes of participation across food systems, pop-up interventions, and community food discourses. We offer a four-part perspective on communicating food justice, which emphasizes engaging communities, mobilizing resources, documenting process, and sustaining conversations.

Part I situates *Everybody Eats* as a contribution to critical organizational and health communication and social justice activism research in communication studies, as well as interdisciplinary studies on food systems. We focus first on a more theoretical and conceptual grounding of food in communication scholarship, as well as tracing the language of food through Greensboro, North Carolina.

Parts II through V bring together a series of case studies to illustrate how communicating not only for food security, but also pushing that conversation toward food justice enabled and constrained how communities in Greensboro organized, as well how partners have documented their processes and faced questions of sustainability in their food justice work. Chapters 3 and 4 follow the Warnersville Community Food Task Force and the Downtown Greensboro Food Truck Pilot Project as instances of engaging communities. The two chapters that follow highlight the Warnersville Community Garden and the Mobile Oasis Farmers Market as examples of mobilizing resources. Chapters 7 and 8 then reference documenting processes with case studies of *Ethnosh*—an innovative restaurant meetup, and *Kitchen Connects GSO*—a kitchen incubator program. Finally, we conclude the case studies with the *Guilford Food Council* and the *Renaissance Community Co-op* as a way to examine how communities sustain conversations around food systems, food security, and the paths to food justice.

Everybody Eats is geared toward audiences with a broad range of interests in food systems and food security, from both scholarly and practical perspectives. As such, each chapter features a set of reflections that are geared toward our scholarly and academic readers, as well as a series of recommendations and resources designed with our practical and applied readers in mind. We have been fortunate to spend over ten years organizing around food in Greensboro, and we look forward to sharing these case studies as examples of communicating food justice activism.

PART I The Language of Food (In)security

Figure 1. The Warnersville Farmers Market. Local farmer Rhonda Ingram (left) and Hannah Harris (right) swap recipes for zucchini at the Warnersville Farmers Market in August 2011. Photo credit: Chris English.

1 Navigating the Language of Food Systems

Everybody eats. To most of you reading this book, that probably sounds like a simple and obvious enough idea. Every one of us must eat to live, and we have no real way around that basic need. Not only do our hunger impulses remind us daily of our need to eat, but we also see food as a foundational concept across our social systems—when food is used as a classic example of a physiological need in Maslow's hierarchy, for example. We also see it in our cultures—when groups of people develop their identities around cuisines, recipes, and how food is passed down from generation to generation. And we see it in our communities—when neighbors organize social events and activities around food. We are beings made of energy, and we require energy to survive.

At the same time, societies need frequent reminders that processes, resources, and practices related to everyday eating do not always operate in just and equitable ways. The World Health Organization estimates that more than 815 million people or 11 percent of the global population experience some level of hunger or food insecurity.[1] In the United States, one in eight people qualify as food insecure.[2] And in 2017, the American food system was labeled for the first time as deteriorating.[3] Communities experience disparities in access to food and health-related resources;

the commercial food sector routinely makes choices that privilege corporate shareholders over community needs; researchers often lack the data, funding, and overall capacity to help make sense of how to improve our food system from a socially just perspective.[4]

With this chapter, we frame food as a systems issue and begin building a case for communication as a way to construct various paths toward food justice. Although everyday eating is certainly an issue of global concern, our approach focuses more on communication and community-level interventions. Identifying and dismantling structures that make inequity possible requires some level of community participation, either through grassroots mobilizing or eventual changes in everyday eating practices. Also, principles of food justice and food sovereignty stress the rights of individuals and communities to construct their own food systems, cultures, and practices.[5] Yet, even the community food efforts that seem the most secure are not immune to the tensions of keeping their advocacy and activism going. The year 2017 saw the end of Growing Power—a model program established by Will Allen in 1993 to promote community development, urban agriculture, and local food systems. The program focused on community food systems and social justice through an urban farm in Milwaukee, Wisconsin. Allen sought to improve the lives of fellow Black men in his community, while also providing hands-on training about growing food and local food systems. At the height of its operation, Growing Power routinely provided food to over ten thousand low-income people and contracted with numerous local restaurants. The program was hailed as innovative, particularly because of how it incorporated a community focus and holistic feedback loops; Allen even received a MacArthur Fellowship (i.e., the "genius" grant) in 2008 to expand his approach. However, mounting financial concerns and a disconnect between Allen and his board of directors led to the dissolution of Growing Power in late 2017. Although Allen has plans to continue working the farm itself, the public and online presence about the organization and its model has virtually disappeared.

For many food advocates and activists, the end of Growing Power became a shocking reminder of the fragility of our food systems and the efforts to promote equity across them.[6] Organizing eating involves complex processes of getting food to people and getting people to food. Those processes include the integration of many people, places, motives and interests, material resources, and communication practices. Before we can offer our perspective on communication and food justice organizing, we must first provide readers with a way to navigate the complexities related to organizing eating; we do so by emphasizing food as a systems issue and the language of food (in)security.

FOOD AS A SYSTEMS ISSUE

Although everyday eating is one of our most basic activities, the process of meeting the food needs of more than seven billion people across the globe has grown increasingly complex. Everyday eating involves an intricate relationship between global, national, regional, and local food systems— all of which intersect to ensure that food gets to people. For example, the average American eats about the same amount of apples and bananas; they are two of our favorite fruits.[7] While thirty-nine of the fifty states can grow apples commercially,[8] barely sixteen states can grow bananas. Only Hawaii and certain corners of Florida can support even moderate-scale commercial farming of bananas , and they specialize primarily in cooking bananas and—coincidentally—a variety called the apple banana.[9] Most of the apples we eat come from either the United States or Canada, while most of the bananas we eat come from Guatemala, Ecuador, and Costa Rica.[10] Just this one example, of two of the most consumed foods in the United States, illustrates how we depend upon local and global producers in order to meet our everyday food needs.

For many of us, food is so readily available that we forget about the complex practices of production and consumption that enable and constrain how we eat. Data from the US Department of Agriculture, last updated in 2014, shows that the average American consumes almost two thousand pounds of food annually.[11] That number translates to a series of intricate relationships between food producers, processors, retailers, consumers, and waste managers. Before readers can fully appreciate the connections between communication and food justice activism, we must outline some of the realities—including opportunities and limitations—regarding how food operates from a systems perspective. In other words, people meet their daily food needs "through a complex set of interdependent processes from seed to table and back again."[12] From a communication perspective, how we organize eating demonstrates many classic features of a system, in that food is:

- Material and social: At its core, food is a natural resource with material and social consequences. People interact with natural and agricultural systems, including growing seasons and climate zones, in order to grow food; therefore, our participation in the food system hinges upon a set of material resources, timetables, and realities that people do not completely control. At the same time, we frequently work in creative and innovative ways to manipulate those material constraints to reflect our social tastes and desires. Consumers select food based on culture, tradition, and routine; producers develop greenhouses and hydroponic systems to extend growing seasons; food scientists and chefs look for new ways to blend different practices and cuisines to keep people engaged with their eating; food writers, marketers, and advertisers persuade us to think about food in particular ways. We generate a good deal of discourse around food, making it inherently social alongside the material.

- Interdependent: Food also involves an intricate network of processes and stakeholders that must work together in order to get food to people.[13] Figure 2 provides an illustration of the many features that influence how food gets created and consumed from a systems perspective. Producers must generate ingredients—either by growing them on a farm or garden or creating them in a lab. Those ingredients must be transported, transformed, and packaged into products that retailers and marketers can persuade consumers to purchase, prepare, and eat. Finally, systems generate waste, which in the case of food, can frequently be incorporated back into the production process. The interdependent features of our food system require a significant amount of coordination and communication among individuals and organizations, and changes in one part of the system lead to direct and indirect changes across the remaining moving parts.

- Enabled and constrained: As part of his theory of structuration, Giddens argued that social systems are simultaneously made possible *and* restricted by the various ways in which human agents interact with structural rules and resources.[14] Applied to food systems, this way of thinking reveals how food is enabled and constrained by the material and social realities of growing food, choosing what to eat, and managing the consequences of our choices. Perhaps most importantly, recognizing this interplay between action and structure also focuses attention on how we communicate about food, particularly how food systems are enabled and constrained by discourse and policy, media, and everyday talk about what we eat.

- Paradoxical: The complexities of how food systems function inevitably lead to tensions, particularly in the form of paradoxes.[15] A paradox often refers to a systemic tension that illustrates the general discomfort that arises when competing perspectives clash.[16] It is where two seemingly incompatible ideas exist at the same time, where the pursuit of seemingly compatible goals begin to undermine each other, or where the pursuit of one goal seems antithetical to its end. Food systems often encounter structural paradoxes, such as the prevalence of both hunger and obesity within a single system.

- Sensemaking activities: Food is also systemic in that we make sense of and learn by enacting the moving parts of a food system and retain that knowledge for future activity in the system. At the same time, our knowledge is always filtered through selected interpretations of how food systems best operate. In many cases, we learn by doing, and this systemic feature of food systems involves a connection to Weick's systems theory of sensemaking.[17] For example, a fledgling gardener might fail their first year at growing tomatoes. Of the many reasons for that failure—including too much direct sun, poor soil quality, inconsistent watering, and countless other reasons—the gardener selects too much direct sun and decides to plant in a different location next year. The enactment of growing (or failing to grow) tomatoes, as well as subsequent choices to move the plant, frames future knowledge about food and the systems that support it. As these kinds of sensemaking practices occur across smaller and larger scales, our food system becomes a space where multiple stakeholders make sense of how to best organize a complicated set of resources.

Taken together, the idea that food systems are material and social, interdependent, enabled and constrained, paradoxical sensemaking activities highlights the complexity of concepts with which we are working. Indeed, these concepts emerged in various presentations, dialogues, and news stories that shaped how food security was framed in Greensboro, North Carolina, when community members began facing high rates of food hardship and food insecurity. For example, much of the foundation

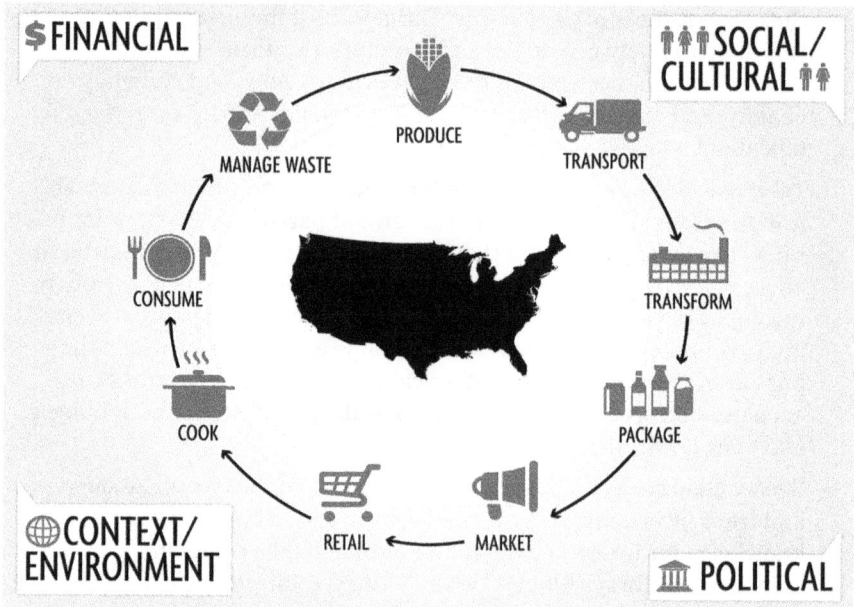

Figure 2. Food as a systems issue. The illustration demonstrates the interdependences between different communities, voices, and stakeholders in most modern food systems. Image credit: Elizabeth Dam-Regier.

for the concepts outlined in Figure 2 was influenced heavily by a presentation that Christy Shi-Day gave in October 2012 for more than eighty-five Greensboro residents who were interested in starting a local food council.

Alongside the core components of food systems outlined in Figure 2 are reminders of other systemic features that deserve consideration. As both a construct and consequence of how food systems operate, they are also social and cultural; therefore, any intervention into food systems—from local to global—must attend to the social and cultural needs of the people eating within that system.[18] They are political, in that people, communities, organizations, and institutions compete for resources in ways that privilege certain interests over others.[19] Food systems are tied to context and environment, particularly when certain regions have easier access to water, good soil, and moderate temperatures or when centers of agriculture experience unexpected droughts. Finally, food systems are also financial in numerous ways, including fluctuations in the cost of food, as well as a common way people earn wages. When food systems are optimized, these features come together to remind us that food is life.

THE LANGUAGE OF FOOD (IN)SECURITY

Inherent within a framework of food as a systems issue is the notion that food systems can be either secure or insecure, sometimes both. Food security often refers to the complex integration of many features of our food system to ensure that food gets to people, while food insecurity regularly focuses more specifically on individual-level factors including income and the ability for people to get to food. This relationship between food security and insecurity provides a crucial framing for how communities might pursue food justice, a term which frequently emphasizes racial and economic equity alongside cultural and structural barriers that communities face as they participate in local food systems and conversations about how everybody eats.

Around the terms *food systems*, *food security*, and *food justice* has emerged an intricate language of food (in)security, which we see evident in policy texts, public health documents and movements, cultural metaphors, and everyday talk about food. From hunger to food deserts to food hardship, the language of food (in)security relies on a dense web of metaphors, discourses, and definitions that both enables and constrains participation in food systems and food justice activism. That language matters in how we use it to construct our talk through food, about food, around food, and as food.[20]

Navigating food (in)security regularly means negotiating some confusing terrain. In what follows, we offer some definitions and conceptual development to equip readers with a basic knowledge of food security and its related terms including insecurity, hardship, and food justice. Throughout, we use the term *food (in)security* to focus on how these terms come together to form a language system that enables and constrains our food system. Food (in)security operates discursively, suggesting that our understanding of what it means to be food secure is both constructed through and a consequence of discourse. At its core, discourse simply means talk and texts. Communication and critical discourse scholars have developed the definition of discourse to focus on the sophisticated process of how we make things (like food) meaningful by talking and writing about them. People talk about food with friends and family, in meetings, at social events, through online and social media, and public speeches. We also encounter a variety of texts about food including advertisements, policies, news articles, blog posts and websites, cookbooks and family recipes, and research reports. Discourse is a relevant and vital part of food justice activism, and we offer this initial definition as a way to consider how individuals, organizations, and communities work through the complex languages around food (in)security.

Some of the most direct and accessible global definitions of food security are available through the Food and Agriculture Organization (FAO) of the United Nations. The FAO includes both the Committee on World Food Security and the World Food Programme. Their definition of food security goes back to the 1996 World Food Summit, which states, "Food security exists when all people, at all times, have physical and economic access to sufficient, safe and nutritious food that meets their dietary needs and food preferences for an active and healthy life."[21] The FAO's approach highlights food as a systems issue by focusing on what they call four pillars of food security: availability, access, utilization, and stability. The concepts of availability and access concentrate on those central processes of getting food to people and getting people to food. While availability addresses the presence or absence of food (i.e., can your local climate and economy support its own local food system or do you need to import food from another region or country?), access focuses on the more precarious concept of whether or not people have the resources (e.g., money and transportation) to secure the food they need.

Further, utilization and stability focus respectively on how people use resources once they are made available and accessible, as well as how the system maintains the availability and accessibility of those resources. These two concepts frequently address questions of affordability, especially when one considers the volatility of food as a resource. Between 2007 and 2017, the basic costs of feeding a family of four in the United States rose 20 percent—from about $124 to about $148 per week.[22] During that time, median wages stayed largely flat, and only in the last three years did wages begin to catch up to the rising cost of food.[23] These changes in the affordability of food in relationship to finances had the sharpest effects on people who earn low-income wages, as they saw more drastic changes to their food budgets without increased compensation from their jobs. At its core, the FAO definition of food security highlights the intersection of these systemic concepts by emphasizing a key question: Is the system stable enough to ensure available and accessible food that people can use to optimize their health and well-being? Also inherent in this definition is the idea that food systems cannot be secure without some degree of equity for the people who are eating.

At a national level, the USDA oversees the language regarding food (in)security. In 2006, the USDA updated their food security definitions to illustrate ranges of severity regarding food insecurity. Table 1 outlines current labels and definitions, as well as their predecessors.[24]

Both the FAO and USDA definitions tend to dominate public discourse about food security. For example, the FAO partners annually with the International Fund for Agricultural Development (IFAD), the United Nations Children's Fund (UNICEF), the World Food Programme (WFP), and the World Health Organization (WHO) to produce an annual report on "the state of food security and nutrition in the world."[25] In their 2017 brief, they highlighted not only a global increase in the numbers of both undernourished and overweight people, they also featured stories of countries facing food systems crises—like South Sudan, where disruptions in agricultural production, trade blockades, and civil discord mean that food is often used as a weapon in ongoing conflicts to secure resources.

Additionally, the USDA definition provides the foundation for the USDA's nationwide survey of food security. The *U.S. Household Food Security Survey Module* is an eighteen-item questionnaire that measures how food insecurity and hunger are related to income limitations.[26] It includes questions such as: "'The food that we bought just didn't last, and we didn't have money to get more.' Was that often, sometimes, or never true for your household in the last 12 months?" and: "In the last 12 months, since last (name of current month), did you or other adults in your household ever cut the size of your meals or skip meals because there wasn't enough money for food?"

The USDA framing of food security also informs a variety of US national, state, and local food initiatives, namely Feeding America and

Table 1   US Department of Agriculture Definitions of Food Security

Language	2006 Label	"Old" Label	Definition
Food security	High food security	Food security	No reported indications of food-access problems or limitations.
	Marginal food security	Food security	One or two reported indications—typically of anxiety over food sufficiency or shortage of food. Little or no indication of changes in diets or food intake.
Food insecurity	Low food security	Food insecurity without hunger	Reports of reduced quality, variety, or desirability of diet. Little or no indication of reduced food intake.
	Very low food security	Food insecurity with hunger	Reports of multiple indications of disrupted eating patterns and reduced food intake.

the Second Harvest Food Bank program. Although Feeding America uses a different methodology to calculate their food insecurity rates, they look at relationships between poverty, unemployment, and homeownership to examine how one's ability to secure food is tied intricately to their income and other financial assets.[27]

The FAO and USDA definitions are also echoed in how major organizations deploy the term *food security* in their own work. For instance, the *Economist* magazine's Intelligence Unit began partnering in 2012 with the DuPont chemical company to further define and measure food security. As part of their Global Food Security Index, they look at three core concepts—affordability, availability, and quality—to rank 113 countries across eighteen parameters.[28] The parameters include both systems-level concepts, like agricultural infrastructure and food loss, as well as individual-level concepts, like food consumption as a share of household expenditures. In its framing of food security, the Index further classifies food systems as showing "improvement, no change, or deterioration" based on their rankings. For the first five iterations of the index, the United States topped the list as the most food secure; with Ireland claiming the top spot in 2017 and dropping the United States to number two. In 2019, Singapore moved into the top spot, with Ireland and the United States ranking second and third, respectively. As a consequence, the United States effectively became classified as a deteriorating food system on the Global Food Index.

In a similar extension of this public discourse, the Food Research and Action Center (FRAC) began charting what they define as "food hardship" in 2010. Comparable to the USDA's definition of food insecurity, food hardship also focuses on an individual or family's financial ability to secure nutritious and safe food. FRAC argues that food hardship is an indicator for hunger, meaning that a consistent lack of nutritious food "harms health, learning, and productivity."[29] To measure food hardship, FRAC draws from the Gallup-Healthways Well-Being Index, which is an annual survey of more than one hundred seventy-five thousand adults living in the United States. The Gallup survey asks a single question related to food security, which FRAC uses as the basis for their food hardship rankings: "Have there been times in the past twelve months when you did not have enough money to buy food that you or your family needed?" Several critics have noted the similarities between the FRAC framing of food hardship and the USDA definition of food insecurity—citing how the USDA's approach provides a more nuanced understanding of food security, but the FRAC data is collected more routinely and with a more precise focus on municipal-level information.[30]

How the institutions and organizations construct and maintain these definitions and public discourses is certainly worthy of critique, but our purpose here is simply to chart the landscape for the language of food (in) security. From a social construction perspective, this language provides the building blocks for how we make food—and our efforts to secure it— meaningful and real. It also imparts us with the resources for critique in later chapters. The conceptualization of food (in)security drives the conversation of how communities ensure they can feed their people, and a constellation of terms, concepts, and phrases has grown around its language. In addition to core concepts like food security and insecurity, and related terms like *food hardship*, this language also includes concepts like

Table 2 The Language of Food (In)Security

Language Category	Specific Term	Definition	Frequently Traced to
Core terms	Food security	Exists when all people, at all times, have physical and economic access to sufficient, safe and nutritious food that meets their dietary needs and food preferences for an active and healthy life	1996 World Food Summit; UN Food & Agriculture Organization (FAO); Global Food Index
	Food insecurity	Household-level economic and social condition of limited or uncertain access to adequate food	US Department of Agriculture (USDA); Feeding America; Committee on National Statistics (CNSTAT)
Related terms	Hunger	Individual-level consequence of food insecurity in which a person is unable to consume sufficient food to meet their nutritional needs; food deprivation	FAO; USDA; CNSTAT
	Food hardship	Experiencing times in the last 12 months when individuals did not have enough money to buy food that they or their family needed	Food Research and Action Center
	Food sovereignty	The right of peoples to healthy and culturally appropriate food produced through ecologically sound and sustainable methods, and their right to define their own food and agriculture systems	La Via Campesina; 1996 World Food Summit
	Food justice	A less formalized but closely related term to food sovereignty; often describes growing local responses to food insecurity and economic barriers to ethical, healthy, and culturally appropriate foods	No formally credited sources

Table 2 (*continued*)

Language Category	Specific Term	Definition	Frequently Traced to
Metaphors	Food desert	Area where low-income residents have limited access to fresh and affordable food; a US census tract where at least 1/3 of the population lives more than 1 mile from a grocery store or supermarket and 20% live below the poverty line	USDA
	Food oasis	Area where residents have access to fresh and affordable food, regardless of income	No formally credited sources
	Food swamp	Area where unhealthy foods are more readily available than healthy foods	No formally credited sources; sometimes traced to Dr. Roland Sturm of RAND Corporation
	Food apartheid	Inequalities in food environments are based on social markers like race and class, and reinforced by public and corporate policies	No formally credited sources; sometimes traced to Community Coalition in South Los Angeles and food activist Karen Washington

hunger and food sovereignty, as well as metaphors like food deserts and food swamps. Table 2 offers further details about the terms related to the language of food (in)security.

Beyond the core terms of food security and insecurity, the related terms and metaphors add layers of complexity to an already complicated conversation. For example, the food desert metaphor gained a great deal of traction when the USDA released their Food Desert Locator in 2011. This online interactive tool, launched in response to former First Lady Michelle Obama's Let's Move! campaign, mapped low-income census tracts where urban residents lived more than one mile from a grocery store, super-market, or source of healthy food options.[31] Renamed the Food Access Research Atlas in 2013, the map continues to connect the food deserts metaphor to access and poverty. The primary conditions for qualifying as a food desert are that one-third of residents in an urban census tract live more than one mile from a grocery store or supermarket and at least 20 percent live below the poverty line. Although food deserts are often associated with the USDA, the term is frequently traced back to Scotland in the early 1990s, when a resident of a public housing scheme used it to describe the community's food landscape.[32] The first formal appearance of the term in public policy documents came in 1995 from a UK policy working group focused on nutrition and poverty.[33]

The terminology of food deserts witnessed a resurgence in popularity and familiarity when the USDA began mapping census tracts in 2011, com-plete with extended metaphors of food oases and food swamps to further describe urban food landscapes. For example, *food swamp* often refers to an overabundance of convenience foods and fast-food restaurants in place of grocery stores and fresh-food access. Food deserts tend also to be food swamps, which means that people have access to food, but it is frequently high-calorie and minimally nutritious food.[34] The once-promising food desert metaphor has faced additional critique—particularly in its applica-tion to the US food system.[35] Critics have argued that, unlike in the United Kingdom where the term emerged from within the affected community, in the United States the term *food desert* has largely been constructed through public policy and used by those who do not live in food deserts to describe those who do. Food activists and writers like Karen Washington and Jacqueline Bediako have begun to reject the food desert metaphor in favor of new metaphors, like food apartheid, to describe the systemic racial and socioeconomic inequalities that exist in our food system.[36]

Even more, the definition of *food desert* might sit at the intersection of access and poverty, but most programming, research, policy, and public discourse continues to privilege the access part of that definition. Early interventions in US food deserts focused on placing grocery stores and farmers markets in low-income neighborhoods or working with existing corner stores to increase their fresh and healthy food offerings. Many of these programs worked to accept SNAP/EBT (Supplemental Nutrition Assistance Program / Electronic Benefit Transfer) as a way to increase access for low-income community members; however, simply placing a grocery store in a food desert rarely translated into changed food purchasing and eating practices for a majority of residents.[37] Poverty, education, and the cost of food are regularly better predictors of people's eating habits. Although the food desert metaphor provides an accessible way for many Americans to understand how poverty and access might affect people's ability to secure food, its language regularly fails to capture the complete phenomenon in meaningful ways and frequently makes the terrain of food (in)security even more difficult to navigate.

Across this variegated field that grounds the language of food (in)security, we also center a definition of food justice that is informed by communication scholarship on social justice organizing and communication activism. Our interest in food justice emerges not only from our interest in navigating food systems, but also working toward social justice. Considering that this book emphasizes communication practices of advocacy and activism as a way to generate pathways to food justice, we rely on a definition of food justice that centers its social components, which both Johnson and Huffman have highlighted as a particular type of interaction. More specifically, "Social justice relies on various modes of action and organizing, including advocating change, building community, improving governance, and reorganizing markets."[38] As such, food justice involves the pursuit of equitable food systems through imagining new infrastructures, economic resources, and community practices around food.[39] Food justice organizing frequently highlights actions including investment in displaced and underserved communities, developing fair trade practices, establishing local food policy councils, advocating for better food access, and a general right to food, as well as practices that attempt to both reform and transform food systems.[40] But that *pursuit* of food justice is what makes a communication perspective on food (in)security and food justice advocacy and activism so important, because it centers our social and community-based practices in organizing and re-organizing, advocating for, and securing food resources. We continue to develop this rationale for a communication perspective on food justice in the following chapter.

CONCLUSION

Developing an understanding of metaphors like food deserts alongside the case for food as a systems issue demonstrates just how complicated the language of food (in)security has become. It also provides us with a shared vocabulary to explore these terms and concepts in future chapters, like when Greensboro media outlets and food advocates regularly conflated food insecurity, food hardship, and food deserts in ways that both clarified and confused local efforts. With this sharper focus on the language of food (in)security, alongside the framing of food as a systems issue, we now have the resources to connect to some of the deeper threads that stitch together the relationship between food, communication, and social justice organizing.

2 Tracing the Discourses of Food (In)security

The late chef, storyteller, and raconteur Anthony Bourdain is often praised for saying, "There's nothing more political than food. Who eats? Who doesn't? Why do people cook what they cook? It is always the end or a part of a long story, often a painful one."[1] Because food plays a role in some of our most everyday activities, questions about who eats, what they eat, who cooks, and how we generally organize eating often reveal connections to contested resources, difficult stories, and systemic inequities. Food is intricately tied to numerous political and social justice issues, and communication scholars have carved out a space to examine the intersections between local interventions and local food systems. Including connections to public discourse, community engagement, and communication activism, this increasingly robust body of literature calls attention to issues of culture and race,[2] the ambiguity of the term *community* in local interventions,[3] and community collaboration to address food insecurity.[4]

By recognizing the important connections between food and communication, we contribute to this space by centering food justice advocacy and activism in a set of discursive processes and practices.[5] We focus generally on what we call communicating food justice, as our work extends from our first-person experiences organizing for food justice from within communities and through community-based frameworks. Communicating food justice draws from critical organizational and social justice activism research to emphasize critical health literacies around food systems, organizing eating to ensure equity, and managing various tensions around community food security. We also offer a more precise set of processes, resources, and practices as this chapter outlines a four-part perspective that prioritizes communication and its connections to food (in)security and food justice through engaging communities, mobilizing resources, documenting processes, and sustaining conversations.

Additionally, this chapter considers how practices of communicating food justice and the discourses of food (in)security, food hardship, and food justice can be traced across local food organizing in Greensboro, North Carolina. We concentrate on the time period between 2009 and 2019, reaching back to before the Food Research and Action Center (FRAC) rankings called attention to Greensboro/High Point's food hardship status, and following ten years of food organizing around the topics of food (in)security, food hardship, and local food systems. The various interventions, policy initiatives, pilot tests, and networks that partners launched during this time also serve as an illustration of the framework we propose. To highlight those connections between the framework and our food work, this chapter concludes with a reader's guide to eight case studies that tell the story of communicating food justice in Greensboro.

COMMUNICATING FOOD JUSTICE

Communicating food justice is grounded in communication activism research (CAR), critical organizational and health communication, and food justice advocacy. We draw inspiration from Frey and colleagues' approach to social justice communication, which focuses on "engagement with and advocacy for those in our society who are economically, socially, politically, and/or culturally underresourced."[6] As a general perspective, Frey et al. emphasize keeping an ethical focus, analyzing structures that reproduce inequity, adopting an activist perspective, and working to identify with others. Communication activism research highlights creating the conditions for the conversation around social justice topics, and both critical organizational and health communication and food justice advocacy help focus that conversation on food systems and food security.[7] Counihan and Van Esterik trace the importance of food, culture, and advocacy back to Roland Barthes's notion that food is itself a system of communication. Barthes famously argued that food is more than numbers and nutrition; rather, when people buy, eat, and even serve food, "this item of food sums up and transmits a situation; it constitutes an information; it signifies."[8] Using this argument as a departure point, communicating food justice and food justice organizing frame food within both agricultural and communication systems.

As an extension of critical organizational and health communication research, food justice organizing centers on structural inequalities in our conversations about food systems.[9] Supporters of structural change from within food systems frequently focus these conversations on the intersections between poverty and access, as well as how those intersections also connect to economy, race, gender, education, housing, and urbanism. Strategies often require analyzing policies, identifying inequities, planning and coordinating activities, and doing so with participation from multiple stakeholders and communities.[10] Perhaps most intriguingly, food justice organizing creates a variety of occasions to learn about and enact democracy,[11] as increased corporatization in food economies and the centralization of power away from communities have steadily separated people from how and what they eat. Communicating food justice enables, and sometimes constrains, how individuals and communities become reconnected to their food and the systems that organize eating.

Centering Communication in Food Justice Organizing

Although food is a systems issue that operates through global-to-local means, and interventions to promote more just food systems can be effective across those levels, our focus here is on local interventions within local systems.[12] The ways in which communities respond to changes, perceived problems, and opportunities within local food systems can provide insight into how people make use of the food resources available to them. Systematic reviews of research on access, local food environments, obesity, and food preferences demonstrate that increasing access to healthier food options does not always translate into changes in food practices.[13] At the same time, facilitating participatory decision-making and policy-making remain vital evidence-based strategies for building more vibrant and secure food systems.[14] In other words, creating the conditions for individuals and communities to participate in local organizing around food has the potential to transform local food systems in ways that are more just and equitable; however, that equitable change is not always guaranteed. Within this space of creating the conditions for equitable food systems is where we situate our focus on communication.

In applying a social justice activism lens that emphasizes organizing and advocacy, researchers are increasingly called to align their work with a variety of communities and partners to facilitate discussions, implement and evaluate interventions, organize and manage institutional memory, and work with partners to create community-driven action. As we continue to refine our focus on communicating food justice and creating paths to food justice at local and community levels, we are guided by four questions:

1. How is community defined in community food interventions? Concurrently, how do food interventions enable and constrain development across communities?

2. As communities face questions about food insecurity and food hardship, how do they organize to ensure that everybody eats?

3. How do communities and their partners coordinate their activities in communicating food justice?

4. How do communities and their partners manage the tensions that enable and constrain efforts to ensure equity in local food systems?

These questions are informed by scholarly and popular literature on food justice and communicating for social justice, media, and social trends in US and Western food systems, as well as our own first-person experiences organizing with communities around food.

To engage these questions, we next outline a more specific set of processes, resources, and practices related to communicating food justice and communicating as communities to ensure food security. We offer a four-part perspective inspired by more than ten years and fifteen thousand hours of organizing with communities, collecting stories and surveys, and constructing resources across eight different food activism efforts in

Greensboro. The four areas we highlight here are also influenced heavily by community-based and grassroots organizing, culture-centered and communication research, and critically reflexive food trends that prioritize food justice.[15]

ENGAGING COMMUNITIES

Engaging everyday community members in identifying, articulating, and solving the problems they face have become a well-documented approach to research and activism—particularly for human communication. Our purpose here is not to articulate community engagement as a field of study, as Dempsey and others have detailed a history of community engagement and its relevance to communication.[16] Still others have argued that researchers need to move beyond the ubiquitous term *community engagement* to focus more on working with communities around communication activism and advocacy.[17] As such, our point is to illustrate that the practice of engaging communities is still important, and communicating food justice activism requires the engagement of numerous communities through intentional and often long-term organizing around food systems. Our need to eat to survive is not likely to change anytime soon; therefore, conversations around food and how communities organize the resources available to them involve regular and routine attention.

Engaging communities involves not only dialogue and deliberation about the ideas, problems, and solutions within a community, but also strategic efforts to coordinate groups and individuals who often hold different priorities.[18] Food advocates and researchers have identified a number of communication-related practices involved in engaging communities around food systems maintenance and change. For example, evidence-based strategies across short, medium, and long-term community engagement in local food systems likely includes the following:[19]

1. Short term: documenting available resources, counseling communities on maximizing those resources; identifying quality and quantity inequities across neighborhoods; educating consumers about food resources.

2. Medium term: connecting partners from existing food programs (e.g., food pantries, urban agriculture projects, farmers markets); creating multi-sector partnerships, networks, and food councils;

facilitating participatory decision-making and policy development; mapping community resources for public use.

3. Long term: advocating for fair wages and housing standards to address poverty; dismantling structural barriers, including racism and sexism, that privilege some community members' participation over others; mobilizing local governments to institutionalize fair land-use policies and agriculture programs, promote community self-reliance to meet nutritional goals, and incentivize business development in low-income neighborhoods.

These strategies speak to the importance of *communicating* in food justice organizing and activism, particularly the ways in which they highlight facilitating conversation, planning and documenting, building relationships between individuals and organizations, and advocating for policy and institutional change.

Coordinating the language and activities of various groups and individuals with different histories, priorities, and missions is an inherently communicative practice. In any given system, numerous communities might be operating—both in isolation and through varying degrees of partnership.[20] Engaging those communities in regular and routine conversations around local food is a necessary initial step in addressing food (in)security and moving toward food justice.

MOBILIZING RESOURCES

Perhaps one of the most crucial practices in working with communities to build more vibrant, equitable, and resilient food systems is to move beyond identifying and critiquing, brainstorming, and simply getting people together to generate ideas. Mobilizing resources entails more direct steps to translate discourse into action and activism. In other words, it involves managing both material and human resources as communities move ideas into implementation. This time period can be particularly tricky because community members, researchers, and partners must connect ideas to details, ensure access to the resources necessary to move forward, and convince people to commit their time and effort to participating. Partners must understand what resources are (not) available to neighborhoods, as well as what resources residents are likely to use, because mobilizing resources involves leveraging that information and creating distribution networks to directly address access.

In some cases, mobilizing resources means developing systems and practices to distribute supplies and capital—such as food and money—directly to the communities, neighborhoods, and families that need them. We see evidence for this approach in the case for food pantries, healthy corner stores, pop-up markets, SNAP/EBT programs, and grocery store incentives in neighborhoods that are characterized as food deserts.[21] In particular, developing resources that are themselves mobile, such as mobile farmers markets and pop-up food pantries, can activate public spaces and create hubs of interaction and communication within neighborhoods.[22]

Beyond the material, mobilizing resources frequently means asking partners to commit their labor, volunteer time, and free time to completing the work and keeping the conversation going. Efforts to mobilize community participation work best when the activism and activity are community driven, not driven by external partners and policy-makers.[23] As such, coordinating the people power around food is critical, especially when working with both community and university partners. Even more so than during the initial community engagement, partners must remain reflexive about how interests intersect, and how human resources are managed and compensated. For example, researchers are often paid through their universities to carry out their work, while community members are frequently asked to donate their time. Attending to the ways in which paid and unpaid labor comes together to carry out the work of food justice activism is an important, if often overlooked, practice.

As with engaging communities, the processes and practices of mobilizing resources are inherently communicative. Community-communication infrastructure, narrative, and communication technologies are all crucial components of these processes.[24] Community-communication infrastructure includes identifying and strengthening storytelling networks among neighborhoods. These networks involve not only narratives about personal experiences, but also a wide range of communication strategies used to construct the story of a community—including sharing stories with the media, policy advocacy, healthy eating campaigns, community celebrations, and documenting neighborhood events. Additionally, new media—like web-based collaboration and smart phone apps—have become increasingly necessary to mobilize community participation.[25] These media channels strengthen communication infrastructure and are increasingly expected in communication about food justice.[26]

DOCUMENTING PROCESS

How we archive community efforts, narratives, and data helps us tell a more complete story of local food systems. Documenting process involves both telling stories and managing data. These practices often cover the more mundane and technical aspects of communicating food justice activism. Certainly, questions about how to collect and manage data around local food interventions do not necessarily inspire most people to think differently about their food. At the same time, knowledge and community memory has become an increasingly complex process.[27] Access to cloud technologies and web-based platforms like Google Drive and Dropbox, social media and websites, and data analysis programs like Qualtrics and Red Hat have made it easier for organizations, researchers, and communities to collect data and track how well their ideas are translating into practice. Public and open-access data systems also create a sense of "who knows what" among community partners, which helps make groups more effective over time.[28]

One of the most useful ways in which researchers and universities can partner with communities is to provide tracking and monitoring data and create repositories for community-level data, stories, and histories.[29] City and county health departments carry out this sort of work through the Community Health Assessment (CHA) process, which is designed to help communities and city and county agencies assess health data, identify barriers, and propose policies and programs to improve local health. Several of the case studies included in this book were either launched, informed, or evaluated through Greensboro and Guilford County's triannual CHA process. Fewer governmental institutions are regularly and routinely collecting data—instead leaving it up to communities, universities, think tanks, and research groups to collect what they need. By filling these data gaps, partners can create transparent touchstones and document the outcomes of their advocacy and activism.

Effectively managing data and documenting processes can also promote communication visibility in that public data and indicator banks, community story sites, local surveys, and social media activity can all provide evidence about the impacts of community food activism.[30] Partners must pay close attention to how promoting food security and food justice can change availability and access, affordability, distribution networks, and how people use the resources that are available to them. For example, a pop-up farmers market in a food desert might fill the access gap; however, when partners introduce new resources, members of the neighborhood may come to rely on them to change their food habits. Communities and their partners need to understand how these new resources change not only access and availability, but also utilization in a system. This kind of information is not only useful for tracking and monitoring purposes, but it also helps communities and partners coordinate work among groups with discontinuous memberships.[31]

Partners in communicating food justice activism often come and go—community members move, community organizations change direction, and life changes for people. Creating shared data resources provides both continuity and visibility as partners change but the work continues. Simple and public documentation can lend greater legitimacy to community voices, show the impacts of partnered work, and ensure that groups are aligned.[32] In recognizing the importance of data, different community groups can begin to stitch together the stories to provide a more complete picture of how local food systems operate in practice.

SUSTAINING CONVERSATIONS

Much of what we have presented about communication and food justice activism has led up to the question of how communities and their partners sustain, and in some cases disrupt, local practices around food. A unique and necessary contribution that communication scholars can make to social justice organizing involves the practice of sustaining conversations. Because food is a systems issue, equitable food systems are frequently associated with environmental, economic, cultural, and program sustainability.[33] Part of communicating food justice means advocating to sustain the agricultural resources, partnerships, food practices, and communication visibility that make food systems more equitable. Cultivating and maintaining positive relationships within and across communities are collective tasks for which we are all responsible.[34] Communication activists and researchers can help communities and grassroots organizers document stories and carry narratives as people and resources change.[35]

At the same time, sustaining conversations sometimes means disrupting systems, especially those processes and policies that reproduce insecurity and inequity, reify racism and classism, and are otherwise in need of reflexive critique.[36] Activism, advocacy, and social change are often associated with disruption, agitation, conflict, and critique of the structures and practices that reproduce inequity.[37] A pop-up farmers market might initially disrupt a local food system by providing resources where there were none before; however, introducing this new resource changes how residents, farmers, volunteers, retailers, and distributors interact with the system. Neighborhoods need to build trust that the market will continue to provide the food they need, just as the producers and farmers need to build trust that the neighborhood will keep buying what they're selling.

Attention to how communities can sustain their activism and advocacy are crucial at this point, especially because of the fragility and volatility of food systems, as well as the unintended consequences of our discourse. Food advocates and activists seem most effective when they can capture a productive tension between sustaining conversations and disrupting systems. In doing so, we recognize, as Spurlock has observed, that relationships between people and food "extend across time and space far beyond the moment of consumption in ways that both conjure the past and shape the future."[38] From a communication perspective, we recognize that resources—particularly those related to food and community—will change over time; however, creating spaces for intentional dialogue, imagining new food and communication infrastructures, constructing shared yet complex narratives, and building platforms for advocacy and activism help communities sustain conversations while disrupting systems that reproduce inequity.

This tension is why engaging communities, mobilizing resources, and documenting process are so important leading up to this point. When attended to thoughtfully and intentionally, the first three parts of our perspective inform communities and their partners about which pieces of food systems need sustaining and which need disrupting. Having committed the time to building local stories and communication infrastructure, engaging multiple voices, and identifying local resources, communities are more prepared to carry forward the narratives they want to preserve while challenging those structures and assumptions that reproduce inequity.[39]

Moreover, this tension also speaks to the concept of resilience, which focuses on how individuals, families, and communities persevere and "bounce back," despite difficult experiences or a poor food environment.[40] Recognizing that disruptions to local food systems can come in the form of social activism, but also changes in weather, the loss of a job, or the closing of a grocery store, the tension between sustaining and disrupting shows how building a truly just and equitable food system is always ongoing and incomplete. As such, we conclude our four-part perspective with sustaining conversations as a way to reinforce that our approach to communicating food justice is not a linear process, but rather a delicate interplay of engaging communities, mobilizing resources, and documenting process to create a necessary and ongoing infrastructure that can sustain and disrupt food systems.

The pieces of this four-part perspective always bring communicating food justice back to social equity and the reminder that everybody eats. Social equity can come in many forms, however, including rural and urban, age, ability, race, social class, local and global, housing status, and gender. We provide this perspective both as a way to reinforce the need to regularly and routinely engage the topic of equitable food systems, as well as a way to capture our participation in food justice work in Greensboro, North Carolina. In the following section, we consider how we traced discourses of food (in)security and food justice organizing across neighborhoods and interventions in Greensboro, and we begin to outline the eight case studies that illustrate our approach.

FOOD JUSTICE ORGANIZING IN GREENSBORO, NORTH CAROLINA

In 2010, Greensboro/High Point first appeared on the Food Research and Action Center's list of Food Hardship in America. By 2015, our community had risen to the top of FRAC's list of major metropolitan cities, with one in four residents reporting an experience of food hardship within the last year. This statistic galvanized a conversation around food in Greensboro/ High Point and Guilford County. At the same time, the numbers did not tell community members and civic leaders much in terms of how to respond to that statistic. The FRAC study asked only one question: *Have there been times in the last 12 months when you did not have enough money to buy food that you or your family needed?*

Despite some level of ambiguity in the question, individuals and groups across Greensboro and Guilford County began organizing information, discourse, research, and resources around the topics of food hardship and food security. Campus and community partners worked to engage neighborhoods, mobilize resources, convene stakeholders, and scale up their efforts to local and regional food systems. We created neighborhood task forces, urban agriculture programs, mobile farmers markets, food councils, and shared-use kitchens—all in a move to ensure not only that people had food, but also that partners were organizing toward a sustainable, equitable, and vibrant food system. Within three years, Greensboro had fallen from FRAC's top ten list, and we saw an 8 percent drop in our food hardship rate. Our response to the FRAC rankings created an opportunity to examine local-level interventions to promote food justice and food security, as well as how those efforts were woven into the fabric of a larger food system.

Greensboro as a Context for Communicating Food Justice

Greensboro has a powerful history of neighborhood engagement, social and racial justice, and higher education—all of which have laid the foundation for cultivating resilience across our communities. Greensboro played a key role in US civil rights history, when four African American male students (and their female classmates from Bennett College) sat down at a whites-only lunch counter in 1960 and sparked the much larger lunch counter movement across the United States. Greensboro is situated in Guilford County, the third-most-populous county in North Carolina and one of the most racially diverse in the state. Guilford is also designated as a refugee resettlement area, with over sixty thousand immigrants and refugees who have made their home here.

As a case study for communicating food justice, Greensboro is unique in its history of social justice activism and perseverance through more than just food hardship. Our community is also very "everyday," in that we are a midsize southern city with vibrant citizens who often struggle to make ends meet. Between 2000 and 2012, the Greensboro-High Point metropolitan area saw among the highest rates of growth of concentrated poverty of anywhere in the United States.[41] Losses in our manufacturing, textile, and furniture industries had drastically changed the landscape of jobs in the available workforce, and people's incomes suffered substantially. During this period, the percentage increase of people living in poverty was 77 percent, growing from 65,798 in 2000 to 116,501 in 2008–2012. In 2000, about a quarter of people experiencing poverty lived in neighborhoods with a poverty rate greater than 20 percent—that number more than doubled by 2008–2012. The poverty rate among African American residents was more than twice the rate than that of White residents (26.5% compared to 10.8%) in 2015, with 25.1 percent of children under the age of eighteen living in poverty.

So when Greensboro reached the top of the FRAC rankings, members of health, agriculture, and research communities had already begun to see the early signs of food hardship. For example, in May 2012, Marianne worked alongside the Guilford County Cooperative Extension, Share the Harvest, a local food recovery group, and the Interactive Resource Center, a day center for people experiencing homelessness, to host a two-part Food for Thought event. Local health officials had recently identified seventeen food deserts in Greensboro, prompting partners to organize the event. Part one of Food for Thought featured a series of short presentations from local nonprofit organizations and social service agencies about their food outreach, followed by a showing of the film *A Place at the Table*. This first event was designed to give community members a starting point to engage in the conversation. Two weeks later, part two of Food for Thought invited community members back for more focused dialogues about how Greensboro might respond to growing concerns about hunger and food insecurity in our communities. Both events were well attended, with over one hundred people at each meeting, and they helped mobilize several interventions across Greensboro, including a mobile farmers market for low-income food deserts and a network of summer meal locations for K–12 students.

The Food for Thought dialogues were just one example of the myriad conversations and interventions that were launched between 2009 and 2019 around the topics of food access, food (in)security, and local food systems. To trace this time period, we constructed an online timeline of the major food related events entitled *Food Security in the Piedmont Triad.*[42] The timeline shows substantial activity around local media coverage of food hardship.[43] Also shown were the launch of multiple pilot tests and pop-ups as invitations for community participation and several instances of engaging people in policy talk around food. Across these numerous points on the timeline are a common refrain—the importance of food, culture, and community in facing food hardship and building vibrant food systems.[44]

Although Greensboro has faced significant challenges in maintaining a secure food system, our community members have also remained nimble in the face of poverty, racial tension, and widening resource gaps. More recent data suggests that Greensboro is making progress. A 2018 report from the Brookings Institute noted that Greensboro's poverty rate dropped 2.7 percent between 2016 and 2017. FRAC now ranks Greensboro–High Point fourteenth in food hardship. Some of this progress can be attributed to the ways in which community stakeholders have collaborated to address concerns across our neighborhoods. Greensboro has implemented participatory budgeting programs, food access initiatives, and health and housing efforts to cultivate resilience in our communities. Because our story focuses on food security, we dedicate the remaining pages of this book to illustrate how Greensboro and its community members navigated the frequently difficult, but often inspiring discourses surrounding food systems.

EVERYBODY EATS: A READER'S GUIDE

Our telling of Greensboro's dramatic rise and fall on the FRAC rankings and our focus on communicating food justice relies on a series of case studies that illustrate Greensboro's food justice organizing in terms of engaging communities, mobilizing resources, documenting process, and sustaining conversations. We conducted the research for these case studies using a qualitative approach called discourse tracing.[45] This approach allowed us, as researchers, to critically analyze the various structures, practices, and power relationships that constructed the food security conversations in Greensboro and engage in a systematic data analysis that is both accessible and transparent. By "tracing discourse," we followed how everyday talk and text about concepts, words, and phrases—like *access* and *food desert*—shaped local conversations and interventions. To do this, discourse tracers scrutinize talk and text along three levels of discourse—the micro level, which emphasizes local instances of community interaction, the macro level, which reminds us of the larger social narratives that enable and constrain us, and the meso level, which connects us together across different contexts and settings. In other words, an intervention to increase access to fruits and vegetables at a local convenience store might be an example of a micro discourse. The narrative that suggests convenience stores only sell unhealthy food is part of the macro discourse, and a policy to incentivize store owners to carry healthier foods might illustrate a meso discourse.

To examine how discourses around food (in)security and food access are deployed at these micro, meso, and macro levels, discourse tracers make use of interviews, observations, archival data, public documents, newspaper articles, policy proceedings, transcripts of public meetings, websites, blogs, cultural artifacts, or campaign slogans. Moreover, data collection can be a lengthy endeavor, as researchers are working with participants as the scene transforms over time.[46] The product of discourse tracing is a case study or series of case studies that provides a snapshot of social change and the mechanisms and discourses that enable and constrain it. Below are additional details about the case studies, including the data represented in each story and the voices that contributed to them. We presented this information as a sort of reader's guide, designed to help readers manage the complexity of information we present in the case studies, and we encourage you to use this guide as a reference point for future chapters.

The Case Studies

Using the guiding questions we outlined earlier in this chapter—that emphasize how community is defined in local food interventions, how communities organize to promote food security, how partners coordinate activities in the pursuit of food justice, and how partners manage the tensions in local food systems to ensure equity—the case studies featured in this book are intended to document the various practices associated with communicating food justice activism. We invite the reader to consider (1) how discourses of food access, food (in)security, and food systems enabled and constrained communication activism, and (2) how each intervention—in whole or in part—might transfer to other contexts and communities.

The case studies represent ten years of dedicated participant observation and communication activism in Greensboro. We offer first-person accounts of eight different interventions, task forces, policy initiatives, and community food programs that were launched in Greensboro through community-based partnerships. Some of the case studies are related, such as chapter 3, where we focus on the Warnersville Community Food Task Force, which laid the foundation for the Warnersville Community Garden and the Mobile Oasis Farmers Market, which we feature in chapters 5 and 6, respectively. Others focus not as much on food hardship and food insecurity, directly, but related questions of food security and food systems—like the Downtown Greensboro Food Truck Pilot Project, Ethnosh, and Kitchen Connects GSO, which we cover in chapters 4, 7, and 8. The remaining cases, the Guilford Food Council and the Renaissance Community Co-op, stand alone, but offer unique perspectives on sustaining conversations about food even when we can't sustain the intervention.

Across these case studies, Marianne served as a primary researcher on those stories featured in chapters 3–9, and Niesha served as a primary community partner on chapters 5, 6, and 9. Chapter 10 was distinctive in that we both served as participants, although we did invite contributions from two organizers involved in the intervention. In addition to chapter 10, we also invite contributions from organizers in chapters 3, 7, 8, and the conclusion, as we believe part of good community-engaged research involves writing with your partners.

In total, these case studies represent 773 hours of participant observation, 3,489 pages of field notes, stories, meeting minutes, and email exchanges, 2,606 interviews and surveys, 1,195 pages of policy and media texts, and 2,918 participants. We share these numbers so that readers understand the deep level of immersion and systematic data collection that we used to construct the narratives. Part of discourse tracing requires an extensive set of qualitative data in order to identify relevant patterns. As such, part of this reader's guide includes a listing of data for each chapter in Table 3, with attention to the micro, meso, and macro sources of data that we crafted into narratives of food security.

A Few Notes on Voice(s)

Our goal in writing this book is to further a conversation about food security and food justice activism. Because we write this text from a communication perspective, we want to invite the reader into that conversation. As such, we adopt both a scholarly and a practical voice. We write primarily from a first-person perspective. At the same time, we occasionally drift into second-person as a way to remind the reader that you are part of this conversation. We also intermittently refer to ourselves in the third person to clarify if the story is coming from Marianne's or Niesha's perspective, or from one of the voices of our coauthors. Whenever possible, we provide additional notes throughout the text to remind readers whose voice is taking the lead.

In addition to our own voices, one of the most significant challenges in writing this book was managing the sheer number of community members, survey participants, civic partners, and researchers that contributed to these conversations. Almost three thousand people participated in various ways, shapes, and forms to the stories included in cases. More than seventy people are directly quoted or referenced across the chapters, and another sixty are indirectly referenced. We have constructed a "Cast of Voices" in Table 4 to be used as part of the reader's guide. This table features the individuals who contributed significantly to each case study, their subject position, and the organizations or groups they represent.[47] The names that appear in bold print are featured prominently in the case study, even if they are not mentioned directly by name. We close this chapter with the Cast of Voices, as a way to prepare for the stories that follow them.

Table 3A   Everybody Eats Data Guide: Chapter 3—The Warnersville Community Food Task Force (2009–2013)

Data Type	Data Source	Level of Analysis	Hours, Pages, and Participants
Participant observation	Community needs assessment • 30 focus group participants • Environmental scan	Micro	• 111 hours of participant observation
	Task force meetings • 12 task force meetings (2010–12) • 11 garden meetings (2011–14) • 14 market meetings (2011–14)		• 642 pages of field notes and meeting minutes
Supplemental texts	Local media and reports • Newspaper and online articles on the history of Warnersville in the *Greensboro News & Record* and the Greensboro History Museum • Guilford County Community Health Assessment		• 75 pages of supplemental texts and local/national media articles • 56 participants
Formal texts	Warnersville Healthy Communities Project Proposal	Meso	• 3 reports/plans produced
Community health data	NC Center for Health Statistics • Mortality rates by race	Macro	
	USDA Food Access Research Atlas • Food desert map		
Supplemental texts	National media and reports • USDA report on *Household Food Security in the U.S.*		

Table 3B Everybody Eats Data Guide: Chapter 4—The Downtown Greensboro Food Truck Pilot Project (2012)

Data Type	Data Source	Level of Analysis	Hours, Pages, and Participants
Interviews and surveys	DGI downtown restaurant survey • 40 pretest surveys • 23 posttest surveys	Micro	• 933 public comments • 32 City Council public comments • 44 hours of observation • ≈ 175 pages of field notes • ≈ 110 pages of online and traditional media coverage • ≈ 50 pages of formal policy text and City Council meeting transcripts • Over 1000 participants • 3 reports produced
	DGI community survey • 458 public comments		
	CST on-site surveys and interviews • 151 public comments		
	CST online surveys • 261 public comments		
Observations	Food Truck Pilot Project • 19 observations @ 2 hours each		
Formal meetings	Greensboro City Council meetings • 9/4/2012; 10 public comments • 11/7/2012; 22 public comments	Meso	
Formal policy texts	Greensboro Land Development Ordinance, Table 8-1 and Section 30-8-10.4 – Mobile Vendors		
Supplemental texts	Let's Roll Food Truck blog posts • 38 posts during pilot test	Macro	
	Media coverage • 8 local news stories about the pilot test from *Yes!Weekly, WXII, WFMY,* and others • 8 national media stories about food truck culture from *New York Times,* the *Food Network,* and others		

Table 3C Everybody Eats Data Guide: Chapter 5—The Warnersville Community Garden (2011–2019)

Data Type	Data Source	Level of Analysis	Hours, Pages, and Participants
Participant observations	Garden meetings • 16 garden meetings (2012–17)	Micro	• 128 hours of participant observation
	Garden work days • 24 work days (sampled; 2012–16)		
Interviews and surveys	Community interest survey • 133 surveys		• ≈ 900 pages of field notes and email exchanges
Supplemental texts	Support documents • Education materials from County Cooperative Extension and NC Department of Agriculture	Meso	• 133 surveys
Supplemental texts	Support documents • Education materials from model programs, including Growing Home	Macro	• ≈ 125 pages of educational materials • Over 250 participants

Table 3D   Everybody Eats Data Guide: Chapter 6—The Mobile Oasis Farmers
Market (2011–2017)

Data Type	*Data Source*	*Level of Analysis*	*Hours, Pages, and Participants*
Participant observation	Warnersville Farmers Market • 28 pop-up markets (total; 2011-13)	Micro	• 307 hours of participant observation
	Mobile Oasis Farmers Market • 65 observations (sampled; 2014-16)		• ≈ 1200 pages of field notes and email exchanges
Interviews and surveys	Warnersville Farmers Market • 71 customer interest surveys		• 948 customers tracked for return visits
	Mobile Oasis Farmers Market • 151 pretest surveys • 30 posttest surveys		• ≈ 75 pages of supplemental materials and support documents
Tracking and monitoring	Farm Fan App • Tracked return visits for 948 people		
Supplemental texts	Local Media Coverage • 18 local news articles on the Mobile Oasis from *Triad City Beat, Greensboro News & Record*, and others		• Over 1200 participants
Formal policies	Greensboro Land Development Ordinance, Table 8-1 and Section 30-8-10.4—Mobile Vendors	Meso	
Community health data	USDA Support Documents • Food Access Research Atlas • Food and Nutrition Services website	Macro	
Supplemental texts	National media and reports • Followed similar mobile market programs, including the Veggie Van out of Buffalo, NY		

Table 3E   Everybody Eats Data Guide: Chapter 7—Ethnosh (2013–2019)

Data Type	Data Source	Level of Analysis	Hours, Pages, and Participants
Stories	Ethnosh stories and photographs • 39 stories with accompanying photos	Micro	• 117 pages of Ethnosh stories and photographs
Observations a interviews	NoshUp event observations • 8 NoshUp events		• 20 hours of participant observation
	Restaurant interviews • 1 interview with Bangkok Café		
Supplemental texts	Local media coverage • Local news articles from *Greensboro News & Record*, *Yes!Weekly*, and *Triad City Beat*		• 40 pages of field notes • 80 pages of media coverage
Supplemental texts	Extended media coverage • News article about Ethnosh: Dayton	Meso	• Over 50 participants
Supplemental texts	Media coverage: international food • News articles and online media about writing and international cuisine	Macro	

Table 3F   Everybody Eats Data Guide: Chapter 8—Kitchen Connects GSO
(2016–2019)

Data Type	Data Source	Level of Analysis	Hours, Pages, and Participants
Surveys and interviews	Kitchen Connects participant surveys • 192 application surveys • 58 exit interviews • 54 6-month follow-up surveys	Micro	• 304 surveys and interviews • 34 hours of program observations
Observations	Process observations • 4 training class observations • 2 kitchen observations • 12 vending observations		• 40 pages of field notes
Supplemental texts	Outreach materials • Kitchen Connects website • Kitchen Connects Facebook page		• 20 pages of policy text • 20 pages of supplemental text
Formal policy text	Local food policy • Greensboro *Fresh Food Access* Plan	Meso	• 200 participants
Supplemental texts	General media coverage • Websites and articles related to model programs	Macro	

Table 3G   Everybody Eats Data Guide: Chapter 9—The Guilford Food Council
(2012–2019)

Data Type	Data Source	Level of Analysis	Hours, Pages, and Participants
Participant observation	Food Council meetings • 7 planning meetings (2013) • 20 task force meetings (2014–15) • 12 food council meetings (2015–19)	Micro	• 117 hours of participant observation • ≈ 350 pages of field notes and meeting minutes
Formal texts	Food Council charters • policy documents from model programs in North Carolina	Meso	• ≈ 500 pages of supplement and formal texts
Supplemental texts	Support documents • web-based documents from Community food strategies and other food council support networks	Macro	• Over 150 participants

Table 3H   Everybody Eats Data Guide: Chapter 10—Renaissance Community Co-op
(2011–2019)

Data Type	Data Source	Level of Analysis	Hours, Pages, and Participants
Participant observation	Observations and interviews • Attendance at 4 owner meetings • RCC grand opening event • 4 key stakeholder interviews	Micro	• 12 hours of participant observation • 25 pages of field notes • ≈ 250 pages of formal and supplemental texts • 4 interviews • 12 direct participants • More than 1300 co-op owners
Formal texts	RCC media package • "More Than a Grocery Store" grand opening document • "We Want a Co-op" video		
	Publications • The Anatomy of a Failed Co-op webinar with *Non-Profit Quarterly*		
Supplemental texts	Local media coverage • 22 news stories with local media outlets including *Triad City Beat*, *WXII*, and the *Carolina Peacemaker*		
Supplemental texts	Transcripts from Greensboro City Council meetings	Meso	
Supplemental texts	Media coverage and research • Articles appearing in *Monthly Review* and *Vice*	Macro	

Table 4A   A Cast of Voices: Chapter 3—The Warnersville Community Food Task Force

Organizations	Voices	Position	Related Chapters
The Guilford County Department of Public Health (GDPH)	**Mark Smith**	Epidemiologist for Guilford County; 50s–60s, white, man	Chapters 5, 6, 9
	Laura Mrosla	Public health specialist; 30s–40s, white, woman	
	Janet Mayer	Registered dietician; 50s–60s, white, woman	
The Warnersville Community Coalition	**Otis Hairston**	Chair of the Warnersville Community Coalition, 60s, Black, man	Chapters 5, 6
	Cheryl Hood	Warnersville resident, 60s, Black, woman	
	Charles Peoples, Lisa Payne	A chorus of Black residents from the Warnersville community, 40s–50s	
Prince of Peace Lutheran Church	**Tim Gamelin**	Pastor at POPLC, 70s, white, man	Chapter 5, 9
	Hunter Haith	Church president at POPLC, 70s, Black, man	
Urban Harvest GSO	**Dawn Leonard**	Director of Urban Harvest, 30s, white, woman	Chapter 5
UNC-Greensboro	**Marianne LeGreco**	UNCG communication researcher, 30s, white, woman	Chapters 4–9
	Zithobile Nxumalo, Beth Archie	A chorus of students from various backgrounds	

NOTE: Bolded names denote individuals who feature prominently in the case study.

Table 4B A Cast of Voices: Chapter 4—The Downtown Greensboro Food Truck Pilot Project

Organizations	Voices	Position	Related Chapters
Greensboro Food Trucks	**Great Escape, Hickory Tree Turkey BBQ, Bandito Bodega, My Dream Cakes,** The Ice Queen, 1618	A chorus of food trucks with owners from various backgrounds	
Downtown restaurants	**Stumblestilskins, Natty Greene's,** Acropolis, Fisher's, Quizno's, Nico's	A chorus of restaurant owners in downtown Greensboro, from various backgrounds	
City of Greensboro	**Mary Vigue**	Assistant city manager; 40s, white, woman	Chapters 8–10
	Reggie Delahanty	City of Greensboro economic development coordinator, 30s, man	
City Council	**Robbie Perkins,** Yvonne Johnson, Nancy Vaughn, **Nancy Hoffman**	A chorus of city council members from various backgrounds	
Downtown Greensboro, Incorporated	**Ed Wolverton**	Director of DGI, 50s, white, man	
UNC-Greensboro	**Marianne LeGreco,** Eddie Chia, Ranata Reeder, Nichole Patino	See chapter 3	Chapters 3, 5–9
Community	**Cecelia Thompson**	Community leader, local blogger, 30s, white, woman	Chapter 7
	Margaret Winslow, Donovan McKnight, Katie Southard	A chorus of local residents; largely white, 20s–30s	

Table 4C A Cast of Voices: Chapter 5—The Warnersville Community Garden

Organizations	Voices	Position	Related Chapters
GDPH	**Mark Smith, Janet Mayer**	See chapter 3	Chapters 3, 6, 9
Prince of Peace Lutheran Church	**John Marion**	Garden manager, 50s, Black, man, physical disability	Chapters 3, 9
	Hunter Haith, Charles Peoples, **Lindora Rowell**	A chorus of Black church leaders, 50s–70s	
	Keyshawn McGirt, Amuarin Watkins, Beyon McGirt, TJ Boyd	A chorus of young, Black church members and garden volunteers	
Warnersville Community	**Otis Hairston**	See chapter 3	Chapters 3, 6
	Niesha Douglas	Warnersville community member and researcher; 30s, Black, woman	
	Lewvenia Parks, Anita Cunningham, Charles Peoples	A chorus of neighborhood leaders from various backgrounds	
Urban Harvest Greensboro	**Dawn Leonard**	Director of Urban Harvest; 30s, white, woman	Chapter 3
Vision Tree, CDC	**Matthew King**	Director of the City Oasis Project; 20s, Black, man	Chapter 6
	Brandon Norman	Coordinator of City Oasis Project; 20s, Black, man	
East Market Street, CDC	Phil Barnhill	Executive VP at East Market Street; 30s–40s, Black, man	Chapter 6
UNC-Greensboro	**Marianne LeGreco,** Patrick Pettiford, Ebony Brown	See chapter 3	Chapters 3–4, 6–9
Out of the Garden Project	Lily Emendy	Urban Teaching Farm manager; 20s–30s, white, woman	Chapter 8
	Don Milholin	Director of OOTGP; 50s, white, man	

Table 4D   A Cast of Voices: Chapter 6—The Mobile Oasis Farmers Market

Organizations	Voices	Position	Related Chapters
GDPH	**Mark Smith, Janet Mayer**	See chapter 3	Chapters 3, 5, 9
Warnersville Community	**Otis Hairston**	See chapter 3	Chapters 3, 5
	Niesha Douglas	See chapter 5	
	Lewvenia Parks	Market vendor; 40s, Black, woman	
	Anita Cunningham	Market volunteer; 40s, white, woman, legally blind	
	Valerie Jones, Adlois Shoffner	Community volunteers; 30s, Black, women	
UNC-Greensboro	**Marianne LeGreco,** Christina Blankenship, Derek Shaw, Hannah Hill	See chapter 3	Chapters 3–5, 7–9
Vision Tree, CDC	Matthew King, Brandon Norman	See chapter 5	Chapter 5
East Market Street, CDC	Phil Barnhill	See chapter 5	Chapter 5
Guilford County Cooperative Extension	John Ivey	Local foods coordinator; 40s, white, man	Chapters 8, 9
	Karen Neil	Director at Extension; 50s, white, woman	

Table 4E   A Cast of Voices: Chapter 7—Ethnosh

Organizations	Voices	Position	Related Chapters
Face-to-Face Greensboro	**Donovan McKnight**	Cofounder of Ethnosh; 30s, white, man	Chapter 4
Triad Local First	Luck Davidson	Cofounder of Ethnosh; 50s, white, woman	
Blue Zoom	**Alex McKinney**	Cofounder of Ethnosh; 30s, white, man	
Local writers	**Tina Firesheets,** Marianne LeGreco	Team of writers from various backgrounds	Chapters 3–6, 8–9
Local photographers	Carolyn DeBerry, **Dhanraj Emanuel, Youngdoo Carey**	Team of writers from various backgrounds	
Ethnosh restaurants	**Pho Hien Vuong, Bangkok Café, Jerusalem Market, Ghassan's, Taaza Indian Bistro, Rice Paper Vietnamese, Taste of Ethiopia, Thai Corner Kitchen, Boba House**	A chorus of international restaurants in Greensboro from a variety of backgrounds; largely immigrant and family-owned	

Table 4F   A Cast of Voices: Chapter 8—Kitchen Connects GSO

Organizations	Voices	Position	Related Chapters
City of Greensboro	Russ Clegg	Planning director; 40–50s, white, man	
Greensboro Farmers Curb Market	**Lee Mortenson**	Market director; 40s, white, woman	
	Angie Blomer, Ashlee Furr	Project managers; 40s, white, women	
Out of the Garden Project	**Don Milholin**	See Chapter 5	Chapter 5
Guilford County Cooperative Extension	John Ivey	See Chapter 6	Chapters 6, 9
	Vincent Webb	Education agent at Extension; 20s, Black, man	
UNC-Greensboro CHCS	**Stephen Sills**	Director at CHCS; 40s, white, man	
	Marianne LeGreco	See Chapter 3	Chapters 3–7, 9
Local food vendors	**Fermentology, Empasta, PaleoLove, Poppy's Pickles**	A chorus of participants in the Kitchen Connects program; from a variety of backgrounds	

Table 4G A Cast of Voices: Chapter 9—The Guilford Food Council

Organizations	Voices	Position	Related Chapters
Guilford Food Council	**Marianne LeGreco**	See Chapter 3	Chapters 3–8
	Julie Lapham	Community member; 70s, white, woman	
	Janet Mayer	See Chapter 3	Chapters 3, 5–6
	Annie Martinie	Community member, Healthy Carolinians; white, woman	
	Odile Huchette	Director, Urban Horticulture at NCA&T; 30–40s, white, woman	
	John Ivey, N'gai Dickerson, Niesha Douglas, Shannon Axtell Martin, Phil Fleischman, George Smith, Joel Landau, Stephen Johnson, Channelle James, Beth Kizhnerman, Helen Robare, Sheri Vettel, Caitlin Romm	A chorus of community members who contributed to Food Council organizing; from a variety of backgrounds	Chapter 3, 5–8
Greater High Point Food Alliance	**Carl Vierling**	Director at GHPFA; 60s, white, man	
	Joe Blosser	Faculty member at High Point University; 30s, white, man	
Greensboro Community Food Task Force	**Jamal Fox**	City council; 20s–30s, Black, man	
	Phil Fleischman	Greensboro Parks & Rec; 30s–40s, white, man	
	Britt Huggins	Greensboro Parks & Rec; 20s–30s, white, man	

Table 4H A Cast of Voices: Chapter 10— Renaissance Community Co-op

Organizations	Voices	Position
Northeast Greensboro	**Concerned Citizens of Northeast Greensboro (CCNG)**	Community group comprising NE Greensboro residents
	Citizens for Economic and Environmental Justice (CEEJ)	Community group comprising NE Greensboro residents and other young leaders
	Goldie Wells	Resident & city councilperson; 60s–70s, Black, woman
	Neighborhood residents	A chorus of residents who live and shop in the neighborhood; from largely Black, working class backgrounds
RCC Board of Directors	**Roodline Volcy**	Board president; 20s–30s, Black, woman
	Casey Thomas	Founding board member; 20s–30s, Black, woman
	John Jones, Eleanor Graves, Erik Fink, Tony Davies, Floyd Guidry, Mo Kessler, Charles Spencer, Leo Steward	A chorus of members from the founding board of the RCC
Fund for Democratic Communities	**Marnie Thompson**	Codirector; 50s, white, woman
	Ed Whitfield	Codirector; 50s, Black, man
	Sohnie Black	F4DC Staff; 50s, Black, woman
Greater Greensboro Community	**Alyzza May, Eric Ginsburg, Michael Roberto, Yasmine Regester**	A chorus of local writers, academics, former F4DC staffers, and volunteers

PART II Engaging Communities

CASE STUDIES

Communicating food justice involves routinely convening, and perhaps more importantly, reconvening people in meaningful and productive ways. Engaging communities emphasizes the social aspects of social justice organizing and activism, particularly the ways we engage people in conversation around advocating for change, building community infrastructure, reorganizing markets, and imagining more equitable structures of governance.[1] As a necessary part of organizing communities around food justice, partners need spaces to synthesize information from multiple sources, share stories, and build communication infrastructure. Drawing inspiration from a communication-centered approach to social justice, Johnson further clarified, "To be social, one must be 'doing' something with others."[2] Useful models of dialogue, community facilitation, and public deliberation abound in the communication literature regarding social justice organizing, advocacy, and activism.[3] By centering communication with communities, these models often prioritize key concepts—such as structure, agency, and culture.[4] Alongside these are key practices—such as the work between communication researchers, oppressed communities, and activist organizations to disrupt unjust discourses and material conditions and develop interventions to create more equitable systems.[5]

Part II grounds food justice organizing and activism in two key communication processes related to engaging communities in dialogue and action: integrating participation from multiple stakeholders and navigating food policy. In chapter 3, we introduce you to the Warnersville Community Food Task Force—by many accounts one of the earlier community-engaged and multi-partnered efforts to address food insecurity in Greensboro. The task force included health agents from the Guilford County Department of Public Health, members of the Warnersville Community Coalition, local nonprofit organizations, members of the larger Greensboro community, and communication researchers. We also feature the Downtown Greensboro Food Truck Pilot Project in chapter 4. As an example of engaging everyday people in public deliberation around food policy, this chapter also reinforces our commitment to studying larger conversations around food systems, without focusing only on food insecurity. The Food Truck Pilot Project demonstrates how engaging communities in policy talk enables and constrains how those communities can work together to reorganize markets and increase access to opportunities within local food systems.

3 The Warnersville Community Food Task Force

With Dr. Mark Smith

We open on a meeting with Mark Smith, epidemiologist for the County Department of Public Health, and Dawn Leonard, director of Urban Harvest Greensboro, alongside Marianne and a graduate student from UNCG. We're sitting in the Green Bean, a local coffee shop in downtown Greensboro. It's November 24th, 2010, at 8:30 in the morning, and it's finally starting to get cold outside. Every story starts somewhere, and Marianne considers this meeting the point where her food story starts in Greensboro. This opening narrative is written from her perspective.

Mark mentioned that he invited us to meet, because he'd seen a local Fox8 news story about the work Urban Harvest was doing to start an urban farm in the Warnersville neighborhood of Greensboro. Urban Harvest was in the early stages of launching an effort to turn unused greenspace into urban farm space—a place to grow food in neighborhoods that did not always have easy access to fresh and local foods. I started partnering with the Urban Harvest team to provide some research and grant support, as well as to connect my students with opportunities to work with community food programs. We had recently hit a dead end with a piece of property in the Warnersville neighborhood, having learned it was a brown field that couldn't grow food safely without expensive land remediation. The timing of Mark's invitation was unexpected but also rather auspicious.

In his role as epidemiologist for the county, Mark had been working with the Healthy Carolinians program to assess needs and to set goals to improve people's health across North Carolina and in Guilford County. During a community health assessment meeting held in Greensboro, community gardens and urban farms had emerged as resources that Warnersville residents wanted in their neighborhood to improve access to healthy food. In an effort to translate the assessment into actionable ideas, Mark invited us to partner in developing some community-based food programs. He was working with community leaders to assemble a task force to consider the possibilities for not only a community garden or urban farm, but also a farmers market and even a community store. At the time of our meeting, membership included local residents and neighborhood leaders, parents and teachers from a nearby elementary school, the director of the recreation center, and neighborhood church representatives. As he explained:

> We had a meeting with groups from Warnersville about developing the task force to take the next steps. Thirty people came to that meeting, and fifteen said they wanted to be a part of the task force. Now we have a need to get with more people from the neighborhood who can take ownership and keep it sustainable. Our role now is to say, "Here are the resources we can bring; now what are you as a community willing to spearhead?"

The emphasis on community-driven leadership and ownership of local food aligned nicely with what both Urban Harvest and I wanted to create in Greensboro. Although we had knowledge about urban farms and communication research, our role was not to tell communities what they needed to do. Rather, we wanted to harmonize resources that could help communities accomplish their own goals.

"Your timing is rather fortuitous," I responded to Mark. "We've recently learned that we can't farm the greenspace we were looking at in Warnersville without about $500,000 in land remediation. So we're interested in reaching out further into the community to see where the momentum is." I explained that Dawn and I had done some early work to engage various groups in Warnersville. Along with some of my students, we attended a handful of local church services and community meetings—attempting to build some connections with residents from the neighborhood. At the same time, we felt like we hadn't quite found the right stakeholders to truly gauge community buy-in. "It sounds like you've tapped into something important in the neighborhood," I continued. "Do you think you've got something that Urban Harvest, my students, and I could join without disrupting what you've already started?"

"I do," Mark replied. "What if you all come to the next meeting in February, and we'll see where it goes from there?"

. . . . .

A CASE STUDY OF ENGAGING COMMUNITIES
TO CONFRONT FOOD (IN)SECURITY

At the heart of engaging everyday people in communicating food justice is a commitment to community. This opening story matters, not only because it highlights Marianne's point of entry into the narratives of food activism and advocacy in Greensboro, but primarily because it reinforces a crucial feature of communicating food justice. Engaging communities in food justice organizing requires creating multiple spaces for different and diverse individuals and organizations to participate in creating food systems, as well as prioritizing community leadership whenever possible. Even the earliest conversations among partners emphasized this responsibility to ground our work in the needs, leadership, and capacity of community members.

The Warnersville Community Food Task Force was assembled in 2010 to work alongside the Guilford County Department of Public Health on a community health assessment. The Warnersville neighborhood is Greensboro's first African American neighborhood and has a long history of community engagement and activism. Residents also experience some of the highest health disparities in Greensboro, particularly around heart disease, diabetes, and other diet-related illnesses. Through an interactive and engaged process, community members generated four key ideas to begin to address these health disparities: increased access to community gardens, a farmers market, a community store, and opportunities for physical activity. The task force's responsibility was to begin building a strategic plan to prioritize and implement those ideas, as well as to identify leaders and members from the community with the capacity to organize in the long term.

This case focuses on the process of integrating multiple perspectives in order to move from generating ideas to implementing feasible practices. With regard to the guiding questions we first outlined in chapter 2, our opening case study most specifically addresses our first two questions: What counts as community? And how do communities organize to ensure that everybody eats? We draw from literatures related to communication activism and public advocacy, especially as community members were given space to construct the dialogue, challenge expertise, assert their own ideas about food in their communities, and articulate their own levels of commitment. We also include contributions from Mark Smith, the now-retired epidemiologist for Guilford County, who organized several early conversations around food insecurity in Warnersville.

Identifying the Early Signs of Food Hardship

Four years before Greensboro appeared in the top four on the Food Research and Action Center's list of communities experiencing food hardship, numerous local partners—perhaps most importantly, our county's epidemiologist—noticed the early signs of food hardship in Greensboro and Guilford County. In 2009, as part of Guilford County's Community Health Assessment (CHA) cycle, Mark Smith started tracking diet-related illnesses and poverty rates across white and Black communities in Guilford County. Using information from the North Carolina State Center for Health Statistics, the US Census, and available Geographic Information Systems (GIS) maps, Mark worked to identify potential health disparities and translate complicated health data into conversation starters with numerous communities and partners. He also coupled his findings alongside food access. Even before the US Department of Agriculture began mapping food deserts, Mark noted at least eight different neighborhoods, which he identified by census tract, with high poverty rates and few grocery stores or supermarkets. Table 5 offers a snapshot of the indicators that Mark shared when he initiated conversations with health agencies,

Table 5 Neighborhood Poverty Indicators, 2009–2010.

Census Tract	Population	% Poverty	% Black	% Unemployed	% Receiving SNAP
010702	6,048	33.2	20.2	5.0	4.1
011101	3,590	32.3	85.3	12.2	25.5
011102	2,643	31.5	99.1	9.3	25.5
011200	4,826	49.1	85.5	9.8	32.4
011400	3,836	57.7	86.7	16.4	47.3
011602	3,387	34.2	33.1	13.6	21.2
012706	3,092	23.2	89.6	7.3	18.7
012707	2,659	34.4	67.8	10.9	19.5

SOURCE: Guilford County Department of Health and Human Services.

educational institutions, and community members. He regularly high-lighted census tract 011400, which mapped out directly on top of the Warnersville neighborhood in Greensboro.

Warnersville has the distinction of being Greensboro's first planned African American neighborhood, and it has historically been a source of prosperity for the Black middle class and civil rights advocacy. Its residents in 2009 now faced the highest poverty and unemployment rates in Greensboro, alongside the highest eligibility for Supplemental Nutrition Assistance Program (SNAP) benefits. Mark regularly communicated these numbers along with supermarket and grocery store proximity to justify his focus on food access as it related to poverty. Figure 3 illustrates an early food access map that he shared as part of identifying the early signs of food hardship. The Warnersville neighborhood is the darkly shaded census tract at the center of the map, one of two communities in Greensboro with the highest concentrations of poverty. The map clearly shows a scarcity of supermarket access in Southeast Greensboro and a complete absence of stores in the Warnersville neighborhood. The underlying argument suggests that limited access to fresh foods, including fruits and vegetables, makes it increasingly difficult for low-income individuals and families to eat in a way that prioritizes health.

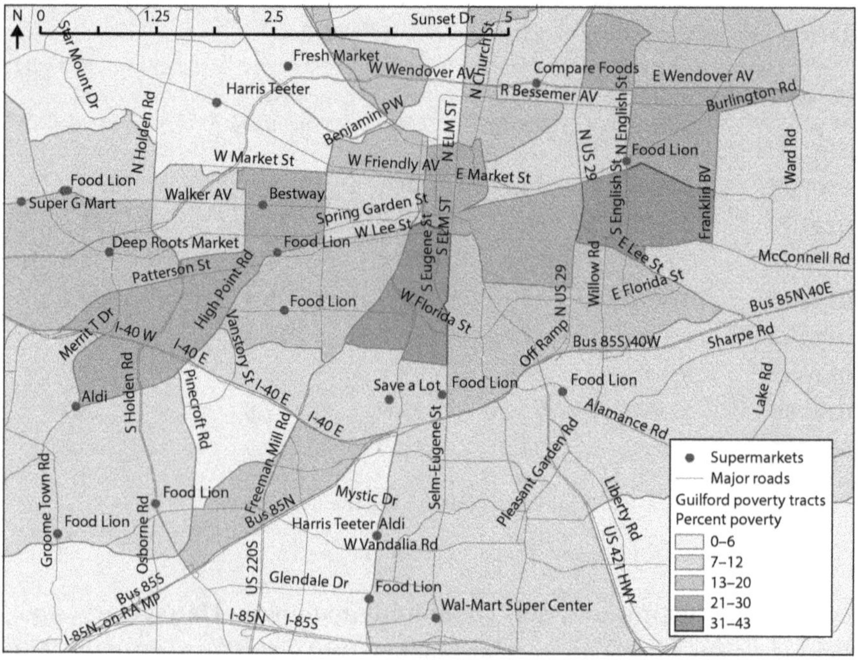

Figure 3. Supermarket and grocery store access in SE Greensboro, 2009. This image shows high concentrations of poverty and limited food access in Greensboro's Warnersville neighborhood (center) and the Cottage Grove neighborhood (right). Image credit: Mark Smith.

In what became a discursively savvy move on his part, Mark added a final piece to the data puzzle around gaps in food access. He linked poverty and access directly to chronic diseases and diet-related illnesses. Rather than always emphasizing obesity rates or body mass index (BMI), Mark turned to county-level data on deaths due to diet-related illnesses including heart-disease, stroke, and diabetes. Table 6 provides a comparison across white and Black communities regarding the top four causes of death in Guilford County. We have included the numbers from subsequent years for additional context, but the initial conversations focused on the data from 2005 to 2009 and eventually 2008 to 2012. By including these numbers as part of the conversation, Mark not only made a statistical case for focusing on food in Warnersville, but he also made some

Table 6 Guilford County Chronic Disease Mortality Rates by Race, per 100,000

Cause of Death	White (Age-Adjusted)				Black (Age-Adjusted)			
	2005–09	2008–12	2011–15	2014–18	2005–09	2008–12	2011–15	2014–18
Heart disease	154.7	147.0	135.4	127.8	205.9	180.4	173.9	165.3
Cancer	162.0	164.0	156.8	151.2	209.4	194.5	181	177.2
Stroke	40.4	39.0	37.2	39.7	57.8	53.1	53.4	54.1
Diabetes	12.1	11.8	15.5	18.8	39.4	30.6	33.2	37.8

Although the table illustrates that rates for heart disease and stroke have improved for both communities, it also demonstrates that deaths due to diabetes are increasing, and the disparities between white and Black communities are sometimes widening. For example, between 2008 and 2012, Blacks were 20.2 percent more likely than whites to die of heart disease. The overall numbers have decreased since that measure, but between 2011 and 2015, the disparity between white and Black communities widened to 28.4 percent and has remained fairly constant since then. Source: NC State Center for Health Statistics, County Health Databook.

initial discursive connections between food access, race, and diet-related illnesses.

The maps and numbers paint a complicated picture—one that emphasizes reducing the disparities around diet-related illnesses through improving food access and community-oriented intervention. In many ways, Mark's research provided a critical point of departure for organizing the early conversations around food insecurity and food access in Greensboro and Guilford County. Certainly, his coordination of data analysis and practices of community health assessment helped frame the early conversations regarding food insecurity and food hardship around key concepts, including access, poverty, diet-related illnesses, and community. How we use talk and text—that is, discourse—to frame concepts like food insecurity and community gives shape and form to the scope of the issue, the possibilities for creativity and change, and the kinds of voices that are included in the conversation.[1] Identifying the early signs of food hardship gave multiple partners—including those from the community and local health agencies—necessary resources to begin engaging in public advocacy and dialogue around food security in Greensboro neighborhoods.

But our food security story grew out of Warnersville, which is where we turn our attention next.

Hanging In with Warnersville

The Warnersville community has a proud history. The neighborhood was established in 1865, when a Quaker man named Yardley Warner purchased just over thirty-five acres of land south of downtown Greensboro. He divided the land into plots, with the express purpose of creating a space where newly freed slaves could purchase land and build a community. As Warnersville historians Dr. Johnny and Brenda Hodge wrote, "It was the first black community in the county where people could own their own homes, build their own churches, own land, run their own businesses and educate their own children."[2] The historical relevance of Warnersville to the city of Greensboro was similar to that of "Black Wall Street" in Tulsa, Oklahoma—an all-Black economic hub that thrived in the early 1900s as the United States forged a new identity after the Civil War.

Warnersville became a model for self-sufficient Black communities across the Southeastern United States.[3] Residents frequently recalled local businesses and a movie theater that lined Ashe Street, one of the main roadways that runs through the heart of the neighborhood. A handful of lifelong residents would also tell you about the J.C. Price School—the neighborhood elementary school atop a hill on the northwest corner of Warnersville, just as you crossed the border from the neighboring Glenwood community. As the civil rights movement also gained momentum, the Warnersville neighborhood would also produce activists including Otis Hairston Sr., the pastor at Shiloh Baptist Church, and Jibreel Khazan (born Ezell Blair Jr.), one of the North Carolina A&T State University Greensboro Four who led the first lunch counter sit-ins against racial segregation at the local Woolworth store in downtown Greensboro. In short, the Warnersville neighborhood served as a thriving example of Black prosperity in Greensboro.

Much of that changed in the 1960s. During a period of federally funded Urban Renewal between 1950 and 1966, local municipalities were given access to federal dollars in order to invest in impoverished neighborhoods, affordable housing, and urban infrastructure. Because of the program, we gained many things—like the Lincoln Center in New York City and nationwide investment in universities and hospitals. But we also lost a lot, especially in terms of progress in Black neighborhoods and communities. In some instances, entire neighborhoods were demolished in order to build new housing, but not all options were the same. Across many large cities, Greensboro included, Black residents were pushed to move to public housing and rental units, whereas white residents were given pathways to invest in becoming homeowners.[4] The Digital Scholarship Lab (DSL) at the University of Richmond has mapped the major cities and neighborhoods most negatively affected by displacement and inequality through urban renewal.[5] Greensboro has two neighborhoods on their map. One of them is Warnersville.

In 1965, Warnersville was razed. Established businesses and above-standard homes were lumped in with abandoned structures and substandard housing when the neighborhood was marked by the City as "an area of blight" in order to receive federal funds. Almost the entire community was demolished to make way for a handful of new homes and an influx of rental units and public housing. As Preservation Greensboro explained, "The process was so thorough that only the J.C. Price School and Union Cemetery survived destruction."[6] Whereas the narrative in Warnersville had once been about ensuring that Black residents had access to resources in order to build self-sufficient communities, the neighborhood's story had changed. The J.C. Price School closed in 1983, many families moved or were relocated to different neighborhoods, and local businesses chose new communities to serve. As roadways and city infrastructure further changed around the neighborhood, opportunities for growth and progress migrated elsewhere. And Warnersville became a somewhat forgotten piece of Greensboro.

Yet Warnersville has remained resilient. In 2015, the City of Greensboro designated Warnersville the first Heritage Community in North Carolina, a distinction they bestowed because the neighborhood is not eligible for the National Register of Historic Places. Too few of the buildings from the original neighborhood still stand for Warnersville to qualify. The neighborhood also celebrated its 150th anniversary with a special exhibit at the Greensboro Historical Museum and a three-day community festival.[7] Many residents—particularly those who had grown up in the neighborhood—remained committed to their activist roots. In 2007, they organized to keep nearby Greensboro College from building a sports complex on the J.C. Price School property. Some community members also fought—albeit in vain—to save the school, which was purchased by the Salvation Army in 2014, demolished, and replaced by a Boys and Girls Club.

Although Warnersville had remained a resilient community that valued the endurance of its history and residents, those residents also faced some alarming disparities in 2009—especially those related to poverty and access to food options. When Mark started reaching out to key leaders in the community, members of neighborhood associations like the Warners-ville Community Coalition were in need of some community and agency partners who could hang in with them as they asked some hard questions about health and food. The neighborhood had seen well-meaning partners come and go, and its residents were looking for people who were commit-ted to translating ideas into action. Alongside the Guilford County Depart-ment of Public Health, community members and partners embarked on a community health assessment and planning process that would lead to the creation of a three-acre urban farm and a mobile farmers market. But a crucial step in building the trust needed to engage members of the War-nersville community required recognizing both the proud traditions and problematic history of the neighborhood, particularly because residents had little reason to trust city and county agencies, researchers, and well-meaning partners.

ASSESSING COMMUNITY HEALTH AND CAPACITY

Equipped with a sense of the early signs of food hardship and a ground-ing in the history and current climate of the Warnersville neighborhood, a loose coalition of partners began to form that would eventually become the Warnersville Community Food Task Force. When Urban Harvest and Marianne joined the conversation in November 2010, engagement with the neighborhood was well underway. Earlier that year, the Guilford County Department of Public Health and faculty from the University of North Carolina at Chapel Hill (UNC-CH) partnered with the Warnersville Community Coalition to host a series of community dialogues about food access. Using questions from the Community Healthy Living Index (CHLI) as conversation starters, their organizational process brought together research expertise with community service experience and neighborhood voices to assess structural barriers and opportunities related to health in Warnersville.[8]

Community members highlighted several key structural barriers to living with fewer chronic diseases. These constraints included a lack of health and wellness programming, particularly geared toward adults; no neighborhood grocery stores or supermarkets; convenience stores that did not carry healthy food options; and limited availability of foods from alternative sources like farmers markets, community gardens, and school-based programs. But these conversations also carried with them an opportunity to name some of the assets in the Warnersville community, especially those that served as an avenue for working through some of their barriers. For example, residents were quick to identify both the J.C. Price School and the Warnersville Recreation Center as potential sites for farmers markets, community stores, and cooking classes. The parent of a student at Jones Elementary School noted that the new principal was particularly interested in food and nutrition programs and community gardens, which opened a pathway for school-based activities. The pastor and church president from Prince of Peace Lutheran Church, which sat on three-acres of farmable land just south of the J.C. Price School, attended meetings to inform community members that their land could be transformed into an urban farm.

The community meetings culminated in a conversation on November 22, 2010, that brought participants from the previous meetings together to prioritize ideas and identify potential members for a community task force. Thirty community members attended this final gathering, where they selected community gardens and urban farms, farmers markets, a community store, and opportunities for physical activity as their top choices. Perhaps just as important as naming those priorities, the final meeting also created the space to consider the future of these ideas through a community task force. Participants were invited to join organizers from the County Department of Public Health, the Warnersville Community Coalition, and local research universities to continue the work through the Warnersville Community Food Task Force. Fifteen of the community members in attendance expressed an interest in joining and agreed to attend a follow-up meeting with some additional partners.

The November conversation also gave early partners an opportunity to ask some needed questions about the leadership and organizing capacity of Warnersville residents when it came to activism and advocacy around food systems and food insecurity. Up to this point, the strongest community voices had come from the Warnersville Community Coalition, and Otis Hairston Jr., in particular. Like his father, Otis was also a key participant in Greensboro's civil rights movement. Although he enthusiastically supported developing neighborhood food resources—especially at the J.C. Price School—he was also eager to cultivate new voices from within the community to take the lead here. But the interest in leadership and organizing had not emerged as clearly as the general interest in seeing farmers markets and community gardens developed within the neighborhood. Consider the following comment from a prospective task force member:

> I really like what everyone is trying to do here, and I will tell everyone when that farmers market gets up and running. But I just had surgery on one shoulder, and they're about to do the other one. So I don't know how much help I'm going to be—I mean, I can't be planting vegetables, and setting up tables, and things like that.

Even residents who wanted to be a part of the task force recognized that they could advocate for more food resources at these community meetings, but they also expressed concern about their capacity, expertise, and commitment when it came to growing and selling food.

These concerns were not isolated to a handful of community members, and the fledgling task force would need to contend with some realities about the community makeup of Warnersville. More specifically, early engagement in Warnersville led partners to two general types of community members—those who lived in family-owned homes and those who lived in public housing like Hampton Homes. The former were often elderly, with many of them in their late sixties to early eighties, and they spoke of physical limitations they faced when it came to growing and selling food. At the same time, they were also more likely to attend community meetings and were genuinely committed to advocating for health resources in their neighborhood. The latter were often more difficult to engage in regular and routine ways, as their public housing situation was sometimes temporary. There were several occasions across numerous engagement efforts when residents attended one event, only to have moved out of Warnersville by the next meeting.

Even more so, early partners also learned quickly that the neighborhood itself did not always speak with a unified or organized voice. When partners first started engaging community members in conversation about food access, they encountered two different community groups—the Warnersville Community Coalition and the Warnersville Beautification and Historical Society. Each group was led by different voices and frequently pursued different priorities. Such features of the Warnersville community brought into sharp relief one of the major challenges of engaging communities in food justice activism. Community engagement and action planning models often privilege the role of community members in leading and organizing activist efforts; however, "the community" is not always a monolithic entity with a shared perspective and unified goals. As with any organized group, communities are made up of a composite of people with some overlapping goals but also varying and divergent interests. We frequently turned to other communication models, particularly those that recognized the diverse knowledge and expertise that is required from multiple partners.[9] As the food justice work in Warnersville transitioned to the task force, the remaining partners would have to decide both what counted as "community" in translating ideas into practice, and in what ways would that community be involved in the various food justice activism efforts that emerged.

Transitioning as a Task Force

The purpose of the Warnersville Community Food Task Force served to translate what the community and Public Health partners learned through the assessment process into a feasible plan for developing health and wellness resources in the neighborhood. Between November 2010 and the first follow-up meeting on February 11, 2011, the task force list had grown from fifteen to forty people. That list included twenty Warnersville residents, four Guilford County health and agricultural representatives, four members of local churches, two parents from Jones Elementary, the director of the Warnersville Recreation Center, and a handful of local food advocates and nonprofit representatives. During this time, the task force members recognized that the type of work was changing; therefore, the makeup of partners needed to change. The research team from UNC–Chapel Hill had committed to this project only through the community health assessment stage, so the overall leadership was now primarily in the hands of the Guilford County Department of Public Health and the Warnersville Community Coalition. At this point, both Urban Harvest and Marianne joined the task force and started regularly attending meetings at the February 11 convening.

At that February 11 meeting of the Warnersville Community Food Task Force, the primary goal was to socialize the members as to the history of work that got us to this point and review the ideas and data gathered during the assessment stage. The bigger moves were made during a meeting on March 31, 2011. Task force members were asked to refine and prioritize six possible ideas or programs that they could put in motion: a community store, a mobile farmers market, a healthy food choice initiative at Jones Elementary School, a community garden/urban farm, a school garden, or a neighborhood walking program. From that conversation, members chose to prioritize the community garden/urban farm and mobile farmers market ideas, and they agreed to continue researching the community store and neighborhood walking programs.[10] The March 31 meeting also marked a key moment when task force members expressed the need to begin moving forward on some of these ideas and plans. As one member stated, "we've been talking a lot about the data and the assessment, and this is the third meeting where we've just talked about some of these things. I think we're all ready to start doing. Let's plant some seeds in the ground or something!"

This transition proved to be a crucial moment in moving the garden and market forward, because it forced us to identify who would actually build the garden, grow the food, and create the market. In other words, how would the task force move from merely visioning a garden and farmers market to seeing the results in the community? The task force continued to meet at the Warnersville Recreation Center, but the focus of the meetings quickly changed. We divided into two working groups, with a "garden group" led by partners from the Health Department, Urban Harvest, and Prince of Peace Lutheran Church, and a "market group" led by partners from the Community Coalition, Urban Harvest, and Marianne providing research support from UNC-Greensboro.

The activities during the meetings also changed. Not only did meetings provide a space where partners could make decisions and strategize the future of a garden and farmers market, they also became spaces to strengthen the momentum around growing and selling food in Warnersville. The garden group quickly moved toward organizing some smaller events, including a backyard container gardening class led by Urban Harvest. The purpose of which was to develop some health and wellness programming about growing fruits and vegetables, as well as to further engage community members about the possibilities for a garden in the neighborhood. Likewise, the market group began exploring opportunities to pilot test a farmers market in Warnersville before investing in a mobile unit that could serve numerous parts of Greensboro experiencing food hardship. Members visited local farms and farmers markets to recruit producers for a Warnersville test market, and they started researching how to upfit an old school bus or food truck to work as a mobile farmers market. These meetings would continue on like this throughout the remainder of 2011 and most of 2012, with the task force organizing a series of test farmers markets and gardening sessions alongside their decision-making and dialogues.

These early activities would eventually lead to the creation of the Warnersville Community Garden and the Mobile Oasis Farmers Market, whose stories we continue in chapters 5 and 6 of this book. But the story of the Warnersville Community Food Task Force was about to change dramatically. As the two working groups continued to connect the ideas generated during the assessment to the details required to implement a garden and market, several needs became immediately apparent. Prince of Peace Lutheran Church had emerged as an early task force partner that was able to provide the land to start a garden, but they did not have the financial capacity or the volunteer labor to do the work on their own. If the task force was going to move forward with both a community garden and a mobile farmers market, we would need materials to build the garden and a vehicle or food truck that could deliver healthier food options safely to the neighborhood. All of that would require funding, and the task force immediately began to research grants that could fund local food organizing and activism. Even more importantly, it would also require people—which meant ongoing community engagement and the socialization of new partners from both inside and outside the Warnersville neighborhood. Although the task force was off to an active and engaged start, many members realized that funding and ongoing community engagement would remain persistent challenges for the partners working with Warnersville.

And then everything changed. In the first year of its activity, the task force navigated three major setbacks that changed the makeup of the partners and the underlying community engagement model that guided our work. The first blow came shortly after the garden group had planted the first four garden beds—full of cabbage and broccoli—at Prince of Peace Lutheran Church. Our partners from Urban Harvest, facing some financial and workforce constraints, put their organization on permanent hiatus as they pursued other work opportunities. And the task force lost a key set of partners who brought needed expertise about growing and selling food. Six months later would bring the next setback, as Mark took the first of two unanticipated and extended medical leaves during the initial pilot tests of the garden and farmers market. And the task force lost, albeit temporarily, an organizational leader who brought several of the pieces together at a crucial time in the development of these projects.

The most significant blow came on October 11, 2012. Our primary connection to the Warnersville neighborhood—Otis Hairston Jr.—passed away very unexpectedly. We were in the midst of wrapping up a series of test markets, and both the garden and farmers market were on the verge of receiving funding to scale up our efforts. After navigating the departure of Urban Harvest and the absence of Mark, the task force had managed to hang together; however, Otis's death would mark a change in the task force as the partners had originally envisioned it. Otis was indeed a gatekeeper for the Warnersville community, and the loss of his leadership—and perhaps more importantly his commitment to cultivating new leaders and organizers from within the neighborhood—certainly left a gap in the task force. He introduced Niesha, whose story we tell more thoroughly in chapter 6, both to the garden and market projects and to Marianne. His loss was felt greatly across both the Warnersville neighborhood and the Greensboro community as a whole.

Although Mark would return to both the garden and market projects and the remaining partners would continue to work with various combinations of community members, nonprofit organizations, and City and County agencies, the emphasis on finding leadership from within the community had changed. We still prioritized community voices and organizing whenever possible, but our model of engagement began to focus more on the integration of partners from multiple perspectives and levels of expertise. These partners continued to meet as both the garden and market groups, and the work in Warnersville now resembled a multi-partnered project as opposed to the kind of community-capacity building that partners had originally envisioned. At the same time, we also recognized the value in what the Warnersville Community Food Task Force had done to move these ideas forward, and we remained hopeful for the garden and market interventions that were about to launch.

REFLECTIONS, RECOMMENDATIONS, AND RESOURCES

As the opening case study for our section on community engagement, we wanted to focus on the Warnersville Community Food Task Force because so much of our subsequent organizing and intervention work was rooted in the discourse that partners generated during these initial conversations. Between constructing a picture through the data, telling the story of Warnersville, and identifying needs and assets within the neighborhood, the task force members established priorities that would become a blueprint for other interventions and conversations around food security and food hardship in Greensboro and Guilford County. To conclude this case study, we offer some reflections, recommendations, and resources for researchers, organizations, and activists to consider as they engage communities around topics of food justice and food access. In appendix A, we also provide a copy of the *Warnersville Healthy Communities Project Proposal*, which was the intervention plan that grew out of the partnership in Warnersville.

Reflections

Our reflections on the Warnersville Community Food Task Force extend from two primary observations—the importance of data in launching a conversation and the need for ongoing engagement with numerous communities. Initially, the data created a discursive foundation to begin building partnerships, which gave way to project development and eventual funding opportunities. By finding the disparities in the data—namely, high rates of poverty and chronic health problems alongside a lack of access to healthy foods—Mark constructed a starting point to frame a conversation around food access. The data gave partners something to work with and make sense of as they identified needs and resources in their neighborhoods. For example, the Community Healthy Living Index (CHLI) to generate conversation around structural barriers and opportunities in Warnersville.[11] Discursively, this particular research tool was useful, because of how it emphasized structures and resources as opposed to advocating that people simply needed to eat more fruits and vegetables. The survey tool asked community members to rate statements like "Food stores in the community carry a variety of fresh vegetables and fruits of acceptable quality" and "Community parks offer on-site gardens and/or farmers markets" as a way not only to identify barriers, but also to start conversations about opportunities for organizing health and wellness programs in Warnersville.

As conversation starters, the data proved useful not only for the Warnersville neighborhood, but numerous communities that were interested in engaging their residents around health, food access, and poverty. The Cottage Grove neighborhood, the other darkly shaded neighborhood highlighted in Figure 3, also used Mark's data to generate local conversations and create community infrastructure to address health disparities.[12] Their partnership has produced resources including a community health clinic and neighborhood marketplace. Communicating social justice and food justice activism means identifying instances of food inequity around which communities can organize. Whenever partnerships can ground that work in communication theory, practice, and data, those partners are able to launch a more structured and focused set of conversations.[13] The Warnersville Community Food Task Force offers a clear illustration of using data, stories, and community history to do just that.

Additionally, we also want to emphasize the need for ongoing engagement in community-based and other forms of participatory research. As the early conversations about food access in Warnersville transitioned to the task force, partners may have initially underestimated the persistent communication required to maintain community engagement and activism.[14] After a strong start during the health assessment and idea generation stage, the partners regularly struggled to keep consistent participation at task force meetings—especially around key turning points such as moving from the needs-assessment stage to the task force, the departure of Urban Harvest, Mark's medical leave, and Otis's unexpected passing.

These turning points in the conversation frequently made that task force partners confront how the group defined community. Although voices from Warnersville residents were routinely prioritized, the community also included people who attended school, church, and work in the neighborhood. Engaging the "community" in Warnersville also meant creating spaces that respected the positions of the people who lived there while also realizing that many individuals, groups, and families had a stake in the health of that community. But conversations around what counts as community must always be revisited. Otis was particularly skilled at reminding partners of the need to cultivate new leadership from within the neighborhood, and he often raised concerns when too much of the organizing was in the hands of external partners. After his passing, the partners had to be much more intentional about how we invited the people of Warnersville into conversations about the garden and farmers market.

Social justice and community-engaged organizing requires strong narrative networks and communication infrastructure in order to maintain a conversation over time.[15] Partners must be prepared not only to convene community members in the early stages of a project, when the ideas are new and exciting, but also to reconvene people across the life of an intervention, when the work often becomes more tedious. This need to reengage communities throughout the process is one reason why the partners changed up our meeting strategy to include backyard container gardening sessions and pop-up farmers markets. As a way to maintain community momentum while the task force secured funding for the proposed garden and farmers market, these meetings infused some life into the conversation as we navigated our next steps.

Recommendations

Engaging communities in conversations to confront food (in)security is crucial to communicating food justice. Communicating with neighborhood networks and leaders to identify community needs should always be a first step to pursuing food security from a social justice perspective. In the spirit of the Warnersville Community Food Task Force, we offer the following recommendations:

1. "Anybody doing work in community needs to have humility."[16] We borrow this first recommendation from food activist Malik Yakini. He argued that when partners start working with communities, they need to learn the history, what they've tried before, what their aspirations are, and which leaders they listen to. Be prepared to take the time to do that work. Partners were meeting and building relationships with people in Warnersville for fifteen months before finalizing the plan for the garden and farmers market, and for almost four years before launching the Mobile Oasis.

2. Pair disparities in the data with stories from the community.[17] We join a chorus of communication scholars in emphasizing the importance of stories alongside statistics in communicating food justice activism. Although Mark's data on food access, poverty, and chronic health problems certainly opened up the conversation, it was learning the history of Warnersville and listening to community members highlight the assets of their neighborhood that gave the task force the foundation it needed to talk about food more directly.

3. Develop a flexible definition of community, but always remember that the people who live in the neighborhood must deal with the daily consequences—both positive and negative—of our organizing.

4. Respect when residents identify limitations within their neighborhood, both individual and structural, while continuing to value what they are able to contribute to the conversation. Although our initial goal was to develop interventions with neighborhood partners who could spearhead leadership from within the community, that goal was never fully realized. At the same time, thirty people from Warnersville helped produce a plan—and more partners emerged to help bring it to life. There is value to the way these different voices came together.

Resources

For researchers, organizations, and activists who are interested in engaging communities to confront food (in)security, we suggest the following resources:

Via Campesina: This organization's *Guide to Food Sovereignty* is a must-read for any organization or individual interested in working with communities around food justice and food sovereignty.[18]

Community Toolbox: When it comes to resources for creating community-based health and food interventions, Community Toolbox has developed the gold standard for helping organizers think about stories and data. They offer an extensive list of strategies for developing needs assessments, interview guides, surveys, and communication plans with a commitment to advocacy and activism.[19]

Community Healthy Living Index: This health assessment tool, also known as the CHLI, is available for free on the YMCA's website. It provides an evidence-based set of questions to help collect data about needs and resources in neighborhoods. These questions can also serve as discussion prompts at community meetings.[20]

USDA Community Food Security Assessment Toolkit: In addition to the CHLI, the USDA's food assessment toolkit also provides numerous resources for designing a local food assessment for neighborhoods and communities facing food insecurity.[21]

County Health Department: Most counties in the United States have a Department of Public Health or a Department of Health and Human Services. Many County Health Departments are required to construct a community health assessment every three years, which is how we got our start in Warnersville. Contacting a local Health Department may grant insight into current conversations about food (in)security.

Neighborhood Coalitions, Associations, and Places of Worship: Perhaps most importantly, neighborhood associations and community coalitions alongside local churches, synagogues, mosques, and other places of worship frequently serve as gateways into a neighborhood's stories about food.

4 The Downtown Greensboro Food Truck Pilot Project

The room was already tense. We approached hour three of what would become a marathon, five-hour Greensboro City Council meeting, and the speakers from the floor were growing restless. The back wall of the council chambers was lined with local restaurant owners waiting to be heard on the topic of food trucks and mobile food vendors in downtown Greensboro. They represented a wide cross-section of downtown restaurants owners—some of them immigrant owned, and others credited with helping to revitalize Greensboro's downtown business district over the past five years. Seated in the audience were supporters of the Food Truck Pilot Project, an equally diverse group clad in bright green shirts that read "Let's Roll Food Trucks into Downtown Greensboro." Marianne and one of her students positioned themselves between the food truck supporters and the restaurants owners, and she shares this story based on their field notes.

The council had just returned from an hour-long, closed-door session, and members had already covered several contentious topics that night—including housing and economic development incentives. The next item on the agenda was a report out from a pilot project to grant food trucks access to the downtown city center. Most of the partners who had been organizing and collecting data around the pilot project had concluded that people in Greensboro were generally supportive of lifting restrictions that had prevented food trucks from operating downtown. Although a handful of downtown restaurant owners had expressed sincere concerns over loss of business, no one was expecting the coordinated efforts by the brick-and-mortar restaurants to challenge the new food truck policy.

I sat with one of my students along the back row of seats, and the unexpected tension between the row of restaurant owners along the back wall and the seated food truck supporters was palpable. When the mayor opened the conversation for public comments, Alexa Bird, perched on her dad's arm, approached the microphone. Alexa was six, and we first met her two months prior when the pilot project was first presented to the council. She similarly spoke first at the previous meeting, confidently proclaiming: "I am Alexa Bird, as you all guys know, and I live in Southside . . . and I would like to have food trucks downtown, because . . . um . . . I haven't yet had any of the kinds that you're talking about in downtown." She was thanked by council and even applauded by a few spectators at that first meeting.

Tonight's meeting exhibited a much different atmosphere. When Alexa took the mic, she froze. "My name is Alexa," she began and then quickly buried her face in her dad's shoulder. Her dad whispered something in her ear, and she turned her face back toward the microphone. "And I'm from Southside," she mumbled before turning back to her dad. She grabbed the sides of her face, embarrassed that she forgot what she wanted to say. After some encouraging from her dad, Alexa finally managed to say, "I want the food trucks here more often, so I can use them because I really like them." I heard some rustling of feet and hushed comments from the row of restaurant owners behind me.

"Oh come on now," one woman sighed indignantly as Alexa struggled to find her words. Her comments were echoed by a quiet boo and a few chuckles further down the line.

"Did they just boo a six-year-old?" I quipped, as I turned to my student.

"I think they did," she replied with a perplexed look on her face.

This long night felt like it was about to get much longer.

· · · · ·

A CASE STUDY OF ENGAGING COMMUNITIES
IN FOOD POLICY COMMUNICATION

Navigating policy is a communication process that can be daunting for community members. Policy research in communication suggests that working with policy is a process inherently related to working through tensions.[1] Food policies within communities operate at municipal, county, state, and federal levels. Although these policies can grant communities access to resources, they also require those who use policy to be skilled at managing paradox, contradictions, and other tensions around engaging communities to navigate policy change. The Downtown Greensboro Food Truck Pilot Project serves as a case study to examine the multiple tensions that community members navigated while working with city government, local nonprofits, and university partners to stage a pilot project that changed local food policy. As an extension of the guiding questions we posed in chapter 2, this case most directly addresses our third and fourth questions—how communities coordinate actions, in this case through policy advocacy, as well as how stakeholders manage tensions as they work to transform food systems.

In 2012, community members approached the City of Greensboro to change a policy that prohibited food trucks from operating in the downtown city center. Partners organized an eight-week pilot project to assess participation and economic impact of allowing food trucks to operate in downtown Greensboro. Additionally, the project also relaxed restrictions that prohibited operation on institutional space, including universities and hospitals. In doing so, the policy changes laid the foundation not only for economic development around local food trucks, but also for the creation of projects like the Mobile Oasis Farmers Market, which we discuss in chapter 6.

Communicating food justice frequently requires everyday people to work with policy. Guttman first challenged those interested in research on policy communication and democratic practice to focus much more attention on the study of engaging "ordinary citizens" in public deliberation about policy.[2] Since then, scholars have addressed ethical challenges of community engagement,[3] theory and method in policy communication,[4] and frameworks for organizing how multiple stakeholders engage in policy talk and navigate policy texts.[5] Taken together, these contributions encourage researchers to concentrate on the interplay between policy structures, everyday expertise, and complex food cultures, as well as the various tensions associated when communities work with policy.

This chapter illustrates how several community partners converged to host the Downtown Greensboro Food Truck Pilot Project, as well as how the City of Greensboro created space for everyday citizens to engage in public deliberation around changing mobile food policies in the community. Considering that social justice relies on "various modes of action and organizing, including advocating change, building community, improving governance, and reorganizing markets," and that ordinary citizens must "attend to the interpersonal, organizational, rhetorical, and cultural realities, possibilities, and constraints" of advocating for change, this case study emphasizes the multiple and integrated forms of community engagement that were required to change food policies at a local level.[6]

Organizing the Food Truck Pilot Project

Street food, mobile vending, and eating on-the-go have been a part of local and global food cultures since people first had the need for convenient and cheap food that they did not prepare themselves. Historians frequently trace street food back to ancient Greece and the first street food policies back to Turkey in the fifteenth century. In the United States, the *New York Times* places the first food truck in 1872, when a man in Providence, Rhode Island, cut a hole in the side of a covered wagon and started selling sandwiches.[7] *Policies* around street food and food carts, however, date back to 1691, when New Amsterdam (now New York City) created regulations for vendors selling food from pushcarts.[8] Street food and food trucks have always been a part of US culture, but popular discourse around food trucks started to ramp up around 2008. Marked by the growing popularity of food truck innovators like Roy Choi, the burgeoning food truck scenes in cities like Austin, Texas and Portland, Oregon, and the 2010 debut of the Food Network's *Great Food Truck Race*, food trucks had suddenly become the centerpiece of hip food culture. With their punny names like "Guac N

Roll" and "Grillenium Falcon," specialty food options, and commitment to low-cost startups, food trucks were quickly emerging as entrepreneurial launchpads for people with viable food concepts and limited budgets. And in 2012, the phenomenon found its way to North Carolina.

Food trucks weren't exactly new to Greensboro in 2012. We had a handful of taco trucks that operated in random parking lots around the outer edges of the city, but we had yet to see the influx of trucks that other communities in North Carolina—Raleigh, Durham, and Chapel Hill, in particular—had started to experience. Food trucks were also prohibited from operating within a one-mile radius of Greensboro's downtown city center, as well as on most institutional properties, like hospitals and colleges and universities. On the heels of the first food truck festival in nearby Raleigh, a small group of citizens—including some downtown business owners, local leaders, and nonprofit voices—started organizing to change those restrictions. For the previous five years, the City of Greensboro had been focusing on revitalization in downtown Greensboro, and this group viewed food trucks as one way to strengthen the growing food culture in the city center.

The Downtown Greensboro Food Truck Pilot Project got its start on August 9 with a blog post from an active leader in the nonprofit community under the tag name modmealsonmendenhall. Titled "Let's Roll 'em In!," the post appeared on a new WordPress site called "Let's Roll Food Trucks into Downtown Greensboro." The author outlined a very specific rationale for allowing food trucks to operate in downtown Greensboro, as well as a specific request of the Greensboro City Council. Posting on behalf of a small, but influential, group of citizens, she wrote:

> As small business owners, residents, and advocates for downtown, we believe food trucks operating with specific regulations would add lively new options in downtown, encourage entrepreneurship and attract young professionals.
>
> Food trucks, with their affordable start-up costs and flexible menus, have a demonstrated ability to turn mobile kitchens into brick and mortar restaurants, providing a path to success for new entrepreneurs. They would showcase our community's cultural diversity in addition to providing much needed jobs.[9]

The post goes on to explain that the group supporting downtown food trucks is requesting that the City reconsider their ordinance (section 26-233) that prevents truck from operating in the city's business district.

Things started moving fairly quickly after that initial post. Modmeal-sonmendenhall continued to regularly submit updates on the need for a change in policy. On August 10, she referenced a City of Greensboro 2022 visioning plan that directly referenced food trucks as part of their recom-mendations, and by August 13, Let's Roll Food Trucks had been officially labeled a movement.[10] In that post, she outlined specific strategies for people to create community and build momentum around changing the city policy. Those strategies included sharing their new Facebook page, being profiled on the website as a "Food Truck Fan," emailing Greens-boro City Council representatives, and writing a letter to the editor at the *Greensboro News & Record* to show support. And Greensboro responded. In the first month, Let's Roll Food Trucks profiled eleven individuals and two organizations that wanted to see more food truck in the downtown city center. They also featured various editorials that were published in the *Greensboro News & Record*—one in support of the food trucks and one opposed. While promoting the food trucks, the supporting letter was also critical of the current policy, arguing: "Greensboro's prohibitive ordinance amounts to protectionism. It blocks one kind of business from compet-ing with another. City ordinances should serve the best interests of the public, not favor some businesses over others. Consumers benefit from more competition, not less."[11] Conversely, the opposing letter highlighted what became a central tension in the policy talk around food trucks: Did downtown have the numbers to support both the current restaurants that served the city center while simultaneously opening the doors to the food trucks? The letter stated: "The truth is that downtown Greensboro lacks enough workforce, residents and tourists to successfully support both food trucks and restaurants. We don't have 60,000 fans pouring from a Panthers game eight games a season or 40,000 supporters from a Red Sox game 81 times a year."[12] Let's Roll Food Trucks had established a platform that engaged communities from a variety of perspectives. While openly supportive of changing the policy that kept food trucks from operating in downtown Greensboro, they also created space to consider alternative perspectives from dissenting voices.

The efforts to change city policy around food trucks in downtown Greensboro started off with a strong communication presence as a way to engage community members. Within a month of announcing their activism efforts, a proposed pilot study was on the agenda for the September 4 city council meeting. The proposed Food Truck Pilot Project was fairly simple. Food trucks would be allowed to operate in the downtown business district for the months of October and November, but the project would have restrictions. The City would close off a section of Commerce Place, a relatively low-traffic side street, for the pilot test on Mondays through Fridays. Four trucks would be permitted to operate at a time, across a weekday lunch shift from 10 a.m. to 2 p.m., and a Friday dinner shift from 5 p.m. to 9 p.m. Truck owners would apply to the City of Greensboro to be considered for the pilot test, and approved trucks would work with the City's small business coordinator to set up a rotation. Beyond applying to participate in the pilot test, truck owners were also responsible for necessary health inspections, related city licenses, and a $20 fee.

Some of the organizers behind Let's Roll Food Trucks had rallied people to attend the city council meeting and speak during the public commentary period. Ten people spoke from the floor that evening—starting off with six-year-old Alexa Bird—and all of them were in support of the pilot project. That night, the nine-member city council voted 7–2 to approve the Downtown Greensboro Food Truck Pilot Project. The yes votes wanted to use the pilot test as an opportunity to work out the details about how a longer-term policy might operate, as well as to get feedback from the community about what was wanted and needed. The two dissenting votes noted that the pilot didn't accurately represent the fair market practices that the trucks would have to follow if the policy was actually changed, and that the City was choosing to host a pilot project without a public hearing first.[13]

On October 1, food trucks rolled into downtown Greensboro. Day one featured three trucks at the Commerce Place stop—Baguettaboutit, a dark blue truck out of Chapel Hill that featured freshly baked baguettes, stuffed with NC-made sausages; Hickory Tree Turkey BBQ, a black truck with bright green letters from Greensboro, serving turkey BBQ legs and macaroni and cheese topped with turkey cracklins; and My Dreamcakes, a cupcake truck whose owner was using the pilot test to see if she could scale up her Greensboro-based business. Over the course of the pilot test, fourteen food trucks joined the rotation in October, and five more were added in November. Although the pilot test did rely on trucks from outside of Greensboro and Guilford County to round out the lineup, with 21 percent of trucks coming from outside of the county in October and 34 percent in November, the pilot test largely served as a platform for local trucks to launch their food concepts. The Food Truck Pilot Project saw the debut of new Greensboro-based food trucks, including the Great Escape, which served five-spice noodles and a combination of sweet and savory crepes, as well as Bandito Burrito, locally famous for their Baja Tacos and Big-Ass Burrito. And while we could spend much of this chapter talking about how much people enjoyed the food, this is really a case study about how the Food Truck Pilot Project was an occasion to engage community in food policy talk, which is where we turn our attention next.

Engaging Multiple Voices in Policy Talk

Part of organizing the Downtown Greensboro Food Truck Pilot Project meant capturing the community's reactions and responses to changing local policies around food access—in this case, related to food trucks. The project would have been little more than a performance of a food trend if several partners had not converged to engage the community and document the process. In addition to the Let's Roll Food Trucks website and Facebook page, which remained active during the pilot test, documenting the Food Truck Pilot Project involved the work of three primary partners. The City of Greensboro's economic development coordinator took on the responsibility of managing the trucks, which was likely the most cumbersome task, as it involved managing the food truck application process, verifying all of their permitting and inspections, scheduling the trucks that were accepted into the lineup, and monitoring the financial side of the trucks that participated. Another partner vital to documenting the pilot project was Downtown Greensboro Incorporated (DGI), a nonprofit entity that works alongside the City of Greensboro to promote downtown businesses and manage Center City Park. DGI targeted downtown business owners, especially restaurant owners, to assess their views on the food trucks and the city policy. They also sponsored a survey on the City of Greensboro's website to gather 458 public comments about the food trucks. Finally, in her research capacity as part of UNC-Greensboro's

Department of Communication Studies, Marianne directed a team of students (CST team) to provide an on-site snapshot of the pilot test with both qualitative comments and 412 surveys from customers at Commerce Place.

The coordinated effort to document the Food Truck Pilot Project provided a foundation for community members to engage in food policy talk from numerous different perspectives. This cross section of voices was necessary, as community views on the food trucks were not exactly unified. The supermajority of people surveyed by both DGI and the CST team were supportive of seeing more food trucks in downtown Greensboro. This did not come as a surprise in the CST team surveys, as we were talking to people who were already coming to the food trucks for lunch or dinner. But the support was also reflected in the DGI data, which showed that 81.9 percent of their 458 respondents thought that allowing food trucks in downtown Greensboro would help downtown businesses. Engaging community voices around the policy was also evident in the qualitative comments from both the DGI and CST team reports. Most of the participants highlighted the need for convenient and affordable food options in the downtown city center. Some comments spoke directly to the perceived benefits for downtown Greensboro:

> If the food is good, it will bring in foot traffic that will bring in more business to downtown. Gives downtown a lively feel. Brings diversity to the food offerings at an affordable price.[14]

> This is a great idea. I feel like I'm supporting the local businesses—both in Guilford County, but also those businesses that buy from local farmers and local Guilford and North Carolina businesses.[15]

> There would be a sorely needed influx to the variety of food downtown. It would also give people another reason to come downtown. Furthermore, I work at A&T, which is in the middle of a food desert. I would like to see the trucks expand to East Market.[16]

While other comments concentrated on how the food trucks made it easier to bring their families downtown:

> This is great for families. We usually don't go to restaurants, because it's just too much with the kids. The food trucks are nice because we can meet up

with other families, and all of the kids can run around, and we're not bothering anybody.[17]

Interesting selection of easy-to-get food. It would also cause me and my family to come downtown more often. I could just grab a bite at a food truck and sit in the park for a few hours. Then we may walk around and visit local store owners.[18]

Finally, a subset of comments made direct connections between the food trucks and creating a sense of community in downtown Greensboro:

Food creates some of the natural conditions of community development. Food trucks are often brightly colored, multi-cultural, and provide a sense of urban energy.[19]

What's great about those food trucks is the little sense of community that's building around it. You come down to the trucks. You get your food. You set up on the curb. You talk to people. I mean, I ran into someone who I haven't seen for years.[20]

At the same time, a very vocal minority of downtown restaurant owners and developers made a strong case against the unfettered access of food trucks to downtown Greensboro. Their concerns stemmed from a perceived threat to the vitality of existing brick-and-mortar restaurants, especially as Greensboro continued to focus on revitalizing its downtown city center. As one restaurant owner stated: "Instead of looking at the concerted efforts of all of us that helped revitalize downtown, add to that heartbeat, the city has now changed its focus on looking to be cool and trendy. At the expense of putting someone out of business? That's not cool or trendy."[21] Another restaurateur explained in the DGI survey:

Food trucks will not bring people downtown. They will only take a part of the existing customers away from the restaurants. Restaurant owners already pay a premium just to be downtown . . . but at least all the restaurants have the same issues. As local business owners we invest in downtown. I don't think a $100.00 permit is much of an investment. All they have to do is start a truck and move on to the next location.[22]

Documenting this kind of policy talk was especially important to the pilot project, as it demonstrated the multitude of communities who had a stake in how revisions to the food truck policy played out in everyday practice.

One of the most prominent ways that community members engaged in policy talk involved navigating policy webs.[23] Policies do not exist in isolation, and some of the more productive conversations that come out of the Food Truck Pilot Project considered how the change in food truck policy was connected to other local practices and local policies. This kind of policy talk was especially important, as concerns started to mount about the impact on downtown businesses, the health and safety of food trucks, and how the policy should be constructed to manage multiple and sometimes competing interests. Navigating policy webs was most evident in how community members diffused arguments that questioned the health and safety of food trucks. We certainly saw some attention to health and safety in the DGI surveys, which included comments from respondents such as, "these trucks don't even have to be inspected by the health dept.," and "[the food trucks will] not necessarily have negative effects, just things that would need to be regulated and/or monitored: health and sanitation, parking, safety, fees and taxation, etc."[24]

Shortly after Let's Roll Food Trucks proposed changing the policy, concerns like this surfaced across online and social media—in some cases as a discursive strategy to undermine trust in the food trucks. Those concerns were first addressed in an August 20 *Greensboro News & Record* article that quoted the County's environmental health director:

> Trucks must be licensed, but once they're inspected they may move freely across county lines. . . . Operators still face potential local check-up inspections though, and are supposed to let health departments know when and where they'll be open in that department's jurisdiction. . . . They also must be associated with a brick-and-mortar restaurant, where they're expected to go for cleanings and to dump things such as used sink water. . . . They face a number of other requirements on par with the ones traditional restaurants must meet, such as having commercial-grade kitchen equipment.[25]

The comments were picked up on the Let's Roll Food Trucks website, which also added:

> Exactly. It's a health department's role to inspect both mobile food trucks and brick and mortar restaurants. They are a valuable player in this

conversation, and it is their responsibility to create systems that work for maintaining inspections—not to discourage a free market. Additionally, section 26-234 #5 in the City of Greensboro Ordinance on Pushcarts, requires "a copy of any approval required by the Guilford County Health Department pursuant to the rules governing the sanitation of restaurants and other food handling establishments and any other approval required by a governmental unit for the preparation and service of food."[26]

This kind of policy talk, specifically concerns of both public health officials and everyday citizens, demonstrates how food activists must consider how policy change often implicates other policies.[27] The Let's Roll Food Trucks site even goes so far as to cite county-level policies to which the city-level food truck experiment would be linked. By showing how the food trucks would not have unfettered access to downtown Greensboro, and that they would be subject to existing health codes, the advocates for policy change were able to diffuse the arguments against their case through savvy policy talk.

The Greensboro City Council took up many of these concerns and productive instances of policy talk in an October 30 planning meeting, where they worked through initial feedback from the pilot test and began constructing a practical policy to vote on at the next council meeting. The policy talk surrounding the Food Truck Pilot Project then culminated at a November 7 council meeting, where more than forty people gathered to engage in public deliberation surrounding the Food Truck Pilot Project and changing food access policies in Greensboro. The meeting was tense, as suggested by our opening story. Summaries of the data reports from the City's small business coordinator, DGI, and the CST team were presented to the council. Six people spoke from the floor in support of the food trucks—one even going so far as to construct a poster with data from the CST team's study.

But the surprise story was the sixteen restaurant owners and downtown developers who had organized in the final hours before the council meeting to speak out against changing the policy. Many of them spoke to significant drops in business, ranging from 10 to 30 percent, compared to both the month and year prior to the pilot project; however, when they were pressed by the council to support some of their claims, they could not provide sufficient answers. For example, in response to statements

that some businesses were down 25 percent and that the only environmental difference was the food trucks, Mayor Robbie Perkins asked,
"How about the weather? Did you check the weather when it was in place
and whether it was walkable weather?" When it became clear that some
speakers had not, council members started questioning the underlying
arguments advanced by the restaurant owners. As Councilwoman Nancy
Hoffman stated:

> What I'm trying to look at, because I tend to be data-driven and analytical,
> is that I'm really trying to get the numbers to work. . . . During the month of
> October about twenty-five hundred to twenty-six hundred meals were
> served at the four food truck locations downtown. I was actually down there
> several times, so I looked at an average dollar-wise, and I think an average
> amount was about $8 to $10. So if you looked at that . . . let's just say we're
> talking about $25,000 for the month of October. Then, when I hear some
> major restaurants say that their business is down 25 percent or 30 percent
> or 10 percent, it's hard to make that equate with $25,000.[28]

As council members continued to piece together data throughout the
meeting, the policy talk that various partners had documented throughout the pilot test gave the council needed information as they navigated
their decision.

In the end, it was a well-researched and artfully communicated case
alongside the extensive documentation of a pilot test that persuaded the
council. In a 6–2 decision, the council voted to support the food truck
advocates and change the policy prohibiting them from operating in the
downtown city center. In what was framed as an extended pilot test, food
trucks would now be allowed to operate in downtown Greensboro under
the same policy provisions as trucks in other areas of the city. That meant
that food trucks could operate on private property and not within fifty feet
of an existing restaurant. They would be subject to County health inspections, as well as various City licensing fees. Food trucks would not have
free rein of downtown, as the private property provision meant that only
a few spaces in downtown were even eligible to host a food truck, but
they would we given a chance to bring some life to downtown Greensboro.
Much of this was possible, because of well-coordinated communication to
engage community members around policy.

Following Food Trucks after the Pilot

In the several years since the City of Greensboro hosted the Downtown Greensboro Food Truck Pilot Project, food trucks have made a recognizable mark on Greensboro's food culture. While they have not radically transformed the downtown city center, they also have not run all of the downtown restaurants out of business. To be fair, not all of the restaurants that spoke out against the food trucks at the November 2012 city council meeting are still in operation—but it's hard to blame that solely on the food trucks. As then mayor Robbie Perkins said in his closing comments for that meeting, "People make choices on food, and everyone here knows that the restaurant business is one of the toughest businesses you can be in. They come and they go." Many of the most vocal critics of changing the policy still have thriving restaurants in downtown Greensboro, while others have closed one restaurant only to open a new one a few doors down, and still others have started food trucks of their own. The restaurant business is incredibly fickle, and finding the right mix to not only open a restaurant, but *keep* it open is almost an art form.

Just as the downtown restaurants saw concepts come and go, so too did the food trucks. Immediately following the completion of the pilot project, several food truck owners organized to create the Central Carolina Food Truck Alliance—a network of owners and supporters that helps food trucks navigate policies and promote events. The alliance was most active in the months following the pilot project, and the group now largely manages a Facebook page to promote food truck rallies. Despite some early attempts at organizing a supportive network, not all of the food trucks owners, even the ones that were most vocal during the pilot test, are still in operation. Both the Great Escape and My Dreamcakes, two of the most highly rated local trucks, didn't make it past 2014. At the same time, we have seen at least one restaurant—Bandito Burrito—move from a food truck to open a brick-and-mortar restaurant, and at least five existing restaurants start up food trucks. Permits for food trucks in Greensboro jumped from fourteen to thirty-nine in the two years following the pilot test.[29] As of 2019, there are sixty-four food trucks registered to operate out of Greensboro.

The advocacy and activism around the Food Truck Pilot Project led to two interesting developments in Greensboro, one related to food access and the other to grassroots organizing. Initially, the change in policy surrounding food trucks didn't just apply to the downtown city center, although that's where most of the attention focused. The change in policy also made it possible for mobile food carts to set up on institutional space. This mostly benefited our colleges and universities in Greensboro, who could now invite food trucks to operate right on campus. But the change also applied to our hospitals. The change in food truck policy made it easier for the Mobile Oasis Mobile Farmers Market, which we illustrate in chapter 6, to partner with a local hospital to provide fresh fruits and vegetables and other local foods directly on-site. Although the advocacy was indirect, the change that mobilized around the food trucks also enabled future partners to increase food access in other ways.

Furthermore, the grassroots organizing that launched the Food Truck Pilot Project infused a spirit of participation in the base of the food truck community. For example, in April 2018, a tornado ripped through northeast Greensboro, damaging hundreds of homes and businesses in lower-income neighborhoods with limited food access.[30] The next day, the food trucks showed up and fed people. King Queen Haitian Cuisine was one of the first trucks on the scene, dishing up free smashed potatoes and chicken and gravy for the people in the neighborhood. Owner Djosen Vilnor told local media that she wanted to serve the same community that supported her local business. "With the earthquake in Haiti, I did have a lot of people who support us," she said. "So now it's my way of giving back to the community."[31] Beyond simply a heartwarming example, the food trucks' support during the first few days after the tornado demonstrated the power of community, and how that sense of community lies at the very heart of democratic participation and engagement.

Engaging everyday citizens in the policy talk necessary to promote this kind of food policy change requires a coordinated effort, but it was an effort that has led to innovative outcomes and creative thinking for Greensboro and its food trucks. In addition to creating a pathway for the Mobile Oasis and grassroots organizing, the food trucks have also helped promote economic development in Greensboro. Many of the food trucks that started during the pilot were minority and/or immigrant owned. Mike

Neal is the owner of Hickory Tree Turkey BBQ, a Black-owned restaurant that launched their food truck during the pilot. "This is great," he told Marianne during a lunch shift, "we've been able to hire three new people." The kind of local economic and community development sparked during the Food Truck Pilot Project is the kind of participation that keeps local dollars in local communities and builds communication infrastructure.

REFLECTIONS, RECOMMENDATIONS, AND RESOURCES

At first glance, a case study about food trucks in a book that largely focuses on food hardship and food insecurity might seem out of place. We remind readers, however, that our goal here is not only to address food insecurity and food hardship, but to communicate about food justice and food systems, as well—perhaps even more so. Part of communicating social justice activism is about reorganizing markets and material conditions, and engaging in policy talk is one avenue to disrupt systems that reproduce inequity.[32] At the very least, the Downtown Food Truck Pilot Project demonstrated that community members in Greensboro had the capacity, strategy, and resources to engage in policy talk around complicated food and access issues. In this closing section, we offer some reflections, resources, and recommendations about engaging everyday people in conversations around food, policy, and participation.

Reflections

In less than three months, more than one thousand voices contributed public comments, survey responses, statements before the Greensboro City Council, blog posts, and newspaper editorials to changing food policy in the city. The Downtown Greensboro Food Truck Pilot Project created an occasion for everyday people to engage in policy talk and public deliberation about local food issues. Our reflections for this case study speak to the readiness of partners to engage in public deliberation and the importance of the pilot test's research and communication platform.

Creating spaces for participation from people with different viewpoints is an essential component of democratic practice.[33] Asking everyday,

ordinary citizens to engage in deliberations over policy and public practice is both challenging and often paradoxical.[34] Communication scholar
Nurit Guttman outlined four concerns that are frequently raised about
the feasibility of public deliberation and policy talk. Fairness—do groups
and communities at the margins have the same kind of access as those at
the center of conversation? Competence—are people even aware of the
issue, and do they have the capacity to assess and discuss it? Discursive
process—will people listen to each other and engage in mutual learning,
or do they just want to debate? Finally, power—do everyday people have
the influence to change the status quo, or does the discourse prevent them
from doing so?

The Downtown Greensboro Food Truck Pilot Project illustrates how
the partners behind the pilot test navigated some of these concerns. The
case study clearly highlights how partners navigated fairness, competence, and discursive process through an intense documentation of voices
and data throughout the pilot test, which was leveraged to produce policy
change. The more interesting conclusions, however, come from a more
thorough reflection on the role that power played across the Food Truck
Pilot Project. The voices that initially launched the conversation through
the Let's Roll Food Trucks into Downtown Greensboro website were
everyday citizens who also had a fair amount of local influence and access
to City offices. They were well-networked coffee shop and local business
owners, nonprofit leaders, and even a few restaurant operators who got
the conversation going. The proposed pilot test might have experienced a
different reception at the city council meeting had the food truck owners
been the voices leading the activism. Instead, the food trucker owners
were able to focus on what they did best—cook food—and the activism
was largely organized by everyday people with the power and influence to
access and change the system. By partnering in this way, the organizers of
Let's Roll Food Trucks were able to move very quickly in terms of organizing the pilot test, expediting the policy talk, and effectively changing the
policy.

One of the ways in which organizers behind Let's Roll Food Trucks were
able to leverage their influence and expedite the policy talk was by facilitating an extensive effort to research, document, and evaluate the pilot
test. The communication platform—including multiple and integrated

media, like websites and Facebook, alongside the extensive documenting of community voices, like surveys and observations—was crucial to the speed in which the supporters of downtown food trucks moved from starting a conversation to changing a policy. In many ways, activists held City offices and related groups accountable for tracking the voices that they represented. The City's Small Business Office followed the food trucks, DGI followed the downtown restaurants, and the CST team followed the customers on-site. Organizers regularly asked for updates from the data, which they then made available on the Let's Roll Food Trucks website and Facebook page. Even the data poster that organizers generated from the CST team's report hung in the front window of a local coffee shop—the Green Bean—leading up to the November city council meeting. The organizers of the Let's Roll Food Truck movement made communication the foundation of their effort, and in doing so, created a space for everyday people to engage in policy talk.

On some level, the Food Truck Pilot Project was an easy testing ground for policy talk and public deliberation around food and access. People like talking about food trucks—even the people who didn't like the food trucks seemed to like *talking* about the food trucks. The pilot project gave them an occasion to discuss the importance of local businesses—and local restaurants, in particular—to the vibrancy of Greensboro's downtown. And although the city council voted to allow food trucks into the city center, they constructed the policy in a way that has still supported and protected restaurants over time. By demonstrating that everyday people in Greensboro have the capacity to engage in complex policy discussions around food, this case opens the possibility for other community-based deliberations around food to commence. Food hardship, food security, and food systems are not nearly as trendy and fun to talk about as food trucks and local restaurants, but by grounding our work in communication practices and policy talk that create space different perspectives, we have available resources to do this kind of work.

Recommendations

Although, at its heart, this case study is a story about the Downtown Greensboro Food Truck Pilot Project, we have equally important recommendations to make about engaging communities in participatory policy talk. As such, we offer the following advice as an extension of this chapter:

1. Get familiar with food service, agricultural, and nutrition policies at a local level. Although policies at the national and state level often outline the generalized parameters for growing, cooking, selling, and eating food, most food policies are administered through the county, city, or township. These policies govern everything from where you can grow food, to health and sanitation codes for businesses, to whether or not you need a grease trap to open a restaurant. An understanding of local food policies can clarify which policies might be the source of inequity and how we can use policy to ensure food justice.

2. Speak at a county board or a city or town council meeting about food issues and inequities that are important to you. Hold local leaders accountable for supporting work around local food systems, food justice, and economic equity. Many boards and councils have select times when they take comments from the floor. Take advantage of those periods of public commentary as key resources for engaging in policy talk. If six-year-old Alexa Bird can do it with a row of twenty angry restaurant owners staring down her back, we believe there is hope for all of us.

3. Seek out local food policy councils. Food councils are becoming more influential as community-based spaces to engage in policy talk. They involve facilitating conversations across different individuals, organizations, and institutions that organize food systems. Many councils operate at the county level, and they frequently involve conversations around policy. We consider food councils in more detail in chapter 10, but their work is relevant here, as well. Food councils can serve as launchpads for activism and advocacy around inequities in our food system, and they are spaces where everyday people can identify policies that need engaging.

Resources

The most useful resources we can offer in relationship to the Downtown Greensboro Food Truck Pilot Project are links to the Let's Roll Food Trucks website and links to the two Greensboro City Council meetings where the pilot project was discussed. These resources provide archives of the comments, data, local support, and opposition for allowing food trucks to operate in Greensboro's city center.

> The Let's Roll Food Trucks into Downtown Greensboro website provides a snapshot of the activism around the food truck pilot test, as well as links to the Let's Roll Food Trucks Facebook page. Neither page is active, so they provide clear archives of how the activism was organized.[35]
>
> Two Greensboro City Council meetings show the full public deliberations over the food trucks in downtown Greensboro: For September 4, 2012, forward to 3:27:11 on the archived video.[36] For November 7, 2012, forward to 2:55:55 on the archived video.[37]

PART III Mobilizing Resources

CASE STUDIES

The term *mobilization* is frequently associated with social justice organizing and activism. The need to motivate individuals, groups, and organizations to use available communication, financial, and other material resources to design interventions and coordinate activities has long been a practical reality. Mobilizing resources frequently relies on engaging numerous communities and stakeholders in discussions around policy change, designing new infrastructure, and launching interventions; as such, this next piece in our four-part perspective should be seen as both an extension from and a continuation of our previous piece, engaging communities.

Theories on resource mobilization date back to the 1970s, extending from studies of the social movements during the 1960s.[1] Mobilizing resources generally involves coordinating activities across numerous groups and organizations as well as integrated and strategically aligned communication. Considering the array of voices involved in organizing food systems, from farmers to retailers to consumers, the need to mobilize people and resources around a common goal is crucial to the success of food justice interventions.

From a communication perspective, mobilizing resources relies heavily on community-communication infrastructure, as well as new media and communication technology. Community-communication infrastructure enables and constrains collective efficacy in communities.[2] When mobilizing resources, this infrastructure operates through four dimensions—a perceived willingness to intervene, local political control, a mix of community and instrumental support, and shared organizational participation.[3] These perspectives suggest that communities with strong storytelling networks and a high sense of collective efficacy have a greater capacity to mobilize material and human resources.

Additionally, despite concerns over digital divides and the capacity of community members to use technology, the use of new media including websites, social media, podcasts, and smart phone apps are ubiquitous across community health campaigns and local food activism.[4] The communication needs here are often technical, like when community groups use programs like SignUpGenius to manage volunteer hours or Facebook or Instagram to promote an event. At the same time, communication technologies and new media also serve organizational and relational purposes. The proliferation of web-based and smartphone apps enables partners to coordinate resources like food pickups and drop-offs and food truck stops. Other programs provide platforms for creating timelines and documenting community activity.

Embedded in these conversations about mobilizing resources is a need to address the concept of access. Marginalized and underserved communities generally lack access to material resources within their neighborhoods and existing infrastructure.[5] Even when these communities have dense communication resources and strong relational networks, they are not always able to translate those communicative and discursive resources into some of the material resources—namely financial—that are required to mobilize change across food systems.

With Part 3, we turn our attention toward two interventions—the Warnersville Community Garden and the Mobile Oasis Farmers Market (Figure 4)—as illustrations of mobilizing resources around food insecurity and food hardship in Greensboro. These two programs grew from the community-engaged work with the Warnersville Community Food Task Force and, to a certain extent, the Downtown Greensboro Food Truck Pilot Project. Chapter 5 highlights the community garden and the challenges involved in mobilizing people to translate ideas into action and managing

Figure 4. The Mobile Oasis Farmers Market. Niesha Douglas (back, left) and Marianne LeGreco (back, center) join Audrey Mangili (back, right), students from Guilford College, and volunteers at a Mobile Oasis stop in Greensboro's Warnersville neighborhood. Photo credit: Michael Dickens.

a shifting landscape of partners. In chapter 6, we focus on organizing the Mobile Oasis Farmers Market, an innovative mobile food project designed to bring fresh produce to neighborhoods without a grocery store. In this chapter, we amplify the importance of pop-up and mobile interventions as a way to reach underserved communities. We add our voices to a growing body of communication literature that suggests that researchers and activists must not only mobilize people to act, sometimes we must also—quite literally—make the interventions themselves mobile.[6]

5 The Warnersville Community Garden

The harvest lunch for the Warnersville Community Garden at Prince of Peace Lutheran Church was fast approaching. We still had a few peppers that Niesha and Adrienne had planted over the summer, and several collard greens and sweet potatoes that Justin and Jenn had tended as summer turned to fall. The broccoli was beautiful—with oversize, dark green leaves that had been spared by bugs and hedgehogs. But it wasn't ready yet. Marianne incorporated many of her courses at the University of North Carolina at Greensboro into her work at the Warnersville garden—namely a Community and Communication course that included a twenty-hour service component. This story is written from her perspective.

My students had been anxiously awaiting the moment the broccoli would finally start to head. They'd been watching most of the semester as these curly green leaves got bigger and BIGGER, but it was like a giant tease. The part most of us eat, doesn't show up until the very end. On a Wednesday in early November, I accompanied three of my students to the garden to harvest the collard greens and peppers. "We've got baby broccoli!" one of them shouted, as she ran up to the garden beds. The students quickly checked both broccoli beds—all sixteen plants had a baby broccoli head, ranging in size from marble to golf ball, growing amid their cascading leaves. My students were thrilled and almost giddy as they examined the deep, dark green heads with a hint of purple and no signs of yellowing around the edges—some of the best broccoli we had grown in our four years gardening in Warnersville.

The plan was to meet the church president at the garden to give her the collards, so she could prepare them for Sunday's harvest lunch, while I would take the peppers and sweet potatoes to do the same. My students and I quickly harvested what was left of the peppers, then we dug through mounds of dirt on a sweet potato scavenger hunt. We finished up by slicing off large, leafy collard greens from their base. We still hadn't seen the church president yet, so we put the collard greens in the refrigerator inside the church, packed up our equipment and the remaining harvest, said good night to the broccoli, and went home.

When I got to my house, I left a message for the church president to let her know that the collards were ready and waiting for her in the refrigerator. As I ended my phone call, a voicemail popped up on my screen. I laughed when I realized that it was the president calling me at that same moment. She had arrived moments after my students and I left, and she was calling to touch base. "Marianne," the voice message began, "I got to the garden and no one was there, so I went ahead and harvested the collard greens. I wanted to let you know that I will have them ready for Sunday."

I paused for a moment. My students and I had harvested all of the collard greens in the garden—four large beds of them. I couldn't figure out where the church president had found some magical collard greens hidden in a bed somewhere. And then it hit me. I gasped a gasp so loud I almost choked. My tone quickly dropped. "The broccoli," I whispered. I grabbed my keys and drove the ten minutes back to the garden. The broccoli beds were the first two garden beds you could see when you pulled into the church parking lot, and the moment my headlights hit the plants, I saw the aftermath. Every single broccoli leaf had been cut. The only thing remaining were the baby broccoli heads sitting on top of a thick green stem. I walked slowly over to beds, hoping somehow my eyes had deceived me. They hadn't. So I snapped off a baby broccoli head, popped it my mouth, got out my phone, and searched "how to cook broccoli greens."

· · · · ·

The language of agriculture is woven into the fabric of North Carolina. Growing tobacco, food, and other commodities has historically been a primary economic driver of the state's economy, with the majority of production centering on rural farms. North Carolina is home to more than 46,000 farms, with a total market value of over $12 billion, annually.[1] Agriculture is one of North Carolina's leading five industries, and our state is a top producer in tobacco, sweet potatoes, pigs, and chickens.[2] The agricultural industry in North Carolina ranks behind only education and health care in terms of jobs, with more than 17 percent of the state—or 663,000 people—employed in agriculture or agribusiness in 2017.[3] Campaigns like the North Carolina Department of Agriculture's "Got to Be NC" initiative highlight our year-round growing season and the diverse crops we can produce with our climate and soil.

Starting in 2010, public discourse in Greensboro and Guilford County increased around urban-centered agriculture, with a particular emphasis on community gardens and urban farming. The US Department of Agriculture explains that "city and suburban agriculture takes the form of backyard, roof-top and balcony gardening, community gardening in vacant lots and parks, roadside urban fringe agriculture and livestock grazing in open space."[4] In Greensboro and Guilford County, the County Cooperative Extension had long served as a resource for people who want to grow their own food, even hosting their own on-site community garden. They also provided organizational advice to neighborhoods and schools who wanted to start gardens, and in 2011, the Cooperative Extension created Community and School Garden Networks to coordinate resources, ideas, and participation across the one hundred community gardens and seventy school gardens in the county.[5] Grassroots groups like Urban Harvest were also a part of mobilizing conversations around urban agriculture. In 2010, they were actively searching for vacant lots and parks that could be transformed into places to grow and sell food in urban neighborhoods that lacked easy access.

The threads of this discourse were picked up by the Warnersville Community Food Task Force in 2010 when they invited Urban Harvest to join their efforts to organize a community garden or urban farm on the property at Prince of Peace Lutheran Church (POPLC). Community gardens and urban farms had emerged as a top priority in a series of community-engaged dialogues with the task force, and partners wanted to build on the momentum sparked through that communication and start growing food. During the task force dialogues, the membership of POPLC offered the use of their property to grow food with and for the Warnersville neighborhood. POPLC sits on three acres of farmable land tucked into the northwest corner of Warnersville—their landscape providing an ideal space to grow food. Task force members saw this as a key opportunity to launch a garden that would serve the community.

With this chapter, we follow the slow growth of a garden in Warnersville. We trace connections between food justice organizing and urban agriculture to emphasize the changing landscape of partnerships. Food justice advocates and activists must carefully consider how to integrate and sustain numerous relationships in order to promote change across food systems. Mobilizing resources often means mobilizing the people and partners who can not only advocate for better food, but who can also (sometimes quite literally) get their hands dirty when it comes to creating new sources of food at the neighborhood level. The chapter weaves together the work of three partnered projects—Urban Harvest Greensboro, the City Oasis Project at Warnersville, and the Warnersville Community Garden—all of which relied on a changing network of partnerships in order to mobilize participation.

ORGANIZING WITH URBAN HARVEST AND THE WARNERSVILLE NEIGHBORHOOD

In January 2012, the future of our fledgling advocacy work with Warnersville was anything but certain. After some purposeful organizing through the Warnersville Community Food Task Force, we now faced the somewhat daunting task of actually growing food that people in the neighborhood would want to eat. That meant translating a lot of sincere brainstorming and idea generating into workable plans and practices. Community members had already invested a great deal of time and energy into identifying priorities for food access in their neighborhood, and they needed support from a broader network of partners in order to mobilize their ideas. Perhaps one of the earliest challenges facing our transition from the planning stages of the task force to launching a community garden or urban farm was mobilizing the human resources behind the project.

The conventional wisdom of community gardening suggests that the most successful gardens are those driven by the residents of the neighborhoods where the garden lives.[6] Indeed, when the Warnersville Task Force consulted with our Guilford County Cooperative Extension, the extension agents mentioned how crucial community leadership was for the success of local gardens. Those residents are responsible not only for managing daily resources—like seeds, soil, water, equipment, and people required to grow the food—but also for constructing the rules for how the garden will operate. Certainly, this model has proven fruitful for many gardens, including those in Greensboro like the Community Garden in the Dunleath Historic District. This neighborhood garden was established in 2009 by our Urban Harvest partners in cooperation with residents from the Dunleath community. The neighborhood features a mix of people from various incomes, races and ethnicities, and abilities, and the garden has thrived in the ten years since its inception—largely because neighbors had an early capacity to take over its leadership and organizing.

As work in Warnersville shifted from identifying priorities in 2011 to mobilizing people and partners in 2012, the task force took this wisdom of past gardens with us—to ensure leadership and ownership from within the community—particularly because this strategy also aligned with what both cooperative extensions and food justice scholars presented as a best practice for working with communities.[7] At the same time, every individual involved also acknowledged that no one partner had the singular expertise to launch a garden and farmers market alone. Even though partners aspired to ground these projects in community leadership, we also encountered some hesitation because of the demanding nature of farm work. These concerns were first expressed by the pastor and the church president from POPLC, where the congregation was small and populated by a majority of older individuals and couples. Some members also experienced significant health limitations that would constrain the types of contributions they could make to organizing around food activism. As the POPLC pastor explained, "We've got such beautiful land. I can look outside and just imagine the rows of vegetables and maybe even an urban orchard. But as we've always said, we can provide the land, but we don't have enough of us who are physically able do the labor."

Other engagement with the community also revealed some conflicting feelings about working on an urban farm—particularly by some of the older members of the largely Black community. As Beatty Petty, a neighborhood resident and POPLC member explained to Marianne, "Well, Doc—I appreciate what you're doing out there in the garden. But I spent my whole life getting off the farm. I don't want to spend my last few years getting back on it." Brother Petty's comments speak to a history of farming and Black communities that in the United States reaches back to structures like sharecropping and slavery.[8] And those structures still leave traces across both Black and white communities. When white organizers—like Marianne and the leaders from Urban Harvest—are invited to become partners in Black communities, we really have to approach this kind of work with humility and recognize the limitations that Black folks identify when white people ask them to grow food.

What we experienced as a task force during this early organizing was similar to what McDermott, Oetzel, and White described as a paradox of participation in community-engaged work.[9] Although some idealized forms of community engagement prioritize leadership and expertise from within the community, this type of activism and advocacy frequently asks community members to push beyond their capacity. In managing this paradox of participation, the garden group started efforts to meet community members "where they were at" in terms of food production. Rather than immediately jumping in to building a garden and planting seeds, we took the time to build relationships within the neighborhood and seek out local leaders. Under the direction of Urban Harvest, we organized some of our task force meetings alongside garden activities. For example, we hosted a container gardening class where Urban Harvest members taught community members how to grow food in large containers on a back porch or driveway. Urban Harvest also helped us take our initial steps in designing the garden. With some research support from Marianne, the task force designed a monthly rotation of community input sessions and neighborhood surveys where residents could share ideas about how the garden should look, what kind of food we should grow, and how folks could get involved. We spoke with 133 residents and learned that community members wanted to see a garden that was well kept, in which the neighborhood could take pride. Residents also had some fairly simple requests when it came to the food—tomatoes, collard greens, cabbage, onions, peppers, green beans, melons, berries, and fruit trees were requested most.

By taking the time to build relationships between external partners and the Warnersville residents, we developed enough trust and support to move forward with building the initial garden. We broke ground on March 17, 2012, with a team from the Warnersville neighborhood, Prince of Peace Lutheran Church, the Guilford County Department of Public Health, and three local universities. Alongside our partners, we planted four small beds of cabbage and collard greens, and we started construction on what would become the first phase of our garden. That day, we also built eight new garden beds and got them ready for a summer planting. In planning for the garden build day, we took great care to design a variety of garden activities to continue meeting community members "where they were." For example, building the eight new beds required a great deal of physical labor—from carrying wood frames that we had reclaimed from an old barn to endless shoveling of mulch and topsoil. We were fortunate to have two crews of students from UNCG and NCA&T who could do some of that heavy lifting, but we also had a team of Warnersville residents who were eager to contribute. Some of those residents were elderly and could not lift heavy materials, another was legally blind, and at least two used wheelchairs. To create as inclusive a garden as possible, we established teams who worked outside to frame out and fill the garden beds, as well as teams who worked inside to plant trays of seeds that would move to the beds once they'd sprouted.

The Warnersville Community Garden was named and dedicated at Prince of Peace Lutheran Church on April 29, 2012. Additionally, the enthusiasm from the community on our build day gave us the confidence to continue growing from a small garden that served the community to an urban farm that could provide food to local markets. Figure 5 shows one of our early garden work days, as we started to expand the garden to grow more food.

Our initial confidence was tested over the next several months. As we first illustrated in chapter 3, shortly after we dedicated the garden, our

Figure 5. A garden work day at the Warnersville Community Garden. POPLC members Charles Peoples and CeCe Mills (pictured top and middle) work alongside Niesha Douglas (pictured bottom) to tear down some old garden beds in preparation to build twelve new plots. Photo credit: Marianne LeGreco.

Urban Harvest partners had to face some funding realities and put their organization on hiatus to pursue other opportunities. That summer, as we started preparing for our fall planting, one of our key project leaders from the Department of Public Health was forced to take an extended medical leave from both his position and the garden. Then, in October of 2012, our key leader from the Warnersville Community Coalition died very unexpectedly. These unanticipated changes in the makeup of our partners also forced the remaining garden members to consider how we might move forward with our efforts to grow food. The community leadership on the project had changed, without any warning, but we were already building beds and planting seeds.

Amid the loss of some partners and the changes in leadership, the individuals and groups who were still attached to the Warnersville Community Garden persisted in their efforts to get a garden going in the neighborhood. A member of POPLC, whose sister lived in the Warnersville neighborhood, wanted to see good food grown in the garden. He stepped up to serve as our first garden manager. Garden team members also worked with POPLC members to apply for grants through the Lutheran Church, as well as grants from UNC-Greensboro and Youth Service America. We slowly started building our capacity to secure funds and a support network in order to transform our initial four beds, at 4 × 4 feet each, into twenty-six 4 × 12 beds. Soon, we were growing enough food in Warnersville to participate in a pop-up farmers market, which we used to test what would become the Mobile Oasis Farmers Market. At the same time, we still lacked a long-term partner who could help mobilize the garden and the people around it in a way that aligned with the original vision. Although we were fortunate to have a very skilled garden manager who stepped in for the interim, his participation and leadership were not guaranteed beyond a couple of seasons. The garden also needed partners who could be committed to the long-term environmental and economic sustainability of the space. Little did we know, the next phase in the transformation of the Warnersville Community Garden was just around the corner.

Launching the City Oasis Project at Warnersville

At the start of 2013, we faced another critical juncture. Our partner from Public Health had returned to full status with the news of a group who was interested in working with the Warnersville Community Garden to help scale up efforts to an urban farm. The City Oasis Project (COP) was an effort organized by Vision Tree Community Development Corporation. The group of young, African American students and professionals hoped to develop community-placed solutions for neighborhoods classified as food deserts. They were particularly interested in designing and implementing an urban aquaponics farm, which featured both fish tanks and garden beds in a system where the fish fed the plants and the plants fed the fish. More than anything, they sought to develop an oasis in a food desert that was rooted in the needs and interests of the community. And so in the fall of 2013, we created a memo of understanding between Prince of Peace Lutheran Church, the Guilford County Department of Public Health, Vision Tree Community Development Corporation, and UNCG's Communication Studies Department to launch the City Oasis Project and begin expanding the Warnersville Community Garden to an urban farm.

Early in our new partnership with the City Oasis Project, we struggled to develop a shared language—even so far as to struggle with what to call the garden in Warnersville. We were no longer technically a community garden, as our connection to the neighborhood was changing with the death of a previous leader. At the same time, we were more than the City Oasis Project, as the garden work in Warnersville had life before the arrival of our new partners. Consider the following excerpt from Marianne's field notes that focuses on a January 2014 strategic planning session for the COP:

As we wrapped up our meeting with the City Oasis Project, I still had a few questions for their director. As everyone else packed up their belongings and left the meeting room at Prince of Peace, I asked Matthew if we could talk through a few things quickly.

He was more than happy to stick around, so I explained to him that I'm a communication person. And I was struggling a bit when it came to naming what we were doing. We'd been talking about the urban farm and mobile market idea for two years before Matthew and the COP had arrived. But City Oasis Project was their name . . . and we weren't trying to take that from them. "So what do you think?" I asked him. "What do we call ourselves?"

After a few moments of reflection, I saw Matthew's eyes light up. He suggested that we call the space at Prince of Peace the City Oasis Project *AT Warnersville*.

I immediately recognized the potential in his idea. I clarified that he meant we were all working on the City Oasis Project at Warnersville, but if Matthew and his team wanted to start something in the Old Asheboro neighborhood, they would start the COP at Old Asheboro. I told him that his idea could work nicely, as we were still recognizing Warnersville, which was really important in this neighborhood, but the COP name was still uniquely theirs.

Matthew confirmed—explaining that each project could do whatever is the best fit for the community. One neighborhood might be a community garden. Another might be an aquaponics farm. Maybe one would become a food hub.

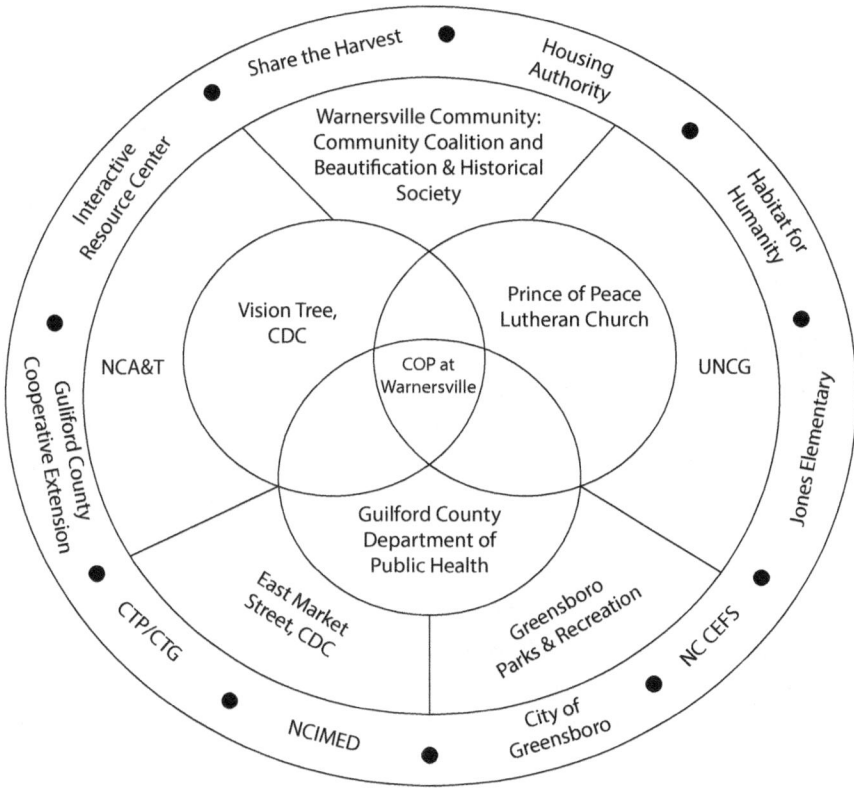

Figure 6. The City Oasis Project at Warnersville. The partner wheel for the COP at Warnersville features a partnership driven by Prince of Peace Lutheran Church, the Guilford County Department of Public Health and Visions Tree, CDC.

The language around the City Oasis Project *at Warnersville* gave us at least some shared level of partnership, at least enough for the various individuals and groups involved to talk about how they each fit in a much larger picture.

This conversation also sparked an idea about creating a visual representation to communicate how the partners of the COP at Warnersville fit together. Marianne designed what we called a partner wheel to illustrate the different ways in which core members and supporting partners worked in relationship. Figure 6 shows the initial partner wheel for the

COP at Warnersville, and we offer a blank model in appendix B. Much more than an organizational chart, the partner wheel also enables two key practices: (1) visually representing how partners are mobilized, and (2) providing a way to adjust partnerships when key members and groups must rotate off a project.

The wheel itself features a core set of three or four partners who are the drivers of the project. In the case of the COP at Warnersville, these partners were Prince of Peace Lutheran Church, the Guilford County Department of Public Health, and Vision Tree. The second layer of the wheel highlights the partners who serve as a support system for the core. These partners included colleges and universities like UNC-Greensboro and NCA&T State University, as well as the Warnersville Community—which included members of two merging groups in the neighborhood. Finally, the outer rim of partners would help translate the ideas into practice and deliver the products of food programs. For example, some of the food we grew in Warnersville was donated directly to people in the neighborhood, while at least 20 percent of what we grew went to Share the Harvest, a nonprofit organization in Greensboro that helps redistribute produce from gardens and farms that grow more than they need.

Over the next two years, we pilot-tested the City Oasis Project at Warnersville as a way to realize the original vision of the Warnersville Community Food Task Force. Our initial plans were to scale up the production capacity of fruits and vegetables in our garden beds and provide resources for a part-time garden manager, and the conversation about an aquaponics farm faded largely to the background. Our partners at POPLC continued to patch together funding from the Lutheran Church and UNCG to buy seeds, starter plants, topsoil, equipment, and a garden shed. Our big break came in March 2015, when the Guilford County Department of Public Health took the lead on securing a $99,997 grant from the Food Insecurity Nutrition Incentive (FINI) program of the USDA. The six months of funding would support both the Mobile Oasis Farmers Market and the City Oasis Project at Warnersville in a comprehensive effort to increase access to local foods, fruits, and vegetables in a food desert.

In many ways, the FINI grant helped give the garden and the City Oasis Project at Warnersville a big push forward. Between 2013 and the end of the 2015, we grew more than two thousand pounds of beautiful red tomatoes, perfectly tender green beans, an array of hot and sweet peppers, the prettiest onions some folks in the neighborhood had ever seen, more collard greens than anyone could count, and enough sweet potatoes to keep a family of grounds hog very, very happy. We were able finally to hire a part-time garden manager, as well as pay folks from the neighborhood for their labor in the garden. We also received front-page coverage from the *Greensboro News & Record*, which reported about how "every now and then, all the right elements converge at just the right time. So it goes with the City Oasis Project."[10] At the same time, our COP partnership faced a number of organizational and communication tensions that would lead us to remobilize our food activism in Warnersville.

The two most central tensions that we faced as the City Oasis Project at Warnersville involved aligning our funding cycles with our growing cycles and embodying the shared language of partnership. Initially, mobilizing people to engage in food justice organizing—especially activism and advocacy that involves growing local food—requires significant time, labor, and money. However, grant cycles and the immediate availability of grant funds do not always align with when urban farmers and community gardeners need to get seeds in the ground. In North Carolina, we have a window starting around April 15 to plant fruits and vegetables for a summer garden. Wait too long, and it gets too hot for the young plants to survive—catch it just right, and you'll have the best tomatoes, squash, cucumbers, and peppers at harvest time. When we received the FINI grant in 2015, we learned of our funding just in time to hire staff for our summer season—or so we thought. While our partners and staff started planting in April, we also learned that our grant award needed a final level of approval from county commissioners before funds could be distributed. That meant several of the partners had to start working months before they were scheduled to be paid. For someone like Marianne, who is paid her university professor salary regardless of external grants, this kind of delay was more like an inconvenience. But for someone like Niesha, who was hired to work on the City Oasis Project as a community member, such a delay could make it increasingly difficult to remain a paid part of the project.

We faced a second central tension in terms of embodying a shared language of partnership. Although we constructed partner wheels and adapted project names to reflect the neighborhood, we sometimes struggled to speak that language of partnership in our everyday talk about the garden. Some of the tension can be attributed to a vision that wasn't always aligned across partners. When Vision Tree joined our partnership and we launched the City Oasis Project at Warnersville, their interest was largely in starting an aquaponics farm as a way to address food insecurity. They set aside that interest to provide support for the Warnersville Community Garden and the Mobile Oasis Farmers Market, which were already in motion when they joined the conversation. But their passion had always been for exploring alternative forms of agribusiness, like aquaponics and hydroponics, as a way to address gaps in food systems. At the end of our FINI funding from the USDA, our Vision Tree partners informed us that they were leaving the partnership to refocus the City Oasis Project on some of their original goals.

Remaining Nimble amid Change

By spring of 2016, the garden was struggling but surviving. Our funding through the USDA had come to an end, and we were searching for new opportunities to keep the food growing. Our partnerships were also changing—again. Our Vision Tree partners put the City Oasis Project on hiatus while their director pursued a PhD studying urban agriculture and aquaponics. The role of our partners from Public Health moved out of the realm of core member and back to serving as part of the support network. We started calling ourselves the Warnersville Community Garden again, and although we remained connected to the community, the garden had become more of a partnered project than what most scholars would call a genuine community-based or community-driven effort.

But much like the Warnersville neighborhood itself, the garden remained rather persistent—almost as if the land wanted food to grow just as much as we did. Partners continued to pursue new funding opportunities and reform the partner wheel as we faced our next set of growing pains. Partners from Prince of Peace Lutheran Church remained committed core members, and UNCG stepped in to provide funding through a new program called the Green Fund, which supported sustainability-related projects decided on by a UNCG student committee. With this

Figure 7. Building the labyrinth. POPLC church members Hunter Haith (left) and Mary Aubel (center) assist garden manager Jennifer Thompson (right) during the installation. Photo credit: Marianne LeGreco.

funding, garden partners secured salaries for a new garden manager and student interns for 2016, and Figure 7 shows a labyrinth walking path that they installed that summer as an entryway into the garden.

Garden partners also recognized the need to make the garden more sustainable both financially and in terms of mobilizing people. We were remaining just nimble enough to navigate the changes in partnership and grow a little bit of food. Our more formal efforts at advocating for food justice and equity had become less central than simply keeping something planted every season. But we also recognized that the land and the community still held so much potential, and partners wanted to consider every opportunity before putting an end to the garden. As such, we also paid attention in 2016 and 2017 to new opportunities for getting food to people and expanding the search for new partners.

The People's Market contacted us in 2016 to begin vending at their new pop-up farmers market in Greensboro's Glenwood neighborhood, which was right next door to Warnersville. The market provided us a platform to sell produce and raise awareness about our food access work in the Warnersville neighborhood. Our farm manager and student interns vended regularly at the market during the 2016 season. We sold mostly green beans—which we'd planted in tomato cages, so the beans grew long and straight—but we also featured the occasional onions, salad greens, and peppers. The People's Market gave us the chance to stay nimble. They helped us keep some life in our work in the garden while our partners managed significant changes, and they created some community infrastructure that helped us generate income for the garden.

Even with access to these kinds of resources, we only sold enough green beans that summer to buy a backpack sprayer. And while that was one of our goals, it wasn't enough to keep the work sustainable in the way the partners were currently organized. We again faced the question of who had the capacity to provide the labor and the sweat equity to make the garden work. Ever since our Urban Harvest partners placed their efforts on hiatus, we had struggled to find leaders with the confidence to grow and distribute food on the scale we originally envisioned. Although that original vision came from the community and we had initial support from the neighborhood, residents also recognized that they did not always have the capacity to take on this kind of work. Because the activity in the garden was starting to wane, so too was the support from the community.

The next option to continue the work of the Warnersville Community Garden came from Out of the Garden Project. This nonprofit organization, which organizes a series of pop-up food pantries across Greensboro and Guilford County, was interested in expanding their mission in 2017 to include an urban teaching farm. They came with their own funding, and after developing an agreement with Prince of Peace Lutheran Church to lease the land for five years, they hired a farm manager and started work cultivating the space. As of 2019, the Urban Teaching Farm team has done an admirable job transforming the property at POPLC. Their farm manager, Lily Emendy, has coordinated volunteers and other farm staff to do many of the projects that we had always wanted to see happen at the garden—including building a hoop house, with hoops that were donated to the farm in 2013, and installing a three-compartment, outdoor wash sink to clean the produce at harvest time. They've grown many of the same standard items that we featured in past gardens—including tomatoes, peppers, and collards—but they have also experimented with other items, like hibiscus flowers, whose dark burgundy seed pods made for a beautiful fall garden.

Although the arrival of Out of the Garden Project provides a tidy and convenient conclusion to this story, we do not wish to give the impression that all of our problems were solved and everyone lived happily ever after. Our new partners in Warnersville have done a commendable job cultivating the land, but both the farm team and our partners at POPLC recognize that work to mobilize participation from within the neighborhood is ongoing. The Urban Teaching Farm started a community-supported agriculture (CSA) program in 2019, a fairly common and well-researched approach to growing and sharing food. Partners asked neighbors to purchase a membership up front, and in return, they would receive a box of produce from the garden each week. The program is still growing and served thirty-three members in its first season. By the second season, the Urban Teaching Farm had become financially sustainable, with a capacity of fifty CSA shares. But the majority of memberships have come from outside of Warnersville, and partners are aware of the ongoing work they need to do to maintain existing relationships and join new networks in the neighborhood. For now, this case study remains a bit open ended, as Out of the Garden Project and Prince of Peace Lutheran Church focus on engaging and mobilizing residents and remain attentive to how different partners fit together—including those potential partners who live right down the street.

REFLECTIONS, RECOMMENDATIONS, AND RESOURCES

The Warnersville Community Garden taught us many lessons—lessons about working with a community to design an idea but needing a larger system of community partners to mobilize it, about how race and class matter when mobilizing Black and white communities around growing food, and about creating a shared narrative without giving the appearance of taking over a community intervention. The story of the garden was never really one about increasing food access and using a community garden or urban farm approach to get people in Warnersville to eat more vegetables. It was about using the garden to start a conversation about food in a community that had been largely forgotten. It was about using food to create relationships that continue to grow and change. Our reflections, resources, and recommendations for this chapter center on strategically aligning partners to mobilize food justice activism and organizing community gardens and urban farms.

Reflections

Any time partners engage in communicating food justice, we must intentionally construct a network of partners who are nimble enough to respond to a variety of changing landscapes, from the physical environment to the makeup of the actual partners. Mobilizing resources—especially the human resources required to do the physically, intellectually, and emotionally demanding labor of growing food at this scale—demands flexibility and adaptability. Partners will come and go. Some seasons will be easier to grow food than others. Partnerships will face gaps in aligning vision, and there will be personality clashes. Partners must be prepared to deal with those tensions, because they will affect the intervention's ability to reach out to the community—even when our partnerships involve residents from that community. Strategically aligning partners requires conversations between neighborhood residents and the partners who live outside the community about the strengths and limitations that they bring to the partnership. We never know or learn to appreciate someone else's background and skill sets, unless we ask. Organizers, activists, and researchers must never forget that there are people behind our interventions, and everyone has a story that has drawn them to this partnership.

It is also important to remind potential partners that growing food at the scale of feeding a community is time consuming, physically draining, and emotionally demanding. Partners must be aware of the time commitments required to grow food as a form of food justice activism. Not only must organizers engage people with a variety of technical and community expertise, but they must also grow food—and grow food on a schedule they do not get to set. This kind of organizing requires precise attention to timing and labor. Much of this type of work can end up falling on a handful of people, who are usually project coordinators and farm or garden managers. But food justice organizing frequently means mobilizing volunteers. Be clear and realistic about the expectations for people who are not being paid to participate. When people commit to volunteering their time, that time has value. Remember that volunteers have families, jobs, school, and other life events that could prevent them from fulfilling some duties. Set realistic goals and over-invite people to participate. Perhaps most important, create a space where people can see tangible results when they do commit their time and talents to pursue food justice.

Strategically aligning partners to mobilize food justice also involves how those partners talk about each other and the intervention publicly. When we work on partnered projects, we often have to train the media and other public voices about how to discuss the community-based nature of our work. Some of our tensions in embodying a shared language of partnership were furthered by various media outlets and public voices that spoke about the City Oasis Project at Warnersville. More specifically, whichever partner the media outlet or public figure spoke with first tended to make that partner the focus of the story. For example, when our Vision Tree partners served as keynote speakers for a Piedmont Triad Regional Council annual meeting, the summary from the event gave the appearance that Vision Tree was primarily responsible for the work in Warnersville—as opposed to the dense network of partners that were building the garden and market. Also, Marianne received a fair amount of publicity from UNCG around the COP at Warnersville and the Mobile Oasis Farmers Market, and despite attempts to emphasize the partnership, one of the early stories overemphasized her role in organizing the COP. On at least one occasion, that story made it difficult for our Vision Tree partners to discuss their vision for the COP with potential partners at future sites.

But rather than focus on the details of the stories that furthered those tensions, we instead offer an example of a story that got it right. In the front-page article for the *Greensboro News and Record*, author Susan Ladd best captured the importance of partnerships in making the City Oasis Project at Warnersville work—even going so far as to make the pieces of our partnership the opening lines of her story. She wrote:

Prince of Peace Lutheran Church was looking for a mission. NCA&T was seeking real-world experience for its horticulture students. UNCG professor Marianne LeGreco wanted to expand the Warnersville Farmers Market. The Guilford County Department of Public Health wanted to bring fresh food to one of the city's worst food deserts. Matthew King wanted to bring urban horticulture to the east Greensboro neighborhood where his father once built houses for low-income families.[11]

Susan is both a veteran journalist and a mid-career graduate of the Communication Studies master's program where Marianne teaches. When Marianne sat down with her to discuss the plans for the above-mentioned story, Susan listened when Marianne stressed the need to emphasize the partnership as a key part of what would make this project successful. Part of communicating food justice means collectively recognizing the contributions of a partnership. Sometimes, organizers, activists, and especially researchers must coach the media and our larger institutions about the importance of partnerships when talking about and assigning credit for our work.

Recommendations

Farming is hard work, and we applaud any group who is able to mobilize the community resources necessary to anchor an urban farm or community garden at the center of their food justice activism.

1. Commit to reciprocity across your labor strategy. Labor is the biggest challenge that food justice organizers will face when launching urban farm and local agricultural interventions—especially those with the hopes of feeding communities and neighborhoods. Organizers and activists must ensure a commitment to mutual benefit at the core of their labor strategy, including both paid staff and unpaid volunteers. For example, many organizations rely on college student volunteers and interns as a source of low-cost or free labor. Without a doubt, the Warnersville Community Garden would not have persisted without student and faculty volunteers from UNCG, NCA&T, and Guilford College. Think strategically about how student work is incorporated into the intervention. If colleges and universities are a resource available for your projects, partner with classes and student groups that have a service-learning focus and explore possibilities for paid

internships and research assistantships. Additionally, be aware of how community members and residents are recognized for their time. Many garden-based interventions trade food when they are not able to provide paid compensation for volunteers. Revisit those labor strategies across the life of the intervention to ensure that people have a reciprocal relationship—based in mutual learning and benefit—with the project.

2. Look for patterns in how partners come and go. The notion that community partners will work together in the same ways over time is naive. Therefore, we recommend developing a way to track the ways that partners move into and out of the network, as well as how they might occupy different roles at different times. Marianne developed the partner wheel as a way to track participation, especially to ensure that we had core partners and support systems at various stages. We can imagine many ways that groups can visualize how their partners fit together—the important point here is to clearly illustrate how partners move within the larger project as a way to identify patterns over time. This kind of work helped us recognize our consistent challenge of finding someone not just with the expertise to grow food, but to manage a *farm*.

3. Speaking of which, we recommend highly that urban farm interventions include someone who knows how to farm. To be clear, many people know how to grow food, but farming is a much finer and more technical practice. Farming takes a person with deep knowledgeability about coaxing food out of dirt to grow quality food that people are willing to eat, let alone pay for. Although we went into this intervention with a solid foundation from Urban Harvest, it took a long time for us to find partners who could bring the resources to manage the farm at the scale originally envisioned. We recommend finding partners with some knowledge of topics like succession planting, row crops vs. raised beds, season extension, high-volume production, companion planting, pest control, permaculture, and organic vs. conventional farming methods. Even if these partners can only serve in a short-term capacity, consult with people who can advise how to scale up a farm.

4. Remember that interventions are about more than food. They're about building relationships and community involvement that can shape the culture at the same time organizers, activists, researchers, and residents change structures. They're about sharing stories around food and getting to know the neighborhood in ways that mobilize participation and bring people together.

Resources

County Cooperative Extensions and statewide Departments of Agriculture are often useful starting points for information about organizing community gardens and urban farms. Additionally, city and county governments frequently have regulations about growing and selling food from community gardens and urban farms. Beyond their recommendations and policies, we also suggest the following resources:

Growing Home: When partners first started work in Warnersville, we started following this program based out of Chicago. They have grown into a model program of not only growing food, but also promoting community economic development.[12]

D-Town Farm: An urban farm initiative based in Detroit that is organized by the Detroit Black Community Food Security Network. This farm has served as a foundation for economic development in Detroit, and they provide detailed insight into how they organize their activism.[13]

Conetoe Family Life Center: Features the work of Reverend Richard Joyner, who speaks about spending most of his life trying to get off the farm, only to begin organizing a food systems program in rural North Carolina that focuses on community building, farming, and increasing food access.[14]

American Community Gardening Association: Provides basic resources for starting community gardens, as well as the conversations required to mobilize them.[15]

Urban Teaching Farm: Readers can continue to follow the progress of the garden and farm space in Warnersville through the Out of the Garden Project, who now manages the Urban Teaching Farm at Prince of Peace.[16]

6 The Mobile Oasis Farmers Market

Before we can tell the story of the Mobile Oasis Farmers Market, we must take readers back to the summer of 2012. On a particularly hot Wednesday in July, neighbors from across Warnersville made their way up to the giant oak tree at the J.C. Price School. The Warnersville Farmers Market had popped up a small group of three white tents, and local farmers had set up tables and truck beds filled with summer fruits and vegetables. But almost everyone's attention was on one of the white tents, which featured an array of peach desserts and other sweet treats, made by bakers from across the Warnersville neighborhood. Amid a series of pop-up farmers markets, which were being used to test the Mobile Oasis, partners hosted numerous special events around the Warnersville Farmers Market—including a Peach Treats Contest in 2012. That neighborhood cookoff was important, not only because it was a celebratory—and delicious—occasion for the community, but also because it introduced Niesha to the conversation about food insecurity in Greensboro. This opening narrative is written from her perspective.

There are only a few things that I look forward to every year: strawberry season in the spring, pumpkin latte season in the fall, peppermint bark season in the winter, and peach season in the summer. Each season fills me with some sort of joy. When peach season arrived in July 2012, I was already planning out a week of delectable baked goods. The Warnersville Farmers Market was also in full swing, and the market group wanted to come up with an event to celebrate peach season while actively trying to draw more traffic to the farmer's market. They decided to host a Peach Treats Contest for the Warnersville community residents. At stake were bragging rights within the neighborhood, your face in the local newspaper, and a gift card.

At the time, I had just started graduate school and was overwhelmed with the amount of time it took to complete assignments. One of my stress relievers is to bake. I make anything from cookies to cupcakes to cinnamon rolls. Otis Hairston, one of the market leaders, knew how good of a baker I was. He seized the opportunity to ask me to participate in the Peach Treats Contest at the farmers market. I was hesitant at first, because I only bake for myself and my family. I'm not used to critiques from strangers. Besides, I wasn't exactly sure what I was going to make. I assumed that peach cobbler, peach pie, and peach cake would be the "go-to" desserts. Otis suggested that I make peach ice cream. Ice-cream? Who actually makes homemade ice cream anymore? Churning salt in a bucket is long gone, especially with access to store-bought ice cream. "I don't even have an ice cream maker," I told him, "and I'm certainly not buying one for this one contest." To my surprise, he said that he won an ice cream maker a couple of years ago and he had never used it. He said that if I participated, he would gift it to me. So I obliged and started looking for peach ice cream recipes online. Deep in my search, I came across a recipe that uses peach brandy as an ingredient. I figured that if I could get the judges drunk, maybe I could win. I quickly realized, however, that you only use a tablespoon of peach brandy in the recipe, so now I really had to rely on the taste. At any rate, homemade ice cream is a delicacy that is no longer made at home. I knew for sure that I had a winner.

July 23 rolled around . . . the day of the contest. I made the ice cream—with local peaches, I might add. And the market loved it. Everyone kept walking around saying, "Well this one is good, and that one is okay . . . but have you had Niesha's ice cream?" I received so much positive feedback from the participants, even Marianne couldn't stop talking about it. I saw how my ice cream had impressed the judges, as well, and thought, "I've got this in the bag." I just knew that I had gotten first place, but alas, it was not meant to be. When Otis took the mic, because of course he brought a portable microphone and speaker to announce the winners, I ended up in second place. The first-place winner made peach "upside-down" cake, which was common, but I guess that is what people expected. Needless to say, I felt that I should have won. I stepped out of the box and made ice cream. But I guess tradition trumps innovation. Even though I didn't win, people still talk about that peach ice cream, and my risky move did lead to my involvement with the Farmers Market and the Mobile Oasis Farmers Market that would soon follow. It all started with ice cream, but joining these efforts allowed me to understand food more and to become involved in a network of food justice advocates and activists.

. . . . .

A CASE STUDY OF MOBILIZING INTERVENTIONS TO MOBILIZE FOOD JUSTICE

In October of 2014, a fifteen-foot trailer filled with locally grown fruits and vegetables rolled into the Warnersville neighborhood of Greensboro, and a partnership under the direction of the Guilford County Department of Public Health (GCDPH) launched the Mobile Oasis Farmers Market. Between 2014 and 2016, this partnership tested the Mobile Oasis as a way to increase access to fresh produce and local foods in Guilford County food deserts. The partnership hoped to inspire other mobile markets, food trucks, and pop-up styles of food distribution to serve local neighborhoods. The Mobile Oasis quickly became a media and health agency favorite, with grant awards from the US Department of Agriculture and the United Way, as well as program and leadership awards from the National Association of County and City Health Officials and the Greensboro News and Record for several of its partners.[1]

One of the hallmarks of the Mobile Oasis was the innovative way in which it flipped the script on access. Rather than expecting people to get to food, the Mobile Oasis brought local produce directly to people who lived in food deserts. Partners established locations in neighborhoods identified as food deserts, including the Warnersville and Cottage Grove communities in Greensboro, as well as at various health and social service centers, such as Cone Health clinics, the County Department of Social Services, and YMCAs. Mobilizing food in this way gave Mobile Oasis partners the ability to test out various models of distributing food and customize the intervention to our various locations.

But the story of the Mobile Oasis reaches back three years before its official launch, when the Warnersville Community Food Task Force started a series of pop-up farmers markets as a way to quickly provide food in their low-access neighborhood while building momentum for a much larger mobile market effort. In doing so, we infused a pop-up structure across what would begin as the Warnersville Farmers Market and become the Mobile Oasis. This pop-up structure would allow us to remain nimble in how we used resources and space, especially as partners worked through a series of questions related to mobilizing our intervention.

Mobilizing resources means not only mobilizing people; in some cases, it also means making the intervention itself, quite literally, move. Mobile interventions have emerged in both health communication and social justice scholarship as flexible and adaptable resources for changing everyday practices. From mobile health clinics as a way to reach people in remote communities to pop-up art therapy as a way to heal communities that have experienced trauma and violence, mobilizing the interventions themselves can shape and drive culture as partners work to reorganize and create innovative structures that invite participation.[2]

The Mobile Oasis Farmers Market offers a particularly useful lens through which to view food justice organizing, because of how it focuses on using pop-up farmers markets as a way to mobilize conversations around food security and invite participation from communities with limited food access. As such, this chapter is shaped by our second, third, and fourth guiding questions—regarding how communities organize to address food insecurity, how they coordinate activities around their activism, and how they manage tensions in their efforts to ensure equity in our food systems. Our discussion of pop-up interventions also emphasizes the need to disrupt dominant narratives of alleviating food insecurity.[3] Mobile interventions, like the Mobile Oasis, bring resources directly into communities, so that residents might imagine new ways of organizing, building trust and relationships, and sharing stories around food.

Pop-Up Markets as Testing Grounds for Mobile Interventions

When we first pitched the idea in 2011 of creating a mobile farmers market that could travel to various neighborhoods experiencing food hardship, the Warnersville Community Task Force was instantly excited: "It's like an ice cream truck . . . but for vegetables," one resident and task force member observed as he enthusiastically endorsed the idea. He continued, "Wait! Can we get an old ice cream truck? Can it play music while we drive it around the neighborhood?" As the task force leveraged this kind of excitement to continue developing the idea, we tried not to get too far ahead of ourselves. Members and Warnersville residents were interested in developing some sort of program, service, or partnership that could immediately start bringing more and better food options into the neighborhood—especially fruits, vegetables, and other local foods like bread and meat. At the same time, we didn't yet have the track record to secure the kind of funding we needed to buy a truck and make our market mobile. So the task force started working on a series of test markets as a way to quickly get food into the neighborhood, while gauging long-term interest from the Warnersville neighborhood, building a foundation for funding opportunities, and testing various features and services of how our market might operate.

FINDING LOCATIONS THAT FIT

We started off with one of our most immediate questions about launching a farmers market in Warnersville. Could we get farmers and shoppers to show up to a market with virtually no budget and only an evolving partnership of community members, health agencies, and researchers? All of our early organizing would be for nothing if we couldn't demonstrate that people in the neighborhood were interested in more than advocating for a farmers market. They would need to actively and consistently shop there, too. To test our belief that people in the neighborhood wanted access to more and better food options, the Warnersville Community Food Task Force hosted a test market on August 3, 2011. Leading up to what would become our first pop-up, the task force spent considerable time building a communication and support network around the market. Our partners at Prince of Peace Lutheran Church organized a visit for community members to the Greensboro Farmers Curb Market, both to shop and to invite farmers and vendors to participate in the Warnersville market. In her research capacity through UNCG, Marianne surveyed seventy-one people in the neighborhood about possible times, locations, and products for the market. The Guilford County Department of Public Health organized a door-to-door flyer campaign to promote the market in the community. And finally, the Warnersville Community Coalition publicized the market to local media, resulting in a front-page article in the *Greensboro News and Record* advertising the market.[4]

Even on the morning of the test market, members of the task force were unsure of how well our networking would pay off. But on one of the hottest days of the summer—climbing up to 94 degrees—120 shoppers and four farmers found shade under a giant oak tree on the lawn of the J.C. Price School, and the community popped up a farmers market. Some folks had seen the story in the *Greensboro News and Record*, while others had received a flyer. Still others had seen a line of people climbing the hill to the J.C. Price School, and they wanted to know what was going on. Shoppers enjoyed squash, peppers, and the tail-end of tomato season. The market featured mid-summer vegetables, flower baskets, starter plants for fall crops, and even some locally raised beef. One farmer brought strawberry and peach ice cream made with fruit from their farm, which made the day that much sweeter. As task force volunteers folded up tables and broke down tents at the end of the market, we considered our efforts a success. We had created a space where farmers and community members came together to share and sell food. We had effectively communicated our market and our mission to the larger public, at least enough to attract some initial participation. We were beginning to build the necessary confidence, as a partnership, to organize a more regular rotation of markets.

The success of the test market inspired the task force to adopt a pop-up approach as an organizational structure for future versions of the Warnersville Farmers Market. The pop-up structure enabled us to test various combinations of resources, including locations and messaging strategies, as well as manage some early tensions and paradoxes of establishing a market. For example, one of the most invaluable opportunities that pop-up organizing offered was the ability to test out both the Warnersville Farmers Market and the Mobile Oasis at different locations across Greensboro.

Between 2012 and 2013, we hosted the Warnersville market first at the J.C. Price School and then at Prince of Peace Lutheran Church. Thanks to some funds provided from the County Department of Public Health, through the USDA's Farmers Market Promotion Program grant, our partnership was able to purchase two pop-up tents, six tables, twelve chairs, and a sign to advertise the market. Along with some volunteer support and four dedicated farmers, these were the main resources we needed to effectively start the markets. From May through October of 2012, the task force hosted weekly markets on Wednesday afternoons at the J.C. Price School. The school provided an ideal spot to launch our early markets, as residents were familiar with and supportive of the space, especially because of its historical significance to the neighborhood. When partners initially surveyed community members about creating the Warnersville Farmers Market, we asked residents to identify preferred spots to host it. Forty-eight percent of our seventy-one participants pointed to the J.C. Price School.

The Warnersville Community Coalition was especially interested in popping up a community-based project at J.C. Price, as talk of selling the school to the Salvation Army Boys and Girls Club had surfaced in the neighborhood. Otis Hairston, in particular, saw our market presence as a message that the J.C. Price School was important to the Warnersville community, and we should do whatever possible to try to preserve one of the last pieces of the original neighborhood. It became quickly apparent, however, that our partnership would not be able to pursue both goals of starting a farmers market *and* saving the school. Over the course of the 2012 season, we struggled to maintain consistent participation for a weekly market—largely because our partnership was not yet set up to take SNAP/EBT. But we also faced a tension in maintaining the market at J.C. Price. Although the task force had permission from the property owners to host our weekly market at the school, we were essentially squatting on the front yard of a space that hadn't been open to the public in decades. Our research into SNAP/EBT also made it clear that the J.C. Price School was not an eligible location, if we wanted to expand our services.[5] Moreover, the talk of selling the school and tearing it down to build a Boys and Girls Club had more than surfaced—by the end of our 2012 season, it was almost imminent.

As this perfect storm of barriers mounted, we faced a challenging structural paradox around moving the Warnersville Farmers Market. If the task force tried to stay and advocate for preserving the school, we risked losing the market. If we moved the market, we gave up the last ground and one of the last connections the community had to the J.C. Price School. And our task force members from the neighborhood did not have a unified voice on the matter. Although our goal with the Warnersville Community Food Task Force and its related garden and market groups had always been to collectively take this effort where the community wanted to go, we still faced a structural tension when the goals to start a farmers market at the J.C. Price School started to undermine each other. Otis was certainly the strongest advocate for using the market as part of the case to save the school. But at a series of late-season meetings in September of 2012, five other Warnersville residents were also part of our task force conversations. Two of them were interested in moving the market across the street to Prince of Peace Lutheran Church, mostly to see if we could align the market with the Warnersville Community Garden. The remaining three were more ambivalent about the market's location, instead reminding the task force that our focus had started to drift from using pop-ups as a pathway to a mobile farmers market. In the end, it was this reminder of our commitment to testing out locations to launch a mobile market that helped the task force resolve the competing perspectives. All of the task force members, including Otis, eventually recognized that we needed to return to that original goal—and that meant moving our pop-up markets to Prince of Peace and continuing to work toward starting a mobile farmers market.

Efforts to mobilize a farmers market in Warnersville would change dramatically over the next two years, as the Guilford County Department of Public Health began to leverage what we had learned from our two years of pop-up markets to secure funding for a fifteen-foot trailer that could make our efforts truly mobile. After a modest, biweekly market at Prince of Peace Lutheran Church—in which we sold $406 of potatoes, onions, broccoli, cabbage, cucumbers, squash, tomatoes, and collards from the Warnersville Community Garden—our partnership had developed enough of a track record to show funders that we could manage a project. With support in 2014 from the United Way of Greater Greensboro and Blue Cross/Blue Shield, the Guilford County Department of Public Health took the lead on a series of grant-funded projects to purchase a trailer, secure a truck to tow it, and sponsor a pilot test. As the partnership grew to become the Mobile Oasis Farmers Market in 2014, the flexibility afforded by our pop-up structure allowed us to continue testing locations for the best fit between space, market, and community.

The market was now on wheels, meaning that our partnership could focus on increasing access to food in more neighborhoods. The composition of our partners had also changed, with Vision Tree Community Development Corporation and East Market Street Development joining the Mobile Oasis to manage the business end of operations and our newly-established SNAP/EBT account. The Mobile Oasis team was now in a position where we could pick up produce from farmers, make numerous stops throughout the week, and make the produce more affordable for our customers living in food deserts. We continued to partner with two of the farmers from the Warnersville pop-ups, as well as the Warnersville Community Garden at Prince of Peace. We maintained stops in Warnersville, this time at the Warnersville Recreation Center, which gave us a more centrally located and visible presence in the neighborhood. In 2014, the Mobile Oasis added its first new stop at the Guilford County Department of Social Services (DSS) Building. The following year, with new funding from the US Department of Agriculture's FINI grant, we added four more locations—a Cone Health clinic and the Hayes-Taylor YMCA in Greensboro, and the Morehead Recreation Center and a County DSS Building in High Point. Partners also made the Mobile Oasis available for one-time pop-up events including health fairs and neighborhood outreach, primarily as a way to build new relationships with communities that wanted to increase their access to food.

POPPING UP INTERVENTIONS TO EXPAND COMMUNICATION

As we expanded our presence across Greensboro and Guilford County, the Mobile Oasis itself became a way to mobilize conversations around food security, food access, and food justice. Every time we popped up a new location, we created the conditions to engage with new community members and partners. In this way, the Mobile Oasis was not only a food access intervention, but also a communication intervention. The

Mobile Oasis gave partners and community members an opportunity to dialogue about food preferences, cooking tips, and barriers to changing eating habits. Consider the following exchange that Marianne had with a Mobile Oasis customer:

> A woman—probably in her mid to late fifties, wearing a track suit and leopard-print baseball cap—approached the table where I was stationed for the Mobile Oasis. I was seated at the end of three long tables filled with butternut and acorn squash, collard greens, cabbage, and apples. She stared inquisitively at the array of produce and eventually asked me, "Now . . . what's a butternut squash taste like?"
>
> Without skipping a beat, I instinctively responded, "like a sweet potato and a pumpkin had a baby."
>
> She cocked her head to the right and gave me a charmed look. "Ooohhhh . . . okay," she replied. "That makes me want to try it." She picked up two small squashes, and we got to talking about different ways to cook it.

Conversations like these were common across Mobile Oasis stops. The market was more than a place to buy food. It was also a space for community members and partners to collectively build and share knowledge, and to reflect on the culture we create around what and how we eat.

Beyond testing out locations, our pop-up approach also helped the Mobile Oasis team gauge a variety of messaging strategies, incentive programs, and social media platforms as a way to coordinate and customize the market with each location and each neighborhood. Now that the Mobile Oasis had multiple stops, the partners needed a way to coordinate communication, marketing, and outreach across a variety of different customers and communities. The County Department of Public Health handled most of the traditional media for the Mobile Oasis—including a logo, billboard and bus advertisements, flyers, and press releases. At the outset of organizing, several partners also worked alongside Marianne to develop basic online and social media—including a website, Facebook, Instagram, and Twitter pages, and email lists specific to the mobile market. We even created a hashtag, #everybodyeats, as a reminder that eating is something that unites us, and everyone deserves access to good, healthy, and affordable food.

One thing we learned from our early pop-ups with the Warnersville Farmers Market was that many of our customers were senior citizens and did not frequently engage with social media. Several of them weren't even fans of getting on the internet. As one of the Warnersville residents who served on the Mobile Oasis team explained in a summer 2014 planning meeting, "These folks aren't on Facebook—or if they are, it's not every day. They want a flyer or a picture with products and the prices and times. Just like you get in the newspaper for a grocery store." Hashtags and Instagram feeds might appeal to the younger generations we were trying to attract to the market, but they would not guarantee us a meaningful outreach to many of the older generations in the communities in which we were also working. At the same time, folks did have cell phones, and many of them could receive text messages—even if they didn't always respond.

To ensure that we were reaching a broad base of community members, regardless of their social media savvy, we also incorporated a text-messaging system called FarmFan to help coordinate our pop-up markets. This web-based program was designed specifically to promote farmers markets through two primary services. With FarmFan, the Mobile Oasis team could send text messages with pictures and price updates to our customers on market days, and we could organize a rewards program to help incentivize return visits. Customers could earn rewards—like vouchers to double their market dollars, reusable grocery bags, and Mobile Oasis T-shirts—by joining the FarmFan program and checking in with their cell phones when they visited the market. Figure 8 provides a glimpse of the FarmFan and SNAP/EBT check-in table at the Mobile Oasis.

As part of the service, the Mobile Oasis partners could track and monitor repeat business. For example, for the 2015 and 2016 Mobile Oasis seasons, which ran from May through October each year, we followed 948 customers who joined FarmFan. For the 2015 market season, we hosted a total of eighty-four markets—twenty-four at Guilford County DSS, twenty-five at Warnersville, thirteen at Cone Health, four at the YMCA, and eighteen in High Point. Through FarmFan, we could track that 29 percent of customers came back at least once, 12 percent came back at least five times, and 3.5 percent came back at least ten times. We also learned that the highest number of repeat customers attended the Warnersville market, with four of the five most frequent shoppers visiting that market.

The multi-site structure of the Mobile Oasis required numerous, integrated forms of communication and media, most notably FarmFan, to

Figure 8. The FarmFan and SNAP check-in table at the Mobile Oasis Farmers Market. A Mobile Oasis customer collects vouchers to double her SNAP/EBT dollars, while volunteers check in customers using the FarmFan app. Photo credit: Marianne LeGreco

coordinate the popping up of each market. At the same time, this structure also gave partners the opportunity to customize the market with partners at each location. One of the clearest examples of customizing the market came at the Cone Health stops. During our 2015 season, with funding from the US Department of Agriculture and Cone Health, the Mobile Oasis offered a voucher program for people using SNAP/EBT to double their market dollars. At the Cone Health stop, we extended this program through a "Prescriptions for Produce" model.[6] In short, doctors at the Cone Health clinic could suggest fruits and vegetables to their patients as part of a personalized treatment, then provide that patient with a "prescription" in the form of a voucher for discounted produce at the Mobile Oasis. When we tracked all vouchers, both the general market vouchers and the Cone Health "prescriptions," the average redemptions were 52.3 percent higher at the Cone Health clinic than the next highest market. These sorts of customization helped the Mobile Oasis improve participation in ways that were unique and appropriate for each market stop. When customers could come out of the clinic and say, as one woman did, "Okay, I get it—it's like I can get my medicine right here at the doctor's office," the market team knew it had a good fit between location and communication.

Pop-Ups as Invitations for Community Participation

The pop-up format adopted first by the Warnersville Farmers Market and later by the Mobile Oasis Farmers Market helped partners extend our reach into the community, and it created the conditions for community members and residents to become involved in organizing the market stops in their neighborhoods. Perhaps one of the more under-realized aspects of the Mobile Oasis, however, was its potential to invite community participation. We say our potential was under-realized, because while we continued to see residents from Warnersville actively participate in organizing and hosting the markets, we did not see that same kind of participation replicated in other pop-ups added during the 2015 and 2016 seasons.

In our early pop-ups as the Warnersville Farmers Market, the task force certainly treated the market as an occasion to bring new voices and potential leaders into the conversation. As the opening story attests, the market became a gateway for Niesha to become a part of the advocacy and activism around food security and food justice in Greensboro. After winning hearts and attention at the 2012 Peach Treats contest, she became a part of the task force for both the garden and market. Niesha has volunteered with the Mobile Oasis since its inception, and she was a staff member with the City Oasis Project at Warnersville in 2015. She has since gone on to serve in developing the City of Greensboro's *Fresh Food Access Plan* and as a member of both the Guilford Food Council and the board of directors for the Greensboro Farmers Curb Market.[7]

People like Niesha were crucial during the early organizing of the test markets that would eventually become the Mobile Oasis. Community members like Valerie Jones and Adlois Shoffner played a key role in organizing some of the pop-ups during our first 2012 season, bringing in local vendors and craftspeople from the neighborhood, and in Valerie's case, designing our first logo. Along with Otis, they came up with the idea to host a special market each month to attract customers and new vendors. This idea grew into the Peach Treats Contest, Children's Day, Fish Fry, and Back-to-School events hosted at the market. These event days became some of our most highly attended markets throughout the summer of 2012. Although Valerie had to move on to other projects, and Adlois and her family moved out of Warnersville, their contributions demonstrated how the market created an occasion to invite their participation. Similar to many other cases in this book, the challenges continue to be maintaining the connections with community members, especially as people and partners change.

Again, we say our potential was under-realized, because as the partnership grew to become the Mobile Oasis, we did remain committed to including community members on our planning, logistics, and communications teams. At the same time, our focus had shifted from organizing the market through community leadership to mobilizing the resources needed to deliver a mobile farmers market. After Otis Hairston passed away unexpectedly in 2012, our relationship with the community changed. And while we continued to connect with folks in the neighborhood, like Niesha, the partnership supporting the Mobile Oasis had grown beyond Warnersville. To their credit, the Guilford County Department of Public Health always kept the topic of community on the table as we organized the Mobile Oasis, but the partnership's attention was now on managing multiple grants, coordinating food pickups across two or three farms, popping up markets across six locations, setting up a SNAP/EBT program, and bringing on new partners who wanted to join the market. Additionally, because both Guilford County and City of Greensboro offices were involved in the project, we were sometimes held to a higher level of transparency in bookkeeping and reporting. All of this took time and effort, and sometimes took attention away from engaging with new communities in ways similar to how we'd worked with Warnersville.

Again, we say this potential for the Mobile Oasis to invite participation was under-realized, which also means it was partially realized. One of the better examples of how we did invite participation is the story of Anita and Lewvenia. These two women are neighbors, who live across the street from each other in Warnersville. Both of them came to the Mobile Oasis after Otis passed away—Anita through her membership at Prince of Peace Lutheran Church and Lewvenia through her interest in gardening and volunteering with the Warnersville Community Garden. Both of them also served as community representatives on the Mobile Oasis organizing team, and they each had specific reasons to advocate for the market.

Anita wanted a market to create a more convenient location to buy fruits and vegetables in the neighborhood. Everyone in Anita's family is legally blind. They rely on public transportation to buy food, and a bus ride to the closest grocery store can take upwards of forty-five minutes. Anita also wanted to support the Mobile Oasis, because she had changed her eating habits and improved her health by swapping out ingredients in some of her favorite recipes. She wanted to share what she had learned with other people in the neighborhood, so she offered to organize a series of taste tests for the DSS and Warnersville market stops. Anita's taste-test table became one of the most popular features of the Mobile Oasis. Her butternut squash macaroni and cheese developed an epic following, and local newspaper *Triad City Beat* wrote about her chocolate zucchini cookies in a feature story on food and transportation.[8] Not only did she offer samples, but she also provided detailed recipes that she and Marianne had put together. We have included copies of Anita's most popular recipes in appendix C. As an extension of her work with the Mobile Oasis, Anita went on to become a member of the City of Greensboro's community transportation board, and she has continued to engage in activism around food access and public transportation.

Lewvenia wanted to see a market in the neighborhood because she hoped for an opportunity for residents, herself included, to become vendors alongside the Mobile Oasis. Lewvenia had her own backyard garden, and she viewed the market as an occasion for all folks in the neighborhood to share and sell food. Anita and Lewvenia didn't always tell the other partners simply what we wanted to hear, and they frequently offered dissenting viewpoints on how we planned to organize various pieces of the market. But those instances of dissent are important when it comes to mobilizing community efforts, and Anita and Lewvenia made sure we knew their perspectives.[9] While the Mobile Oasis created the conditions to invite their participation into a larger conversation about food, perhaps more importantly, both of these women also carved out their own contributions to the market—Anita with her taste-test table and Lewvenia with her own produce table. They still vend together at the People's Market in the nearby Glenwood neighborhood—about a mile from where they got their start with the Mobile Oasis.

Pop-up structures help social justice and food activism scholars launch ideas while continuing to invite community participation and customization. Although the Mobile Oasis did not replicate the same kind of community engagement as we did with the Warnersville neighborhood, our pop-ups did inspire a long-term partner to step forward to manage the market. From the outset of our partnership, the Mobile Oasis team knew it was not in the business of running farmers markets beyond the startup of the idea. Rather, our goal had always been to work with communities to see what kinds of projects we could help them launch. At the close of our 2016 season, Mobile Oasis partners began working with Guilford College—a private, Quaker-based college in northwest Greensboro—to hand off the market. Guilford College had a long history of working with immigrant, refugee, and low-income families on the topic of food security, and they were in the process of starting a sustainable food systems major. The college also had a farm.

The Mobile Oasis gave these new partners an opportunity to extend their reach with the communities they were already working with. For example, Guilford College took the Mobile Oasis into the Cottage Grove neighborhood, another high-poverty, low-food access community in Greensboro. There, the Mobile Oasis helped anchor the creation of the Cottage Grove Marketplace, a market where neighborhood entrepreneurs can sell their homegrown and handmade items.[10] Thus, the Mobile Oasis continues to realize its potential, both as pop-up food market and as a community and communication intervention that invites participation.

REFLECTIONS, RECOMMENDATIONS, AND RESOURCES

We could have told many stories about the Mobile Oasis Farmers Market. This intervention involved an extensive list of community, civic, and research partners and over five years of organizing and popping up markets. Moreover, as of January 2020, the Mobile Oasis continued to operate and had received new funding and research interest through its base at Guilford College.[11] Although operations for the Mobile Oasis were suspended in March 2020, due primarily to COVID-19, the first five years of organizing it taught us something important. The pop-up style of interventions can invite community participation, thereby addressing the relationship between culture, structure, and agency as a part of social justice organizing.[12] We emphasize the potential for pop-up interventions as a form of community advocacy and activism in our reflections, recommendations, and resources.

Reflections

Pop-ups are useful approaches for launching ideas in food systems. From mobile farmers markets to food trucks to pop-up restaurants, this kind of organizing can disrupt and potentially transform food systems through low-cost interventions and business models. In terms of mobile and other forms of pop-up farmers markets, these kinds of interventions are generally about mobilizing access. The mission of most mobile markets, like the Veggie Van out of Buffalo, New York, or the Fresh Truck from Boston, is to increase access to fruits and vegetables by making access more convenient. By bringing resources, information, and food directly to people—be it where they live, where they work, or where they go to the doctor— mobile markets increase *convenient* access to fruits and vegetables, making it more likely that people will buy (and hopefully eat) what the market sells. This argument is reflected in similar mobile market interventions out of Buffalo, New York, and Eastern North Carolina, where a randomized controlled study of mobile farmers markets showed that by the end of their intervention, 95 percent of the people they surveyed were familiar with the mobile market in their neighborhood, two-thirds of participants shopped at the market, and customers had increased their fruit and vegetable intake by 1.6 cups since the mobile market started operating.[13]

But mobile markets and pop-up interventions are about more than mobilizing access. As a structure, pop-ups give food justice partnerships some needed flexibility to test out ideas, relationships, and locations as they scale up from planning and pilot tests to larger scale interventions

and community outreach. Many grassroots and community-based interventions start off with limited financial and material resources as partnerships build track records and working relationships. Since pop-ups don't
rely on long-term spaces and rarely require complex permitting from city
and county offices, unlike other food systems interventions like opening
a grocery store or restaurant, they allow partners to begin reorganizing
resources and get food to people without having to raise tens and hundreds
of thousands of dollars to do so. Simply put, pop-ups can move. In this way,
partners can stage interventions across a variety of venues and mobilize
conversations about how we eat throughout numerous communities.

Mobilizing these conversations and interventions, however, often relies
on the strategic use of material resources—namely, grant funding and
social media—in order to launch ideas. With the Mobile Oasis, we were
able to leverage the flexibility of our pop-up markets into grant funding
from Blue Cross/Blue Shield and the US Department of Agriculture, and
that initial funding was crucial to scale up from pop-up markets to a fully-
realized mobile farmers market. The FINI grant, in particular, gave us
the opportunity to pay for people's labor and purchase produce in ways
that would not have been possible otherwise. Between 2010 and 2016, the
USDA infused millions of dollars into local economies through their FINI
grants, as well as their Local Food Promotion Program, Community-Based
Food Programs, and Farmers Market Promotion Programs. For many communities facing food insecurity, these funding streams created vital pathways to implement innovative ideas and mobilize conversations around
food, such as those illustrated around the Mobile Oasis. However, grant
funding is not a permanent solution, and since 2016, funding mechanisms
out of the USDA have changed—meaning that communities must also
attend to the material realities of making their innovations and interventions sustainable over time, and that frequently means moving beyond
grant funding for initial pop-ups and startups.

Additionally, this project was also indebted to the strategic use of
media in order to mobilize participation. From the first news story about
our first pop-up in Warnersville to the use of FarmFan to the bus advertisements that we created to promote the Mobile Oasis, both traditional
and social media played almost as important a role as funding in mobilizing resources around the Mobile Oasis. In many ways, the proliferation of

programs like FarmFan—which has now grown into a new, more robust program for managing community-support food programs, now called Harvie—enables organizers and activists to tailor their media strategy to communities in ways that are much more accessible and appropriate to that community. As such, organizers cannot underestimate the importance of a well-researched media strategy to mobilize resources within and around communities.

Pop-ups also create spaces to mobilize culture as partners simultaneously navigate structural change. This case has clearly illustrated how pop-ups can assist partners in managing tensions and structural paradoxes that arise as they design and implement interventions, and even more so, we have highlighted the importance of culture in terms of organizing. From a communication perspective, research on social justice frequently relies on theories that emphasize both material and social structures and human agency as the necessary components when organizing for social change. As part of his Culture-Centered Approach to communication, Mohan Dutta has argued that culture is an equally necessary component, and that interventions must be grounded in the culture of the community as opposed to levied by outside voices that simply reproduce the status quo.[14]

Early in our organizing, one of our advisors from the County Cooperative Extension worried that we had launched the Mobile Oasis to soon, saying that we hadn't done enough work to change the culture of people's eating habits in Warnersville before expecting them to buy fruits and vegetables at a farmers market. This kind of thinking, however, reproduces a paradoxical situation that imposes outside definitions of eating in which people are expected to change their routines, based on cultures and practices that are not always their own, and without necessary access to the structures to support any changes they might make. What she failed to realize was that the Mobile Oasis wasn't about *changing* people's culture as much as it was about mobilizing a conversation around food access with a community that had identified that need within their neighborhood. We saw this in the grassroots organizing that gave rise to the Mobile Oasis, and we saw this when Anita and Lewvenia carved out their own spaces for participation through the market.

Mobile Oasis partners recognized the market's purpose to increase individual agency by changing the structural barriers to better food in their neighborhoods. But what we didn't always realize was the Mobile Oasis's potential as a cultural driver, as well. This intervention was about more than simply increasing access to food. It was about furthering a conversation about secure food systems across our communities and neighborhoods. In terms of providing food resources and improving food access, the Mobile Oasis was sufficiently successful. In terms of mobilizing people to talk about food and advocate for changes they wanted to see in their communities, the Mobile Oasis has only scratched the surface in terms of its potential.

Recommendations

For this case study on mobilizing interventions, we offer the following recommendations for organizing both pop-ups, in general, and mobile farmers markets, more specifically:

1. Start with an environmental scan. Many community-engaged and social justice scholars stress the importance of the environmental scan as a way to document the assets, barriers, histories, and geographies of a neighborhood and its people.[15] Environmental scans are especially important for pop-ups and mobile interventions, as they also help partners to map potential locations for pop-up events, as well as community interest in the idea or intervention.

2. Develop a system for selecting sites that involves community customization. Interventions like the Mobile Oasis work best when partners take the time to invite participation from community members and create a space for them to customize the market to their neighborhood. Mobile farmers markets can serve as anchor vendors that help neighborhoods launch their own systems for community and economic development, as we saw with the Cottage Grove neighborhood. In this way, a system for selecting sites can be aligned with the culture, structures, and media practices that are important to residents.

3. Create a space that is about more than food. The Mobile Oasis is often recognized for how it increases access in low-income food deserts, but the better stories come from the times that people swapped ten different recipes for squash or started popping up their own tables to share and sell food. Sometimes partners can get so lost in the organizing, the data collecting, and the business operations that we forget to enjoy the community that is building around us.

4. But don't forget that you're still running a "business." Part of communicating food justice means reorganizing economic markets to more equitably serve communities. Mobile farmers markets have the potential to disrupt food markets and distribution systems in some unique and creative ways. At the same time, even cooperative food structures still rely on some sort of economic model to manage their resources. Be prepared to manage those resources in a way that is transparent and accountable to the community, especially when addressing concerns like the cost of food and access to SNAP/EBT in low-income neighborhoods.

Resources

The Veggie Van Study: This site started off as a research project around mobile market access in Buffalo, New York, and Eastern North Carolina. The research team have now transitioned to providing technical assistance for mobile farmers markets, and their website offers toolkits and other resources for starting mobile farmers markets.[16]

The Fresh Truck in Boston, Massachusetts: Another model program featuring a mobile farmers market, the Fresh Truck team offers insight about their nonprofit approach to organizing.[17]

Market Umbrella: Early in our organizing, we relied on Market Umbrella to help us craft some initial survey questions and other strategies for designing pop-up markets.[18]

Harvie: We mentioned FarmFan as a resource we used to help launch the Mobile Oasis. FarmFan grew into a different program, now called Harvie. They provide many useful resources for increasing traffic for local agriculture programs.[19]

The Justice Fleet: This group follows communication scholar Amber Johnson as they launch a pop-up art exhibit to mobilize conversations about trauma, forgiveness, and healing.[20]

Eventbrite: As a social media platform, Eventbrite has positioned itself as a go-to resource for pop-up events. They have created a playbook for organizing pop-ups for everything from entertainment events to social activism.[21]

PART IV Documenting Process

CASE STUDIES

One of the most substantive contributions that communication researchers can make to conversations around food justice organizing is documenting the stories and data involving community-based and community-engaged interventions. A primary component of communication research for social justice activism involves documenting the processes, practices, and outcomes of our work and making that information available to multiple publics.[1] How we weave together stories and numbers to show our work provides crucial details and support for food activism efforts.

Frameworks for tracking and monitoring require key decisions, including those captured by the following questions:

- What do we want to know?
- What will we look for?
- What will we gather?
- How will we gather it?

By focusing on these questions, communication researchers can help communities and activists create a composite picture of the partnerships, practices, and processes that define our interventions.[2] Documenting process gives researchers and communities a narrative to share with people in power who can further influence change and other activists and advocates who might replicate their work. In this way, documenting process also works alongside mobilizing resources in that well-documented interventions can mobilize further conversations and actions.

Part 4 focuses on telling stories and managing data as essential practices related to documenting process. Chapter 7 emphasizes the importance of multi-mediated storytelling around food as it relates to Ethnosh—an innovative program that highlights the contributions of immigrant-owned restaurants on local food systems. Ethnosh tells the story of over twenty international cuisines in Greensboro through stories and photographs of the restaurant owners who come from those cultures. Chapter 8 offers a perspective on managing data through the lens of a multi-partnered kitchen incubator program called Kitchen Connects GSO. This intervention involved a systematic data collection process that tracked the communication and business practices of applicants, participants, graduates, and partners associated with the program. The emphasis on documenting process helped partners to improve the services they offered and to appreciate the importance of good data in designing food systems interventions.

7 Ethnosh

With Donovan McKnight

At the center of Bangkok Café are sisters Ad Griffin and Yim Thepsoumane. Ad and her husband, Jeff, bought the restaurant in 2013. Yim had previously owned the space since 2005, and you can still find her managing the front of the house and bustling back and forth between the dining room and the kitchen. Even though she's the younger sister, Yim also carries the narrative of the restaurant and her family's connection to food. This opening story was featured in the *Greensboro News & Record* on June 14, 2017, written by Marianne for an innovative community program called Ethnosh.

Ad and Yim's story is printed on the closing pages of their menu. Their approach to food is influenced heavily by their family—especially their mother. They grew up on the edge of northeast Thailand, in a small town on the Mekong River. From the front porch of their mother's home, they can look across the river and see the neighboring country of Laos. As such, their food is influenced not only by their roots in Thailand but also their proximity to Lao food culture.

Beyond the menu, I also learned that Yim and Ad came to the United States from Thailand in 1993 and 2005, respectively.[1] Yim had previously worked for Tyco Electronics, but she switched over to restaurants after moving to Greensboro. When she was ready to start a family in 2005, she thought owning her own business might give her more time to spend with her children. I asked her how that worked out for her, and she just laughed.

Nevertheless, she bought the Bangkok Café in 2005. Shortly thereafter, she asked her older sister Ad if she knew how to cook. "Yes, yes. I'm a very good cook," Ad assured her. But Yim quickly learned that while Ad was an excellent cook for two people, getting up to speed on feeding an entire restaurant took a little more time. They laugh about these stories much in the same way that my sister and I banter with each other, all in good fun with a hint of truth.

The community around these sisters has continued to grow, especially as Ad became more skilled and experimental in the kitchen. The sisters also take great pride in cooking food to order, which has become a great way for the sisters to connect with the many Thai and Lao families in Greensboro. Yim explains, with a sly grin, that they cook food a little differently for their customers from Thailand and Laos. "How so?" I ask. Sweet, sticky rice. Lots of vegetables. Smelly fish. Strong herbs. And very spicy. (Pro tip: if you want your food really spicy, and I mean really spicy, order it "Thai hot." They'll take you there.)

Perhaps one of the best stories comes from Jeff Griffin, Ad's husband since 2012 and co-owner since 2013. Jeff had been a regular at the Bangkok Café for several years—he's a big fan of the Pad Thai. Jeff and Ad also became big fans of each other and eventually married in Thailand. "So you started out as a fan and became part of the family?" I asked him. "I guess so," he said.

·   ·   ·   ·   ·

A CASE STUDY OF SHARING FOOD STORIES

In 2013, three local organizations partnered to create Ethnosh, which is a semimonthly meetup and menu tasting at an immigrant-owned restaurant in Greensboro. The word itself is a mash-up of the Greek work *ethno*, alluding to culture, and the Yiddish word *nosh*, to emphasize the eating. As a way of "eating culture," Ethnosh focuses not only on the food, but also the families, communities, culture, and most importantly the stories behind it.

Greensboro is home to vibrant immigrant and refugee communities, with many members of those communities involved intricately in local food systems. More than sixty thousand immigrants and their children live in Guilford County, and these families bring with them rich food traditions and cultures that are celebrated across the city.[2] Greensboro is home to more than one hundred fifty immigrant-owned restaurants and food businesses—Ethnosh alone has covered fifty-one of these locations, including thirty-nine restaurants, three food trucks, and two markets where individuals and families sell food that reflects their cultures. These restaurants and markets represent over twenty different cuisines, largely from Central and Southeast Asia, Latin America, the Middle East, and Northeast Africa. Often using family recipes that have been passed down and refined over generations, these local food businesses make up a substantial part of Greensboro's food culture. Ethnosh emerged as an opportunity to highlight this asset in Greensboro's food system, help introduce people to new cuisines, and build community around food.

Ethnosh coordinates a range of resources to promote restaurants. Before the meetup, they invite both a local writer and a local photographer to interview the families and take photographs of the food, both of which the owners can use for future advertising. The photo-essay is turned into a cover story for a local newspaper's food section. The photographs and stories are also featured on Ethnosh's website and social media platforms, which serve as an online resource for learning about international cuisine in local places. Finally, at the meetup itself, attendees receive a sampler plate of food for ticket prices that have ranged anywhere from $5 to $13 to $45. Meetups regularly sell out of seating, and because Ethnosh events are hosted on the restaurant's slowest night of the week, the family owners regularly cover costs and typically have a "good night" for a Tuesday.

This chapter creates an opportunity for us to examine questions one and three from our set of guiding questions—specifically, what counts as community and how neighbors work together to coordinate resources for food justice activism. In some ways, Ethnosh's process operates like a variation of photovoice, a popular community-engaged method that asks research participants to take photographs within their communities and everyday activities as a way to facilitate dialogue and policy change.[3] The use of photographs and narratives opens up a space that is different than traditional methods of documentation and reflection, in that the images and stories also spark conversations that can help communities unpack difficult issues—like food insecurity, racism, and classism. Ethnosh, and their unique way of promoting their partners, represents a savvy way of building social and economic support for immigrant-owned restaurants in Greensboro.

This chapter provides additional detail about Ethnosh's communication activism, as it highlights the importance of immigrant-owned restaurants on Greensboro's food system. We also invited Donovan McKnight—one of the cofounders of Ethnosh—to offer some reflections on the continued appeal of this program. We begin with an overview of how Ethnosh is rooted in a communication approach to documenting their process. But the beauty of this program is truly in its simplicity—how it uses narratives, pictures, and events to create genuine community. In this way, Ethnosh advances a culture-centered approach to communication that focuses on telling stories.[4] As such, we spend the majority of the case study sharing stories of food and family that Ethnosh has woven.

Cuisine, Culture, Community

Three words articulate the essence of Ethnosh: *cuisine, culture*, and *community*. These words appear along the top of their website and beneath their logo. They are a reminder of why Ethnosh was started—to celebrate the diverse cultures that make up Greensboro, introduce people to the variety of cuisines available in our city, and create a sense of community by building relationships between diners and the individuals and families behind the food. Ethnosh was launched in August 2013, when three local Greensboro organizations partnered to highlight local restaurants and food establishments that are frequently immigrant or first-generation-owned. As outlined on the website:

> Ethnosh is an organization created to get you in the know and out to eat at all of the excellent immigrant-owned international food businesses in your area.

Pairing a rich online experience with real-world events, Ethnosh works to foster cross-cultural discovery and enrichment, and to drive business to potentially underserved areas within your community. It's a really delicious way to get involved.

Ethnosh represents cultural food traditions and recipes from people and families with that heritage. Triad Local First, a nonprofit organization that emphasizes supporting local businesses; Face-to-Face Greensboro, a group dedicated to building communication through sharing information, conversation, and culture; and Bluezoom, an advertising and media company, brought their collective talents together to create the model.

Ethnosh's model focuses on hosting a semimonthly meetup, or "NoshUp," at a featured restaurant. As the website further clarifies:

> NoshUps are casual tasting events held at select restaurants. . . . Our events bring people together . . . to sample authentic international cuisine and meet the families that bring the deliciousness to their communities. The people, flavors, and stories come together to create uniquely rich and memorable experiences for patrons and restaurant families alike.

A typical NoshUp features two or three seatings over the course of a weeknight evening. Hosting NoshUps on a weeknight is essential, as they are often slower nights for the restaurant owners. Ethnosh typically charges diners anywhere from $8 to $13 for a sample plate of popular items from the menu. Diners can try numerous foods to help them decide what they might like to come back and try again. In this way, Ethnosh's model is committed to generating repeat business for the restaurants.

Ethnosh has evolved its model over time. In its earlier versions, events featured open seating with a first-come, first-serve approach. The sample plates were $5, and people sometimes had to wait in long lines for food. In early 2016, Ethnosh partners started selling advanced tickets for a limited number of seating at each event. They also increased the ticket price from $5 to $8, not as a way to exclude people from the experience, but as a way to bring a greater and more realistic value to the food. In late 2018, partners announced, via website and email, that ticket prices would increase to $13, emphasizing that "after three years of hosting ticketed tasting events, we have decided to increase pricing for this and future NoshUp events. This increase will allow us to provide more revenue to our partnering restaurants, and it gets Ethnosh a little closer to covering the cost . . . to organize monthly NoshUps."

The NoshUps started as a way to introduce the diverse cuisines in Greensboro to people who might not otherwise be familiar with the vibrant Vietnamese, Thai, Lao, Ethiopian, Korean, Latin American, and Middle Eastern foods available in the city. They have grown to facilitate a sense of community at each meetup. The first NoshUp was hosted on August 27, 2013, at Pho Hien Vuong—an incredibly popular Vietnamese restaurant that has been a Greensboro staple for decades. Known primarily for their pho, a soup revered as a comfort food in Vietnam, Pho Hien Vuong was a recognizable place to launch Ethnosh. Since that first NoshUp, Ethnosh has continued to host events—almost monthly—at more than thirty restaurants across Greensboro. In November 2019, Ethnosh hosted its fortieth NoshUp—a special event at Boba House, a vegetarian restaurant featuring live music; the $17 ticket price included a 10 percent donation to SPCA of the Triad.

Although the NoshUps are often the most exciting part of Ethnosh—not only because of the food, but also the sense of community and conversation that emerges at the meetups—the necessary core of the program lies in the stories from the restaurants. The foundation of Ethnosh is rooted in communication and ethnographic practice—which focuses on documenting culture as a way to promote understanding about a community. About two weeks before each event, Ethnosh works with local writers and photographers to construct a story with the restaurant owners about their heritage, their families, and the nuances of their menus. At the NoshUps, themselves, the owners are also invited to speak at each seating and share their story more directly with their customers. Coupled with photographs of the food, the people, and the process, these ethnographic tales provide a window into the background and history of the families.

The way Ethnosh partners document the process is quite elegant. The stories and photographs appear in the *Greensboro News & Record* on the front page of their Wednesday food section. Many restaurant owners have framed the articles to hang in their restaurants, and they have used the stories and pictures as part of their in-house advertising. Prior to 2016, Ethnosh partners relied on Facebook and Instagam to push out

information about NoshUps, the stories, and pictures, but over that summer, they reached a critical mass of restaurants to launch a website. The
website features a unique interface to learn more about the restaurants,
the twenty different cuisines featured, and the stories of the owners. Using
photographs to create a gateway to learn more about the restaurants, each
restaurant profile includes directions to their location(s), a copy of the
story and photographs, links to the restaurant's website and menu, and
a share link to let others know about the food. The website also contains
an archive of past Ethnosh events, as well as promotions and tickets for
upcoming NoshUps.

The simplicity of the program's design alongside the detailed documentation makes Ethnosh highly replicable. For example, Ethnosh Dayton
launched in 2019 to highlight the diverse cuisines, cultures, and communities in Dayton, Ohio. The satellite program is off to a strong start,
and Ethnosh has remained open to working with other communities who
would like to organize NoshUps and tell some ethnographic tales that
feature local cuisines of color. At the same time, Ethnosh's minimalism
also makes it highly poachable. At least one copycat program emerged
that focused primarily on the meetups, choosing to forego the stories and
pictures. But without those pieces, the spinoff program fell flat. The conversation that Ethnosh builds through the stories and pictures—especially
as they appear in local newspapers and other media—provides a crucial
component to what has made this program successful. Ethnosh doesn't
work without the stories.

The Stories and Pictures of Ethnosh

A surface-level critique might suggest that Ethnosh walks a line very close
to cultural appropriation—a misguided example of cultural voyeurism
that materially benefits the primarily white organizers behind the original model. That sort of critique would make it easy to miss something
important—something that communication scholar Osei Appiah might
argue is noteworthy progress in cross-cultural communication and the
benefits of cultural voyeurism.[5] Appiah's research suggested that mediated interactions between groups from different cultures, especially those
interactions that allow a window into the culture that would otherwise

Figure 9. Bangkok Café. Co-owner Ad Griffin prepares for the lunchtime rush in a photograph by YoungDoo Carey.

be hard to observe, can unite people who otherwise see themselves as different. Ethnosh anchors its model in a communication framework that privileges photographs and stories, and when those stories are published on the front page of the *Greensboro News & Record*, they open that mediated window that invites people to learn more and maybe have a meal that supports that local business.

Considering how strongly we feel about the importance of the stories and the pictures that make up a large part of Ethnosh's model, we would like to use the remainder of this chapter to highlight some of those ethnographic tales that have been crucial to its success. In the opening pages of this story, we introduced you to a story that Marianne wrote about Bangkok Café—a Thai restaurant operated by sisters who grew up on the border between Thailand and Laos. Figure 9 shows Ad preparing kapow—a dish they make with chicken, bell peppers, broccoli, carrots, chili paste, garlic, and basil.

Food and family are common threads across many of the stories that Ethnosh writers have collected. Leading up to the inaugural NoshUp at

Figure 10. Ghassan's. Khaled Fleihan at work on the grill at Ghassan's Mediterranean restaurant in Greensboro. Photo credit: YoungDoo Carey.

Pho Hien Vuong, co-owner Trang Trinh told writer Harvey Robinson, "To us, this place is everything. It's our family's livelihood." Another early NoshUp was hosted at Ghassan's, a restaurant that introduced Greensboro to Mediterranean food more than forty years ago. The title of their article read, "A Place of Food and Family," and it told the story of Khaled Fleihan, who fled Lebanon during its civil war and opened a restaurant with his brother in Greensboro in the 1970s. His family grew up in the restaurant, which has four locations across Greensboro, and two of his children are managing the next generation of Ghassan's. Figure 10 shows Khaled Fleihan working the grill wearing Ghassan's signature "YALLA!" T-shirt, inviting everyone to come on!

The story of Jerusalem Market (Figure 11)—with the iconic Saliba Hanhan and his sons Easa and Omar—picks up on several similar threads. Saliba was a trained chemist, who came to the United States in the 1960s to escape violence from the Arab-Israeli war. When he relocated to Greensboro, after earning a degree in chemistry from Miami University

Figure 11. Jerusalem Market. Saliba Hanhan watches over the array of international items at Jerusalem Market. Photo credit: Laath Martin and Natalie Abassi.

in Ohio, he opened a market on the west edge of the city that specialized in Middle Eastern groceries, with a sandwich counter in the back. Saliba is known across Greensboro for his spicy falafel, which years later his sons have spun off into a full-service restaurant in the downtown city center. Ethnosh has visited Jerusalem Market three time, both at the grocery and market in November 2013 and then twice at the downtown restaurant after it opened in February 2017 and again in 2019. Again, this notion of family creating space for the next generation is frequently reinforced across Ethnosh narratives.

Many of the restaurant owners and operators also tell stories of how they hope to educate diners about the importance of their food and culture. In a story on BBQ Nation Indian Grill (Figure 12), co-owner Sri Edupuganti says, "We want to make sure people here enjoy authentic Indian food. . . . We want all cultures to understand what we are about and what we are trying to do." Her restaurant features a unique twist in that each table houses its own grill, so diners can grill their own skewers with chicken and vegetables. Similarly, Timmy Vasasiri—owner of Thai Corner Kitchen (Figure 13)—speaks of educating his customers about Thai food in a story by Tina Firesheets, who writes:

> When it comes to the food . . . they use some of his mother's recipes—with his own twist. "I add just a little bit of my taste," he says. He likes a perfect

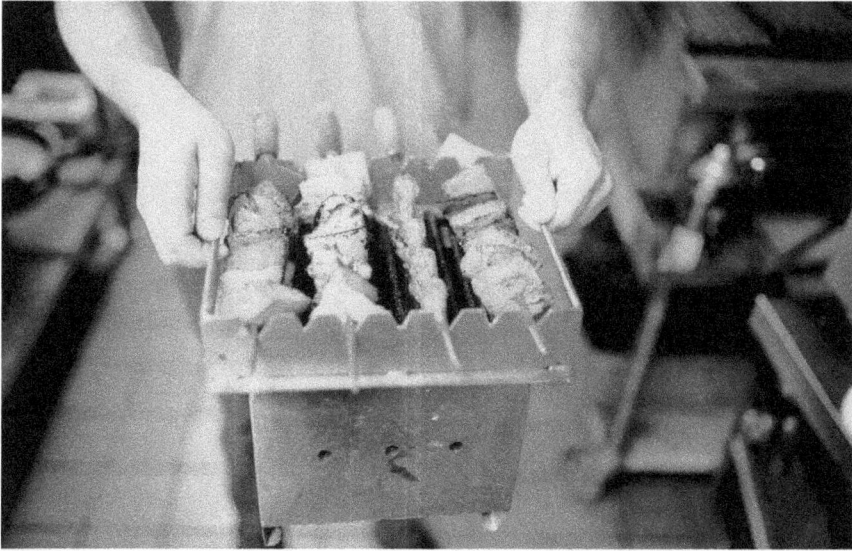

Figure 12. Skewers atop a portable grill at BBQ Nation Indian Grill in High Point. Photo credit: Daniel White.

balance of sweet, spicy, salty and tangy . . . for the most part the Vasasiris stay true to their Thai roots. The combination of flavors and the foundation of their soups, rice and noodle dishes are strictly Thai. And he's noticing that people are coming into his restaurant more educated about Thai food.

The stories of Ethnosh also feature writers and photographers who have used this platform to express the importance of their culture and heritage to the food scene in Greensboro. Local writer Tina Firesheets has contributed more content to Ethnosh than any other writer. As a Korean American adopted by a Japanese American mother and European American father, she uses her writing—Ethnosh included—to explore her love of food from other countries and cultures. Another example is seen in a story about Taste of Ethiopia, where author Aden Hailemariam writes with her friend, Sarah Ivory:

For people like us, a first-generation immigrant growing up in an Eritrean household (Aden) and a longtime friend and advocate of the resettled Ethiopian/Eritrean refugee communities (Sarah), the restaurant's promise was

Figure 13. Thai Corner Kitchen. A view from the kitchen, where owners Timmy and Tanyawat Vasasiri hope to expand Greensboro's palate for Thai food. Photo credit: YoungDoo Carey.

more than culinary. An authentic Ethiopian restaurant would offer a taste of home for those who've settled far from their families. It would be a place to bring American friends and loved ones to share in a familiar cultural tradition. It would be a fond reminder of youthful travels and adventures past and more importantly, could serve as a symbol of hope for our city's newest immigrants who dream of one day having a place of their own.

Finally, photographer Dhanraj Emanuel, whose work is featured in Figures 14 and 15, has partnered with Ethnosh not only to showcase food from his native country of India, but also to express his artistic side by hosting a NoshUp in his photography studio.

The photographs, stories, and events curated by Ethnosh weave together a sense of community, not only for the restaurant owners, but also for the writers, photographers, and diners. By documenting the process—both through traditional print media like newspapers and online media like their interactive website and social media

Figure 14. Taaza Bistro invites customers to experience the many shapes, sizes, and textures of Indian cuisine. Photo credit: Dhanraj Emanuel.

Figure 15. A story in pictures. Pasta making by Dal Maso Pasta on the left and a signature noodle soup at Rice Paper Vietnamese Cuisine on the right. Photo credit Dhanraj Emanuel.

sites—Ethnosh has created a platform and a process that can be repli-cated in other communities that want to highlight both the stories and the food from their cuisines of color. Organizers recognize that the com-munication pieces of social justice activism are about more than web-sites and social media. Although these forms of communication and media are certainly crucial to the success of a program like Ethnosh, organizers have also acknowledged the pervasiveness of communica-tion in the design of their model by emphasizing dialogue, narrative, and photographic storytelling. That model is simple and elegant, and it reinforces the importance of communication and storytelling to food justice organizing.

REFLECTIONS, RECOMMENDATIONS, AND RESOURCES

Ethnosh illustrates a more subtle example of communicating food justice. Similar to the Downtown Greensboro Food Truck Pilot Project, whose story we told in chapter 4, Ethnosh does not tell a story of food access and food insecurity. Rather, this program focuses on the larger food sys-tems and culture that are an important part of building food security in communities like Greensboro. Even more so, Ethnosh pursues their mis-sion by grounding their work in cohesive communication practices and detailed storytelling. In addition to providing ethnographic tales and photojournalistic insights about the restaurants and families featured at their NoshUps, Ethnosh operates almost like a variation of photovoice. An increasingly popular research approach, photovoice uses photographs, usually taken by community members, as a way to share stories and open up conversations with civic leaders about important social justice issues.[6] Indeed, cofounder Donovan McKnight has taken the stories and pictures to speak publicly about Ethnosh at numerous meetings of the Greens-boro City Council, who voted in December 2014 to adopt a resolution sup-porting Ethnosh's mission and goals. In this section, we concentrate on some reflections about the program from Donovan's perspective before providing recommendations and resources for organizing programs like Ethnosh.

Reflections

Ethnosh has experienced some level of success in a specific area where many other community-based efforts have sometimes struggled: they have built a collection of stories from communities that are often hard to reach. As we mentioned previously, Ethnosh doesn't work without the stories, but the process is not so simple as walking into a restaurant and asking an owner to recount their life history. Soliciting stories from first- and second-generation immigrant families requires a great deal of trust building. Moreover, writers and Ethnosh organizers must take great care of those stories once they hear them—which can bring up particular challenges as food writing evolves as a form of activism. We consider both of these reflections here.

First, we offer the following account from Donovan about the importance of trust and humility while inviting restaurants owners to participate.

Gaining trust with many of the immigrant-owned restaurants we've worked with takes work. And 90 percent of that work is showing up. These business owners get bombarded with Groupon-type outfits trying to get them to buy all kinds of advertising. So when I walk in and tell them I'd love to work with them, most of the time, they are skeptical. I would be too. I'm a white male, so there's that layer too. I've been turned away many times. I've even been escorted off the premises after a few repeat visits.

When we first decided to launch this program, I asked people in the community if it was a good idea. Was there a need there to justify the program? Could I, as a white guy, do this work legitimately. The best answer I got, the one that sticks with me came from my wife. She's half Colombian and worked in refugee resettlement for several years. She told me, "Donovan, as long as you are approaching this work from a place of always honoring these families, their businesses, and their culture, you'll be okay." And so I take that with me wherever I go with Ethnosh. I show up, time and again, with a sense of humility.

Some of the restaurants I work with are very savvy marketers. When I walk through the door and give them my elevator pitch, their eyes light up and they ask when we can make it happen. Others, frankly, have no interest in an unfamiliar client base that's going to complicate their process. Many of these restaurants exist to serve their respective communities. Going out of their way for Ethnosh just isn't of interest. A ton of attention from a crowd of demanding patrons just isn't worth it. Others still are so lightly staffed that they simply can't fulfill a spike in demand. In some cases, it's a mother and her son who aren't ready to hire more staff.

It's a complex situation, and it takes a lot of restaurant visits to make this project happen. Humility, honor, respect, empathy, and yes, just showing up. The owners need to know you're for real. We're about to embark on a partnership together, trust is everything. We're not just hosting an event together, I'm asking them to open up their hearts to us and share their history, their struggles and successes, the intricacies of their menus. None of it would be possible without first establishing trust. And 90 percent of the time, that happens face-to-face, on opposite sides of a counter.

Second, we also see an opportunity to reflect about Ethnosh in the context of social activism and food writing. More specifically, we have taken great care—almost to the point of hypervigilance—about the language we've used to write this chapter. As food writing continues to evolve as a form of social activism, many writers have justifiably critiqued the use of words like "ethnic" and "foreign" to write about international food.[7] We have avoided them in this chapter, and we have played around with phrases like immigrant-owned, cuisines of color, and international food after consulting with some professional food writers from various backgrounds. At the same time, we also recognize the need to manage various paradoxes, dilemmas, and tensions as food writers continue to find language that is more representative of the cultures and people behind the food.

Consider the following account from Donovan's perspective about how Ethnosh managed the tensions surrounding the language of food writing.

Yes, "ethnic." It's complicated. In May of 2018 I sent an email to Alex McKinney, co-founder of Ethnosh, with the subject line "Ethnic." The email begins with a list of five or so URLs all linking to articles about why that word is dated.[8] I go on to write:

I think our work here is to continue to include the vast majority of people who use that term in search and in conversation, but help them begin to change up that term for something like "international" or "global."

I've heard this argument with film and music too, right? Like global music means music that's not western. Or foreign film means not from US or England?

It's complicated. And we can't solve it or walk the line perfectly. But we can continue to evolve on it.

When we started Ethnosh in 2013, I ran the term "ethnic" by a few people in the immigrant services industry and their response was: "It's not great, but it's what people use for the most part."

But that was 5 years ago. And I think it's time to adjust.

Alex, who built our website from scratch, revised the content and switched out "ethnic" for terms like "international." From a communication standpoint, we want people to find our website through simple searches, obviously. The folks we spoke with in the search engine optimization field, recommended keeping the term, because that's primarily what people use if they're searching for global food. So it creates a bit of a paradox. People won't find our site as easily if we strike "ethnic" from our language on the site—but if we leave the term, we're perpetuating the misnomer, which is irresponsible.

Complicating the matter further, the hashtag #ethnicfood has 68k uses on Instagram. A quick scroll of those uses and you can see that the accounts posting that hashtag are, in many cases, international food accounts. To manage our way out of this dilemma, our SEO consultants advised incorporating the term "ethnic" into our metadata. In other words, the term shows up in search but not on the website itself.

If what Appiah argued about mediated experiences as a potentially positive form of cultural voyeurism applies here, and Ethnosh can serve as a way for people who are unfamiliar with a particular cuisine to test out something new and begin to support an immigrant-owned, local restaurant, then they need a way to open the window.[9] Using media strategies, like hiding terms in metadata, are one way that organizers and activists can avoid reproducing problematic language while still attracting the people who may need to hear their messages and stories the most.

Recommendations

This chapter furthers the conversation about food justice activism by focusing on story and research-based advocacy in support of immigrant-owned, international restaurants. Our recommendations are geared toward readers who might be interested in organizing a program like Ethnosh in their community.

1. Explore your community. It all starts by researching what's in your community. Many international food businesses exist along the

seemingly forgotten corridors and shopping plazas of every midsize city. Jump in a car and go find them. Bring a friend and get out of your usual patterns. Discover for yourself the areas of your city you hadn't before noticed.

2. Think about your position and enter into these spaces with a little humility. If it's your first time trying out these cuisines, some of your visits are likely to be uncomfortable, and that's what makes it so important. Be open to the new experience. Go with the flow of the place. If you're trying to gauge their interest in partnering to host a NoshUp, get to know the owners and families, and let the partnering develop organically.

3. Start Ethnosh in your city—Ethnosh is replicable by design. We started this program as a way for communities to drive business toward their immigrant-owned and international restaurants, and as a way for writers, photographers, and everyday eaters to join together in celebrating the stories of these families. We are committed to ensuring that this model is used to honor these kinds of stories, and the Ethnosh headquarters team is at your service to help you launch the program wherever you are.

4. Read Saru Jayaraman's book *Behind the Kitchen Door*.[10] This book focuses on the political and economic implications of dining out. While she doesn't focus on immigrant and international food specifically, she does raise some provocative thoughts about where we choose to eat.

5. Consider the possibilities of using photographs and narratives as a way to document process and carry out basic data collection, network assessments, and environmental scans with communities and neighborhoods who are experiencing food hardship and/or economic barriers to participating in food systems. Photovoice offers an excellent set of strategies and ethics for designing, implementing, and documenting community-based processes through photographs, dialogue, and policy change.[11]

Resources

If you plan to start organizing with immigrant and refugee communities in your city or town, and you are not a member of that community, we recommend that you consult with local organizations and nonprofit groups that have an established and well-respected reputation for working in these areas. We can share some resources here:

Refugee and immigrant resettlement and service organizations like the Center for New North Carolinians and the Montagnard Dega Association.[12] Many of these organizations will be unique to your community and may require a little searching.

Welcoming America is a nonprofit, nonpartisan organization that aids communities in becoming more inclusive toward immigrants and all residents with a focus on social entrepreneurship.[13]

We also invite you to our website, ethnosh.org. Learn more about the photographers and writers, check out full-color versions of the photographs, and read up about the families who are driving Greensboro's international food scene.[14]

Both Community Toolbox and Photovoice.org provide excellent resources and support for designing and implementing photovoice projects in your community.[15]

8 Kitchen Connects GSO

With Dr. Stephen Sills

The necessary components for a proposed shared-use kitchen program were almost in place. The City of Greensboro's Planning Office had secured funding from a USDA Local Food Promotion Program grant to launch ideas from their Fresh Food Access Plan. First up was an effort to coordinate a kitchen incubator program to help new food entrepreneurs develop the skills and capacity to bring new food products to market and create their own small businesses. For a small set of program and kitchen fees, applicants would be guided through the process of starting and certifying a food business, as well as given access to space in a shared-use, low-risk kitchen where they could create, package, and market their products.

Three core partners stepped forward to help drive the program—the Greensboro Farmers Curb Market, the Out of the Garden Project, and the Guilford County Cooperative Extension—with the City and UNC-Greensboro's Center for Housing and Community Studies providing organizational and research support. Seven people representing these partners were gathered at the Farmers Curb Market to begin connecting the ideas to the details, and we had just finished brainstorming a pathway to delivering the program. Each step was written on large sheets of butcher paper, taped to the meeting room wall:

Participants. Project Intake. Certifications.

Kitchens.

Entrepreneurship Training. Retail Outlets.

Beneath each piece of the puzzle was a list of possible resources, partners, and details that the group would need to consider. For Participants, the core partners wanted to focus on young startups, immigrant and refugee communities, older retirees, as well as food desert residents and people who were under-connected in the food system. Project intake involved both recruiting people to the program and managing their applications. Certifications would require partners to check with the North Carolina Department of Agriculture to determine if participants needed Safe Plates or ServSafe certificates. Kitchens meant upfitting space at both the Out of the Garden Project's and the Guilford County Cooperative Extension's respective shared-use kitchen spaces. Entrepreneurship training would entail partnering with East Market Street Community Development to cover branding, marketing, and managing a business. Retail outlets asked the Farmers Curb Market to consider how program participants might become vendors at the market.

As the discussion turned from Participants to Project Intake, the core partners started to consider the application process in more detail. What would they ask applicants? What would be the criteria for selection? Who would get scholarships? Why might some people start the program, but not others? The County Cooperative Extension's shared-use kitchen was already open to the public, and our partner from Extension mentioned that they already had an application to use the kitchen. "That's great," another one of the other partners interjected, "we'll just use the same application."

"But we don't have an application to the program—just the kitchen," the partner from Extension continued, "and we might want to know some different things. We've also got pre and post surveys that we'd like to do."

In his role as the director for the Center for Housing and Community Studies, Stephen saw an opportunity to clarify the kind of support that he and Marianne could provide in their program evaluation. "So, these are the sorts of things that we can help organize and manage out of the Center," he said. "You *are* going to want to know *a lot* of things with the application. Any demographics we can get are great. For those who apply and get in. For those who apply and don't get in. For those who drop out. We can follow-up with all of them."

"Forgive me," one of the partners questioned, "but I don't quite see what following up with the people who *don't* participate in the program is going to get us. Is that really the best way to spend our limited resources?"

"Talking to the people who don't get in will help you refine the program," Stephen responded. "It will help you know if you're marketing well, if you're reaching your target audience, or what you can do to help the people who are close but not quite ready yet. And that's what we can do—we can handle the applications, the pre and post surveys, the interviews, all of that. So then everything is standardized across all of your sites, and it frees you up to focus on running the kitchens, and the classes, and the outreach—all of the things that you're really good at."

．　．　．　．　．

A CASE STUDY OF MANAGING DATA

Building the infrastructure for food systems that are equitable and resilient frequently requires having the space to test out new and innovative ideas. As we have illustrated in previous case studies, ideas like the Mobile Oasis, Food Truck Pilot Project, and Ethnosh create new opportunities to engage communities, consider the constraints of our food system, and communicate about food justice. One of the most substantial ways in which food justice researchers can contribute to food justice organizing is through documenting process and managing data around these novel, albeit often untested, programs and interventions. We realize that "managing data" doesn't always get people excited—especially people who get to talk about something as creative and engaging as food—but tracking and monitoring our work with community partners is a crucial part of activism and advocacy.[1] Managing data and documenting processes are often underappreciated—if not frequently underestimated—pieces of communicating the work we do across food systems. They help us tell stories, through both narratives and numbers. They help partners leverage their successes to secure future funding and support. They help us make sense both of what we should take with us and what we should leave behind as we move forward to the next iterations of our work. Such is the case with Kitchen Connects GSO.

When Greensboro reached the top of the Food Research and Actions Center's list of cities experiencing food hardship, the City of Greensboro's Planning Office and Parks and Recreation Department began networking community members, researchers, and agencies to produce a Fresh Food Access Plan for funding consideration by the US Department of Agriculture.[2] Partners and citizens representing City and County health and agriculture agencies, local nonprofit organizations, colleges and universities, and Greensboro neighborhoods collaborated to produce a plan that highlighted the need for shared-use and community kitchens, as well as training on how to launch local food businesses. Kitchen Connects GSO emerged from that planning process as an incubator program that helps everyday people navigate what can be a complicated commercial food system. Although anyone using local foods from Greensboro or Guilford County could apply to the program, partners designed the program specifically to attract low-income and low-access community members. The intervention provided educational and communication resources to novice food entrepreneurs in order to test out local food products in a supportive space. In doing so, Kitchen Connects focused not only on issues of food access and economic development, but also on building a supportive local food system.

This chapter uses Kitchen Connects GSO as a backdrop for a case study on the importance of managing data across multi-partnered projects involving food justice, advocacy, and activism. As a case, Kitchen Connects also helps us directly address questions two and three from our initial guiding questions, with regard to how communities organize to address food hardship and how they coordinate their actions to promote food justice. The Kitchen Connects GSO program featured a robust and systematic data management strategy that aligned strategically with delivering a shared-use kitchen initiative. Much of the credit for managing the data goes to Dr. Stephen Sills, the director of the Center for Housing and Community Studies at UNC-Greensboro, whom we have invited to contribute to this chapter.

Plotting the Points with Kitchen Connects

Part of organizing, when it comes to communicating food justice or virtu-ally any activity involving the pursuit of common goals, means managing flows of communication and information—especially when working on a multi-partnered project.[3] At any given moment in the Kitchen Connects GSO program, different partners were managing various workflows to recruit participants, train and certify them, get them set up in a kitchen at the Out of the Garden Project or Cooperative Extension, and eventu-ally prepare them to guest vend at the Greensboro Farmers Curb Mar-ket. To provide the most useful feedback during the project, researchers with the Center for Housing and Community Studies (CHCS) needed to strategically align these workflows with a mixture of data collection prac-tices. Aligning the pieces required the partners to plot out the points of the Kitchen Connects program so that CHCS could design an appropriate data strategy.

The Kitchen Connects program asked participants to commit to four primary components: certification, education, production, and test mar-ket. With certification, the Guilford County Cooperative Extension pro-vided a two-day Safe Plates food safety training, where participants could also take a state-level exam. This gave them the credentials they needed to work in the shared-use kitchens. Education involved three basic business courses: Plan for Success, Marketing Your Product, and Selling Your Prod-uct. Once the fledgling food entrepreneurs had completed the certification and education pieces, they were eligible to work in one of two shared-use kitchens—with most participants opting for the kitchen at the Out of the Garden Project. The kitchen provided access to prep spaces, cold and dry storage, ovens, sinks—everything but a grease trap. Kitchen space was available for $10/hour, and Kitchen Connects provided the first three hours at no cost. Finally, within about a month of starting the Planning for Success class and Safe Plates certification, participants could begin sell-ing their products at the Greensboro Farmers Curb Market. Although the program did not guarantee they could become full-time vendors, the Curb Market allotted three Saturdays for participants to test their products.

Beyond these specific pieces, Kitchen Connects also included a two-month recruitment and application period for each cycle of the program.

The core partners were able to administer the program in about three to four months, meaning they could host three cycles of Kitchen Connects each year. Eight total cohorts of participants went through the kitchen incubator program between March 1, 2017, and July 20, 2019. This enabled the CHCS to design a data management strategy that collected surveys and interviews early in the program in a way that could help core partners refine their application process, the education and training, and the test market.

To mirror the workflow of the Kitchen Connects components, the CHCS plotted occasions to collect data across six distinct points in the process. Table 7 summarizes the six data flows that informed our evaluation. First, the CHCS used the application to collect some basic demographic information about each applicant, background about their business and the food product they wanted to create, if and how they were using local ingredients, any past experience working with food, and their financial and business goals for their food venture. The next three data points involved observations by the CHCS team during the Kitchen Connects classes, production days in the kitchens, and the test market days at the Curb Market. Upon completion of each program cycle, CHCS researchers contacted participants for an exit interview. This included interviewing applicants who had not been selected to enroll in the program—in some cases because of program fit, in other cases because their product couldn't be approved for a low-risk kitchen. Finally, every four to six months after completion of the program, participants are interviewed again to see how their business has progressed. To manage these six data flows, we relied on Qualtrics online software to manage the application process and follow-up surveys. This allowed the CHCS to share application information with the partners quite easily, as well as create a standard repository or bank for the data we managed. We have included some samples of our data collection materials at the end of this chapter.

The CHCS team shared data updates with the Kitchen Connects team in three annual reports, as well as in some of the meetings where the core partners reviewed applications. From these reports, The Kitchen Connects team was able to make some slight revisions to their process as the incubator program progressed. For example, it became clear after the first two cohorts that the application needed to do a better job capturing

Table 7   Managing Data for Kitchen Connects GSO

Source of Data	Type of Data	Total Numbers	Sample Data Tracked
Application	24 survey questions embedded in an online intake application for the program	192 total applications	• basic demographics • business background • financial information • local ingredients
Classes	1 set of observations for a complete cycle of Kitchen Connects classes (1 certification class; 3 training classes)	4 observations for a total of 18 hours	• program alignment • education components • experiential data
Kitchen	2 observations of vendors using the Out of the Garden Project kitchen to prepare Kitchen Connects products	2 observations for a total of 4 hours	• program alignment • usefulness of kitchen access and resources • experiential data
Test market	12 periodic observations of Kitchen Connects vendors during their three test market days	12 observations for a total of 12 hours	• program alignment • vending strategies • experiential data
Exit interview	11-question, semi-structured phone interview with participants upon program completion	58 interviews	• program expectations • program effectiveness • future plans
Six-month follow-up	6-question, online survey for those accepted into the program and those who were not	54 surveys	• current vending • current sales • program effectiveness • future plans

participants' financial expectations about their businesses, especially so the Kitchen Connects instructors could help participants make those expectations as realistic as possible. Two-fifths (44.7%) of applicants wanted to make their food product a primary source of income, and the Kitchen Connects team wanted participants to think practically about their food ventures without limiting their potential. Not only did the CHCS team modify some questions on the application, the Kitchen Connects partners and instructors adjusted some of their training to more directly address financing a food business.

Setting up our various data flows also meant creating space for the core partners to engage in some of their own documenting and data collection. For example, as we moved further into the program, and participants started making food, the partners identified a need to begin profiling some of the people and products that were coming out of Kitchen Connects. Not only did they want to feature stories on their websites and social media, but they had also begun to develop relationships and a sense of community with the people who were using the kitchens and vending at the market. At first, Marianne offered to fold this kind of story collecting into the data that the Center for Housing and Community Studies was managing. But the partners were also interested in capturing these stories on their own. Out of the Garden Project hosted a potluck with their Kitchen Connects participants, and they talked about what kinds of stories they wanted to tell around their products and the program. Our partners requested that they be able to write the profiles as a way to let the community guide how they wanted their stories to be told.

The Farmers Curb Market also documented stories of vendors who had come through Kitchen Connects, which they posted on the program website. Beyond helping customers learn more about the people behind the products, the posts also gave the Kitchen Connects partners another opportunity to capture data about the program. For example, when they asked vendors to talk about how Kitchen Connects helped them, Wolf Daddy—purveyors of pimento cheese made with local dairy products—commented, "Having access to a larger commercial space at Out of the Garden Project's kitchen, through Kitchen Connects, is allowing us to build our business without going into debt, and to grow the business at our own pace." And Fermentology Foods—who creates a variety of kimchi, sauerkrauts, and other fermented items—also added:

> The most important part of the KCG program for me was the business class with Candace from S.E.A. and the Safe Plates Program. Even though I had learned a lot about running a small business on my own, Candace brought a great deal of information to the class about pricing, costs, overhead, trademarks and more. The Safe Plates class, while taught by Vincent Webb, also featured a Microbiologist from NC State who was able to answer all the hard questions about safety in the production of fermented foods.

By carving out a space for the core partners to document process, we collectively created additional data points that gave insights into the program—particularly the pace at which it helps small businesses grow and the training it provides on food safety and production.

A Snapshot of the Program

Across eight cohorts of the Kitchen Connects GSO incubator program, 192 people applied to participate. More than 100 applicants were selected, and approximately 50 percent of those who started went on to complete the program. Some of the vendors featured in the program included the aforementioned Wolf Daddy Pimento Cheese and Fermentology Foods, both of whom rose to a quick success after completing the program. Kitchen Connects also introduced customers to vendors and products like PaleoLove, who transforms paleo granola into various mixes like Gingerbread and Blueberry Bliss; Poppy's Pickles, who pickles everything from cucumbers to okra to green beans; and Empasta, who might win the clever name award for their vegan cheese sauce.

The Center for Housing and Community Studies' multi-method and systematic approach to tracking these 192 applicants and 100 participants helped the Kitchen Connects partners refine their approach and better reach the communities they hoped to serve. Although data management can be tedious, we wanted to walk through some of the highlights from the Kitchen Connects evaluation to demonstrate the value of good data. Data can serve as a valuable, if sometimes underestimated, communication

resource in the service of food justice advocacy and activism, and we consider each point that CHCS plotted for Kitchen Connects.

APPLICATION

The application served us well by helping us understand the people and
products the core partners were attracting to the Kitchen Connects incubator. The CHCS asked a broad range of demographic questions, which
gave us key insights into who was coming to the program based on race,
age, education, and income level. For example, in the first cohort, the
majority of the twenty-six applicants were white/non-Hispanic (58%),
while 31 percent were African American. By the time we got to cohorts
5–8, those numbers virtually switched—with the majority of the ninety-
one applicants identifying as African American (49.5%), and 38 percent
as white/non-Hispanic. We also learned that applicants' ages ranged
from eighteen to seventy-two, with a median age of forty, and most of
the applicants had either some college/technical training or an associate's
degree.

Embedding some of our data collection into the application process
also enabled the CHCS and Kitchen Connects teams to answer some key
questions about both the reach of the program and how applicants had
learned about the program. For instance, the partners were eager to learn
if Kitchen Connects was reaching low-income and under-resourced members of the community, which was the top objective of the program. The
median income for the first two cohorts was $22,000 and $17,500, respectively, which gave us some early confidence that the program was reaching its target communities. This trend continued across the ninety-one
applications from cohorts 5–8, where the median income did increase,
but was still near the federal poverty line at $28,400. In these last four
cohorts, many applicants (n = 66) received other forms of assistance including SNAP/EBT (25.4%), WIC (5.1%), housing assistance (5.1%), and
SSI (5.1%). Nearly a third, (30.5%) were single parents and 61.0 percent
of applicants were the head of household.

The data suggested that the Kitchen Connects partners were attracting the folks to the program that we'd hoped for, and both the core partners and the research teams also wanted to pair that information with how

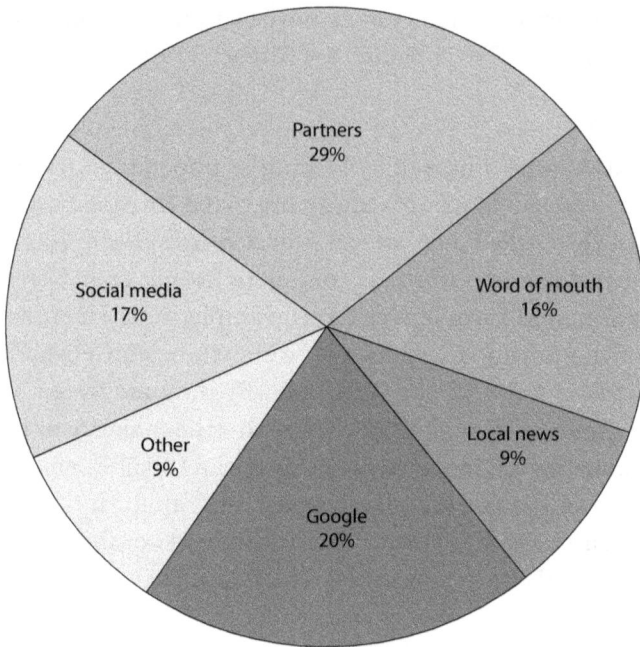

Figure 16. Media and marketing reach for Kitchen Connects.
Image credit: Stephen Sills.

these particular communities were finding out about the program. Start-ing with the third cohort, participants were asked—directly on the applica-tion—how they learned about Kitchen Connect GSO. The program drew in applications across a broad range of media and recruitment hits. Of the 122 people who applied to Kitchen Connects between cohorts 3–8, 29 percent of applicants were recruited by the core partners, 20 percent found the program through Google searches, 17 percent through Facebook and other social media, 16 percent through word of mouth, and 18 percent through other sources, including local news and referrals from nonprofit and busi-ness development agencies. Figure 16 shows how Kitchen Connects drew in applicants from multiple sources, suggesting the importance of a broad media and marketing reach.

CHCS was also able to observe how the marketing and recruitment response changed over time, so partners could adjust advertising and outreach as each cohort cycled through a program. For example, the research team noted how the biggest gains in media and marketing strategy were made through word of mouth, which saw a 38.5 percent increase between cohorts 1–3 and 5–8, and simple Google searches, with a 200 percent increase in responses between these same groups. We can attribute some of this growth to increased community awareness and local media attention around the Kitchen Connects—but our larger point here is about how we managed data as a communication resource, so we could learn from it along the way. By building this sort of data collection into the Kitchen Connects GSO application process, the CHCS communicated some key indicators to the core partners early in the program. This allowed each group to refine and adapt Kitchen Connects to how the community responded to the resource.

OBSERVATIONS

The observations of the Kitchen Connects classes, kitchen work days, and test market days provided essential qualitative and narrative support for the kitchen incubator program and its partners. Observations of the four certification and training classes helped the research team and core partners learn how the participants were adjusting to the instruction, as well as document where some of their gaps in knowledge might linger. For example, in an observation during the Marketing Your Product class, participants were asked to pitch their food items to the rest of the room. The first person to take the stage was trying to scale up his pickle business. He approached a table at the front of the classroom and spread out an assortment of pickled vegetables—from cucumbers to green beans. Each type of pickle was packaged in a 32 oz plastic tub, which the participant buys wholesale. He sells his pickles for $7 per container. Immediately, the marketing instructor realized that pricing could be an issue: if packaged and marketed correctly, these pickles could sell for much more. The instructor explained that if the pickles could be packaged in glass jars and made shelf-stable, they could easily sell for $12. This observation surprised the participant, as he had been selling pickles for nine years at his $7 price point. While he was initially uncomfortable with the idea of selling his pickles for $12, he absorbed the information and considered how it might improve his product.

Figure 17. Sharing the kitchen. Marianne observes Mary Bryan-Stewart from PaleoLove Company as she prepares her Momma's Mammoth Munch granola. Photo credit: Michael Dickens.

Additional observations at both kitchen work days and test market days also proved insightful for the CHCS researchers. Figure 17 illustrates an observation that Marianne did with Mary Bryan-Stewart from Paleo-Love Company in September of 2017. During a bit of prep time, Marianne learned about Mary's inspirations for making grain-free granola, including her daughter who suffers from an autoimmune disorder but can eat Momma's Mammoth Munch every morning for breakfast. The observation gave the opportunity to document how Mary moved through the kitchen, used various pieces of equipment—mostly sheet pans, bowls, and cooling racks—and how she navigated her entire process of producing and packaging her granola. We also saw how she followed the rules of sharing the kitchen, as Amy from Fermentology Foods was making her purple cabbage sauerkraut at the next work station over. Both cooks respected

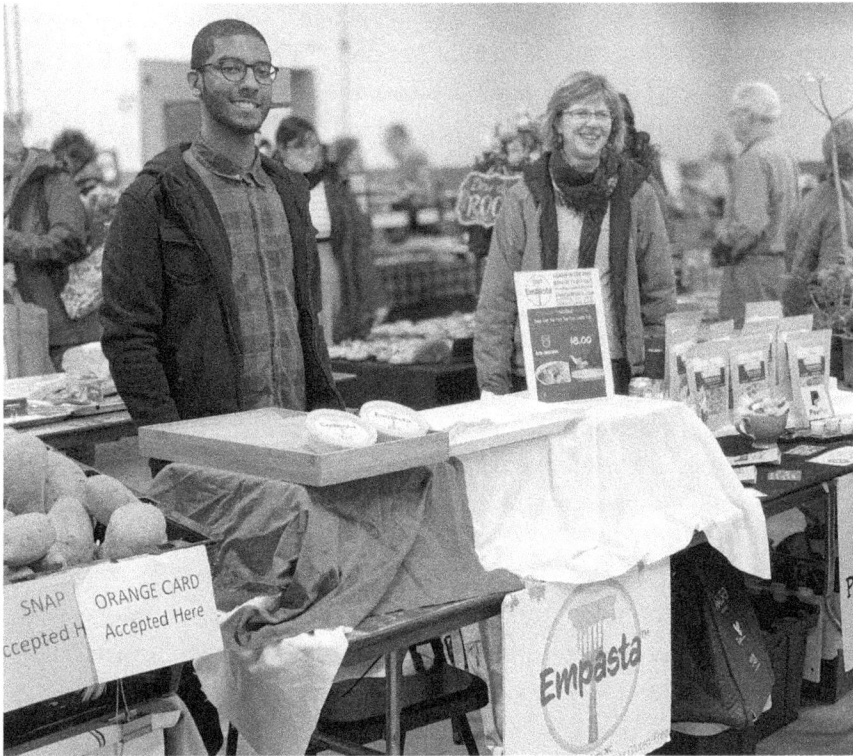

Figure 18. Selling at the market. Mary from PaleoLove (right) joins Matt from Empasta (left), as she sells her paleo-friendly granola alongside his vegan cheese sauce. Photo credit: Marianne LeGreco.

each other's prep space, announced when they were moving through common areas, and kept a friendly conversation going.

Observational insights were furthered as participants moved into the test market stage at the Farmers Curb Market. Figure 18 shows Paleo-Love and Mary out of the kitchen and into the market, where she is seen vending alongside Matt from the cleverly named Empasta vegan cheese sauce. Both graduates from the Kitchen Connects GSO program went on to become full vendors at the Farmers Curb Market. One of the core partners from the Curb Market noted that observing the Kitchen Connects participants *at the market* helped her realize just how important a good story was to the success of certain vendors. When they had the right combination of personality and narrative, they were much more likely to engage with customers at the market and increase their sales.

EXIT INTERVIEWS

Upon completing the Kitchen Connects certification and training classes, getting access to the shared-use kitchens, and taking part in their test market days, participants were invited to share their experiences in an exit interview with the CHCS. These interviews gave both the research team and the core partners the most direct reviews of how well the Kitchen Connects program met the expectations of the people who completed it. We interviewed fifty-eight participants across the first five cohorts regarding their personal background, expectations prior to participation in the course, perceptions and feedback from the class, and if their expectations were met.[4]

Information compiled from these interviews created a narrative of the Kitchen Connects program—its participants, their expectations, and later successes. For example, one participant had been making salsa for a few years as a hobby. She explained:

> Our friends really encouraged us to turn it into a business. A friend of mine told me about the program at the GSO Curb Market for new food entrepreneurs to come and take classes and have access to a kitchen to prepare my product. Because it is a fresh product, I am not able(ethically) to make it at home and serve at the market. This program was perfect for me to open that door of opportunity for me to be able to do that.

Another interviewee had been selling baked goods to family and friends. Living in High Point she has few options for shared use and commented, "the City of High Point makes it hard to open your own business under a kitchen that is Department of Agriculture regulated." A third participant to complete the program had not sold prepared foods and was developing a line of jams and jellies. She explained her reasoning for applying to the program, relating that Kitchen Connects GSO "would get me the safe plate certification, make me and customers more confident in my product, networking opportunity, marketing learning about, and to be able to sell it at the market to see if it was a viable business." Since filing the application to attend the Kitchen Connects GSO program, most participants feel as though their goals have not changed. Those who have completed the classes feel like the program has helped to make their goals more feasible and reasonable.

The exit interviews also gave participants a chance to share possibilities for improving Kitchen Connects with the researchers in a way that aided core partners in aligning and tightening their objectives. For instance, one suggestion from program participants in the second cohort was more instruction on marketing—especially social media. While marketing was the most praised workshop, many wanted even more training on how to tell their stories. In other instances, participants in the fourth cohort reported feeling overwhelmed by the volume of information being shared in the courses, and they requested handouts or other communication materials to make the training more manageable. CHCS reported these findings to the Kitchen Connects partners at the end of the second and fourth cohorts, thereby giving partners the opportunity to adjust the next marketing classes to sharpen their focus on social media and provide more explicit instructional materials to accompany the classes.

SIX-MONTH FOLLOW-UP

While not everyone who was accepted into Kitchen Connects GSO completed the program, about 50 percent of them did—and many are still involved in making their new food businesses work. With the previous points of data collection, the CHCS concentrated on using data to help improve Kitchen Connects and get participants ready to launch their food businesses. The six-month follow-up gave us the information to focus more directly on the outcomes for participants after they started cooking up a storm.

Most of those who completed the program—around 68 percent—started vending their products and 81.6 percent of those selling said things were going somewhat to extremely well. Half (55.9%) of the respondents indicated that their profits had increased since taking the cycles of classes and certifications. For those who had not yet started selling, the primary barriers were financial with 34.9 percent of participants saying they did not have access to resources or ingredients they needed, they did not have money to cover kitchen expenses, or they did not have money to purchase ingredients or supplies.

The follow-up surveys also gave participants one more occasion to share feedback about their time with Kitchen Connects GSO. This meant soliciting comments from those folks who were accepted into the program and those who were not. The insights from the people who were not accepted into Kitchen Connects were sometimes rather curt. One woman who was not selected called it a "terrible program" and hung up when CHCS attempted to interview her. Other applicants who were not selected realized that they were not a good fit for the program—that they did not have a product that was suitable for a low-risk kitchen, they needed more knowledgeability about operating a business, or they were not using local products in a sufficient way. But others were frustrated that they had to be further along in their business in order to be selected. As one applicant stated, "I was under the understanding that the program was supposed to help me with improving my skills. I was told that I don't have enough experience, skills, and knowledge. I thought that was what the program was supposed to help me with."

Although some folks were frustrated that they were not selected, those who did participate overwhelmingly stated that Kitchen Connects enabled them to take the next step with their business—or not. Some vendors who completed the program were able to leverage what they'd learned and launch their food concepts. As one participant noted:

> Things have been going great! I have become a permanent vendor at the GSO Curb Market, I am beginning to get established in retail establishments. The only thing I am really struggling with now is taxes and keeping up with receipts. Now I am able to work 3 full days a week on my business instead of two. I now have 3 retail establishments I work with. My products are sold in the "House of Health," "Deep Roots Market," and the "Summerfield Farms Market." One thing I still haven't done is paid myself. I still seem to put all my money back into the business.

Similar ideas are echoed in feedback from another new food entrepreneur:

> The program has reiterated the potential for me to make this bigger than I ever thought it could be. I now have the tools to make that happen. I now want to be able to have my own kitchen/space, even if it's in my own

backyard. I would like to eventually have a greenhouse so I can grow my own products.

At the same time, Kitchen Connects let some participants realize that owning and operating a food business was *not* the next step for them. One potential vendor put his reaction very succinctly, claiming that Kitchen Connects showed him that his business would not work for him:

> Too much time and effort required and not enough (financial) gain. Using the kitchen and being able to sell at the farmers market for free was great, but after that . . . the cost barriers were just too high. Especially for the amount of time and effort required. I was able to break even plus a very, very small profit, but I was exhausted. That, plus . . . I really didn't know how to even begin to get my foot in the door with local restaurants (which was where I thought I'd have "the best" chance of being able to sell my product.)

Too often, would-be food entrepreneurs attempt to start up a business before understanding what it's like to work in food systems—without understanding the policies and regulations, the sourcing, the pricing and promotions, and the exhaustion that this kind of work can bring. Perhaps one of the most important things that the exit interviews showed was that Kitchen Connects GSO gave some vendors the confidence to get off the ground, but it also prevented some fledgling food businesses from taking flight too soon.

REFLECTIONS, RECOMMENDATIONS, AND RESOURCES

At the start of any intervention, partners inevitably experience a great deal of excitement and anxiety upon launching a new and innovative idea. Amid the flurry of conversations about program design, creative potential, managing funding, and building community, most partners are not immediately thinking about systematic approaches to data collection and tracking and monitoring participation.[5] Not only is this a reason why community-university partnerships are important to managing community-based organizing, it also demonstrates the strategic benefits of framing data management as a central communication practice.

Documenting process can help partners strategically align their roles, refine the scope and reach of their program design, and use data across the life of the intervention to strengthen the organizing. As such, conversations about data management are necessary early steps for communicating food justice, and we gear our reflections, recommendations, and resources in this regard.

Reflections

One way to read this case study of Kitchen Connects GSO shows how partners worked together to refine a kitchen incubator program that reaches underserved communities in Greensboro. But we think a more important story to tell with this chapter is how partners used data as a communication resource to organize their intervention, and how the CHCS's emphasis on data management has helped them organize some of their next steps. As the opening story of this case study suggests, community partners and non-profit organizers do not always understand why data should be prioritized as part of organizing food or other social justice interventions. For many of these partners, their focus is on providing direct services or engaging community members on the ground. They are thinking about installing ventilation hoods and obtaining their kitchen certifications, about potential products that can be created and sold at the market, and about myriad other decisions that need to be made to launch an intervention like Kitchen Connects. At the outset of partnerships and alliances, conversations about data can sometimes feel awkward—especially when partners want to focus attention and resources elsewhere. Nonetheless, Kitchen Connects GSO has reinforced the need for community-based researchers to partner with local interventions to offer systematic data supports.

As the Kitchen Connects GSO partnership progressed, those involved developed a deeper understanding and appreciation for the systematic and centralized data management that the CHCS provided through the application process, observations, and interviews. As Don Milholin, the director of Out of the Garden Project and our partner in their shared-use kitchen, explained:

The data collected was helpful to have a better perspective on what the food entrepreneurs were hoping to accomplish with our Kitchen Connects program. I gained a sincere appreciation for data. When used effectively, [they're] a very helpful added tool in our toolbox, as an organization working to alleviate the root causes of poverty.

Additionally, Lee Mortenson, the director of the Greensboro Farmers Curb Market and our partner in both project management and test marketing, spoke of how the data helped them more quickly identify some early indicators for launching a product by the end of the program. She clarified, "The data helped us see just how important it was for people to have a story. The people who came through who could tell a good story about themselves and their products were the ones who made the most out of the program."

The emphasis on systematic data collection to refine the Kitchen Connects GSO program also gave partners some necessary resources to extend their programming beyond the initial grant period. Both the Out of the Garden Project and the Greensboro Farmers Curb Market have continued their respective pieces of the partnership beyond the USDA funding. In November 2019, for example, the Greensboro Farmers Curb Market launched a variation of Kitchen Connects aimed at supporting women-led food businesses. Participants receive similar training and product development as they did with Kitchen Connects, and they are given information about the Out of the Garden Project kitchen as well as certifying their home kitchens. Although the program was paused due to COVID-19, Lee mentioned the value of the data system that CHCS created for the Kitchen Connects program, and how the CHCS systems helped the Curb Market extend their programming. "The data gave us a really solid foundation to launch this next step," she said. "We're using a simplified version of the application. We're not using Qualtrics, but we are using Survey Monkey—and that's helping us track a few things. It was really helpful to have a structure that we could borrow from." Although conversations about data can be tedious, and partners do not always understand the need to prioritize data collection alongside the launch of an intervention, the conversations are crucial to work through in the early stages, as their benefits can be lasting.

Recommendations

Because this case study focuses on both data management and a kitchen incubator program, we provide recommendations primarily about data, but also about kitchens:

1. Develop a data management system that is easily shareable with partners. The Qualtrics online system worked in our case because we could provide partners with observer status for the data we collected. After some quick instruction with the project manager, partners were able to access data reports and application materials when they needed them. This flexibility made it easier for the partners to agree to a centralized data system for all applications and data collection.

2. Consider a multi-method approach to tracking and monitoring data. The CHCS team relied on a combination of qualitative and quantitative methods of data collection, and each one provided useful insights. When brought together, the survey/application, interviews, and observations helped create a more cohesive picture of Kitchen Connects GSO for both within-project and outcome evaluation.

3. Include the people who don't participate. The people who do not participate, either by choice or for some other reason, can tell you a lot about a program, intervention, or effort to organize. They can help you understand if you're reaching your community, if your message is salient, and if your ideas match what the community needs. The people who don't participate frequently tell us what we don't want to hear, but that insight is valuable as partners refine their approach to organizing.

4. Know your kitchens. A brief note about kitchens: Learn the differences between high-risk and low-risk kitchens, shared-use and community kitchens, and commercial kitchens, as well as the regulations governing each one in your community. Each kitchen is different, and some are regulated by the state's Department of Agriculture, while others are monitored by the county's Department of Public Health. Each community is different, and some cities must also consider city-level policies, as well. Consult with local and state regulating bodies before organizing shared-use, community kitchen efforts.

Resources

Community Toolbox: We first mentioned Community Toolbox in chapter 3 as a resource for designing community-based data collection. We reference it here again, as it provides an excellent starting point for both researchers and community members to consider how they will incorporate data into their interventions.[6]

North Carolina Department of Agriculture and Consumer Services: This page provides insights into opening food businesses with related links in North Carolina.[7] The page also illustrates the process for certifying a home kitchen to produce food for sale. Each state will differ, but this site helps narrow the kinds of information that food systems organizers will find useful.

PART V Sustaining Conversations

CASE STUDIES

Recognizing the importance of sustainability is nothing new to conversations around food justice and communication activism. In his book *More Than Just Food*, communication scholar Garrett Broad argued that programmatic and financial sustainability should be priorities—not only for social justice activism in general, but also for food justice activism in particular.[1] Additionally, because we are dealing specifically with food systems, environmental and economic sustainability are also integral to conversations about how people eat.[2] These perspectives tend to privilege the ongoing sustainability of programs, projects, and practices across food systems—as if to suggest that only long-term, sustainable economic, environmental, and programmatic change holds the potential to reduce inequity in food systems.

But from a communication perspective on sustainability, we argue that an equally critical point worth examining is sustaining the conversation.[3] Sometimes, projects and interventions become so focused on sustaining the programmatic elements of their work that they lose sight of how food access, cooking habits, food preferences, and environments are always changing. Programs, projects, and organizations commonly fail—especially when they focus on the ever-changing landscape of food systems. But that does not mean that important organizing did not occur leading up to a failure, and a communication approach to sustainability grants insight into how well partners sustain conversations when things do not unfold as intended or planned.

Moreover, this position on sustainability also opens the possibility to consider the importance of disrupting conversations as a way to disrupt injustice across food systems. Communication theory and practice can help researchers, activists, and communities disrupt systems and reimagine organizing processes.[4] When we focus on sustaining conversations, as opposed to sustaining systems, we have the potential to disrupt the routines and habits that reproduce injustice. At the same time, we also reinforce the ongoing importance of maintaining conversations about food in our communities.

When it comes to sustaining the conversation, organizational and health communication scholars tend to focus on two strategies—do it yourself or build a partnership and hand it off. In both cases, the conversation generally keeps going across communities as planned. With part V, however, we focus on sustainability when organizing does not progress as intended, and what community partners must do to sustain conversations when they are forced to step aside or make an exit. In chapter 9, we present a case study of the Guilford Food Council—a countywide effort to organize a local food council for Guilford County. After launching a conversation around food systems, the council made the decision to step aside as other council-like groups emerged to emphasize hunger and food insecurity. Chapter 10 provides insight on the Renaissance Community Co-op, a neighborhood-based movement to open a cooperative grocery store in a northeast Greensboro food desert. Just two years after opening, the co-op closed, and organizers were confronted with sustaining and making sense of their conversation amid an exit.

9 The Guilford Food Council

Malik Yakini had just taken the stage at the 2013 Come to the Table conference. Hosted by Rural Advancement Foundation International and the North Carolina Council of Churches, the conference focused on networking local food stakeholders including farmers and faith-based organizations. Yakini was delivering one of two keynote addresses for the Come to the Table audience. His talk focused on equity and justice in food systems, with a particular focus on his work with the Detroit Black Community Food Security Network, which he founded in 2006. Marianne had worked with the conference organizers to host Come to the Table at UNC-Greensboro, and she writes this account of the keynote event.

Yakini has a rare stage presence. With his long, black locks, salt-and-pepper beard, and clear-framed glasses, his look is smooth and relaxed, yet he demands your attention. This quality served him well on stage, as his talk emphasized difficult topics like racism in food systems, dignity amid food insecurity and hunger, and environmental justice. Yakini exuded his calm yet commanding style as he explained in the opening moments of his talk that he "unapologetically focuses on Black folks."

After a few hushed laughs from the audience, he went on to introduce his work with the Detroit Black Community Food Security Network

(DBCFSN), describing how food insecurity in urban areas—like his home-town of Detroit—is often disproportionately higher in African American neighborhoods and other communities of color. Yakini explained his emphasis on cultivating leadership from within the Black community, stating that "it's imperative that those who are most impacted by food insecurity and food injustice have agency to change the conditions in their communities, rather than being subjects who are simply acted upon by others." He went on to highlight some of the agricultural aspects of the DBCFSN, showing pictures of the D-town farm, a seven-acre urban farm that they helped establish in 2008, as well as illustrating plans for a cooperative grocery store in the urban center.

As his talked progressed, Yakini also discussed how the DBCFSN pursued its mission through policy development. Leaders pressured Detroit's city government to create a local food policy council, arguing in 2006 that Detroit did not have a comprehensive food security policy and desperately needed one. Moreover, they needed guidance and expertise from within the Black community to draft that policy and establish the food council for the City. DBCFSN's underlying rationale for focusing on Black leadership was that Detroit was a city of seven hundred thousand people, and 83 percent of them were African American. As such, that kind of representation should be viewed as an asset and reflected in the conversations that create the policies.

"Let me be clear; we think what's most important is community self-determination," Yakini continued. "We shouldn't wait for the government. We shouldn't wait for the corporate sector. But we think that government should behave in a responsible manner." In October 2008, the Detroit City Council unanimously voted to approve the DBCFSN's food security policy and recommendations for the food council, which was established the following year. "We can't have food justice without social justice," he concluded, "and because everybody eats, it's a great uniter. It becomes a way to build a broad consensus for justice. We need to use the momentum we're building around food justice and food sovereignty to build a movement for social justice, generally."

As I watched and listened from the audience, I couldn't help but think how he made things sound so easy. Just forty-five minutes earlier, I had facilitated a breakout session over lunch where I asked my guests if we needed a food council for Guilford County. When everyone responded "yes," I realized we had a lot of work ahead of us to connect the people we'd need to launch this idea. We wanted to construct a network of organizations and individuals who could disrupt some dominant narratives around food across the county and build a more equitable and sustainable food system at a local level. After hearing Yakini's keynote, I now realized the much broader potential for food councils and strong local food systems in moving toward social justice generally. And I wondered if we had it in us to do this kind of work.

·   ·   ·   ·   ·

A CASE STUDY IN SUSTAINING (AND DISRUPTING) CONVERSATIONS

Striking a balance between navigating, disrupting, and sustaining conversations is an important part of both social justice activism and communicating food justice. Food systems are tricky and often fickle structures with sometimes unpredictable pieces. Navigating them requires cooperation across many people who are connected to how everybody eats every day—from producers, to distributors, to consumers. Disrupting them involves identifying parts of food systems that reproduce injustice and working to change the narratives. Sustaining them means integrating the structures, cultures, peoples, and practices that make up a food system in ways that are equitable and socially just.

Since the 1980s, community-based food councils have operated as local structures that diverse groups can use to navigate, disrupt, and sustain conversations around food systems. Starting in 2008, however, work on a national scale by food activists like Mark Winne and Malik Yakini took the food council structure to a much larger scale.[1] Whereas food councils had existed in scattered pockets, usually at the county level, communities in North Carolina saw a notable increase in the number of food councils at the municipal, county, regional, and state level.[2] According to Community Food Strategies, an extension of the Center for Environmental Farming

Systems (CEFS) based out of North Carolina State University (NCSU), the number of local food councils tripled between 2010 and 2019, with about thirty-eight councils registered across the state.[3]

Our contribution to this story involves organizing the Guilford Food Council, a grassroots council dedicated to connecting organizations and individuals in Guilford County to build stronger and more secure local food systems. After a strong start in 2013 that brought together more than 115 voices over two years to create a county-level food council, the conversation changed in 2015 when two other council-like groups emerged in High Point and Greensboro to address our combined cities' high rate of food hardship. With a more specific focus on food access and hunger, the Greensboro Community Food Task Force and the Greater High Point Food Alliance reframed the conversation as a response to Greensboro/High Point's ranking atop the Food Research and Action Center's food hardship list.

As structures that communities can use to disrupt and sustain various pieces of local food systems, food councils help everyday people navigate the complicated discourses involved in getting food to people. At the same time, simply convening people using a series of best practices does not guarantee that food councils can reach their full potential. Meetings can just as easily fragment communities as they attempt to unite them.[4] Using the Guilford Food Council as a case study, this chapter offers insight into the importance of sustaining (and disrupting) conversations through food justice organizing. On some level, this chapter touches on all four of our guiding questions, with allusions to what counts as community, how communities organize to respond to food hardship, how we coordinate our actions to promote food justice, and how stakeholders manage tensions to ensure that everybody eats. Our focus on the Guilford Food Council illustrates how, sometimes, a group of people converges to start a conversation, only to have it go in an unexpected direction. To sustain the work that went into building that conversation, sometimes the best thing we can do is simply step aside.

A Quick History of the Guilford Food Council

The conversations to build a local food council for Guilford County got their spark in February 2013 at the Come to the Table Conference on the campus of UNC-Greensboro (UNCG). At a lunchtime breakout session, a table of twelve Guilford community members and organizers—including local church leaders, nonprofit representatives, agricultural extension agents, and a handful of researchers agreed to take some initial steps to gauge community interest in organizing a council. Those initial steps involved consulting with CEFS, which focuses on promoting sustainable agriculture and community-based food systems. Connecting with this research center also connected us with Christy Shi-Day, who was leading up a subset of CEFS that would eventually become the more formally named Community Food Strategies. Christy was developing a model of creating food councils at the local level, and she had partnered with several cities, counties, and regions in North Carolina to construct some best practices.

These best practices were rooted in a dynamic governance model that identified key members across local food systems and invited them to a community meeting to learn about food councils. If, at the end of that meeting, community members agreed to develop a council, the next step involved recruiting a task force who could commit to a six-to-nine-month process to design the structure, mission, vision, charter, and membership. In total, we were looking at a twelve-to-fifteen-month process just to get a food council off the ground.

INVITING THE COMMUNITY

After consulting with Christy, we were off to a pretty textbook start. Of the twelve people who attended that first breakout session, seven us of began meeting regularly at the Guilford County Cooperative Extension to plan the community meeting. Alongside Marianne, these organizers included Julie Lapham, who was representing an immigrant and refugee group called the Center for New North Carolinians; Janet Mayer, a registered dietician with the Guilford County Department of Public Health; and Annie Martinie, a community member who was also working with neighboring Alamance County to develop their food council.

We recognized immediately that we were a room full of white people. Like we said, textbook start. Janet was the first to call attention to it, but everyone quickly agreed that we could not proceed if we only included white voices in building the council. At the same time, we also realized that while we could not speak for Guilford County's Black communities and other communities of color, the people in the room were not completely disconnected from the very diverse neighborhoods and people across the county. For example, Julie had close relationships with immigrant and refugee communities across Greensboro, and she had managed the campaign that elected Greensboro's first Black woman mayor. If we could leverage some of our networks to carve out a space for Black voices and other communities of color, we still had a chance to build a council that represented the greater diversity of Guilford County.

These kinds of conversations were important to have early on, as Guilford County is made up of a unique and diverse set of people. In 2019, Guilford County became a minority-majority county, with 49.8 percent of residents identifying as white, 35.1 percent as Black or African American, 8.2 percent as Hispanic or Latino, and the remaining as Asian, multiracial, or American Indian.[5] Guilford is also designated as a refugee resettlement area, with over 140 countries of origin and 120 languages represented in county schools and 13 percent of residents speaking a language other than English at home.[6]

Not only is Guilford County unique in terms of its people, but also in terms of its structure. We have about twice as many major cities and towns as our neighboring counties in the Piedmont Triad. While Greensboro certainly anchors the county, we also have the metropolitan areas of High Point and smaller towns such as Jamestown, Summerfield, Gibsonville, Pleasant Garden, and Climax, among others. As we moved toward planning the community meeting, we had an opportunity to create a space that could celebrate this diversity. At the same time, we also needed to find people who represented different pieces of our local food system. Part of the success of the model encouraged by Christy Shi-Day and CEFS hinged on bringing together voices from farmers, distributors, nonprofit organizations, educators and researchers, retailers and business owners, and everyday consumers. Different stakeholders brought different expertise to the conversation, and all voices were necessary to mobilize the conversation. So we went to work assembling as many voices as possible in preparation for a community meeting on October 25, 2013.

The community meeting was an important starting point in organizing the Guilford Food Council. By the time we hosted the community meeting in October, the diversity in the room had grown. The early organizers had

Figure 19. The Guilford Food Council community interest meeting. Future Food Council members Niesha Douglas (pictured right) and Odile Huchette (pictured left) listen along with county epidemiologist Mark Smith (pictured center) as community members discuss organizing a food council. Photo credit: Marianne LeGreco.

assembled a room of eighty-five people across eight different sectors of our local food system, including producers, industry and restaurant connections, community organizations, faith-based organizations, government offices, and our school systems. Moreover, 27 percent of the voices represented on the list were from Guilford County's Black communities and other communities of color. Statewide organizers would later tell us that this was the largest community meeting for a local food council to date. Christy joined us to give a presentation on the purpose of food councils, where she emphasized their potential to facilitate connections across people in the food system, focus attention on local needs, and drive action through policy. Figure 19 provides a glimpse of the short discussion sessions that followed her presentation, where attendees overwhelmingly spoke of the need to network all of the existing groups and agencies that focused on food. At the end of that meeting in October, everyone in the room recommended moving forward with developing a food council, and thirty-two people committed to working on a task force to design it.

CREATING THE COUNCIL

Although we had managed a relatively textbook start to organizing the Guilford Food Council, the six-to-nine-month planning process that followed unfolded during a very precarious time. Initially, the community members who volunteered to participate in the newly formed Guilford Food Council Task Force agreed to reconvene in January 2014. In that time, however, we lost a key voice in organizing the food council. At the end of 2013, Julie took her own life. The news came as a shock to everyone in Greensboro, but this had been a very intentional choice on her part. Julie had been a chemist in a previous career—she helped develop the formula for permanent press fabrics. But an accident in the lab ended all of that, and she spent the rest of her life with a lot of pain and related health problems. Knowing Julie, she simply wanted to end things on her own terms. Members of the task force felt her loss greatly, as she provided mentoring and motivating for the early organizers. Many of us had hoped that she might lead the task force in finding the right structure, mission, and people for the Guilford Food Council.

The social support we received from CEFS also changed during this transition. At the time, CEFS was still growing its Community Food Strategies program. Although the program is now better positioned to provide both broader and more detailed support, their resources in 2013 and 2014 were more limited. This meant that Christy had to spend time with other cities and counties that were working toward the community meeting stage of the process. The task force had a rough sketch of some best practices and a couple of key activities, but as Christy said at the end of Guilford's community meeting, "Now, the fun begins. Now, you're on your own."

On our own, we admittedly struggled. At first, the task force struggled to find a rhythm to the meetings. Julie had provided a lot of early guidance on how to structure the process, and without her, our first few meetings tended to wander. We needed to begin making decisions about what form and shape the council could take, what to prioritize in our charter, and how we might recruit members. And although we built a list of thirty-two people who could help design the council, many of them were in the room because they wanted to talk about food, not organizing.

These members wanted to jump ahead in the process to discuss specific policies, garden initiatives, and food access problems that the council might address—but we weren't there yet. Based on the model from CEFS, those were the kinds of decisions that the Food Council, itself, would make. Our job as the task force was to build the infrastructure for the council. That meant creating a purpose statement and charter based on priorities in our food system, an organizational structure for how the council would be governed and how members could join, and a process for selecting the first council leaders. But early task force members frequently pulled conversations toward what we could *do* as a council, rather than how we might organize.

The task force also struggled in terms of adopting best practices. When we started organizing in 2013, Cabarrus County was one of the first local councils to suggest models and best practices for developing councils. Their most central recommendations involved recruiting a city council or county board member for a seat on the food council and advocating for the City or County to fund the food council as a line item in their budget. This strategy had worked well for Cabarrus County, whose food council advocates had leveraged this approach into a salaried position for their council chairperson and the creation of a County-funded incubator farm. In June 2014, however, the Cabarrus County Commissioners abruptly cut funding for the council, leaving advocates scrambling to reorganize the food council and save the farm.[7] Suddenly, best practices had become cautionary tales, and members of the Guilford Food Council Task Force became wary of aligning ourselves that closely with a city or county government.

Over the summer of 2014, the Food Council Task Force seemed to get back on track. Annie had been attending food council meetings in neighboring Alamance County, where she learned more about facilitating council development from CEFS and Community Food Strategies. She offered to walk the task force through two workshops designed to identify the critical functions and focal points of a food council. Each workshop asked members a series of questions, such as, "how important is it that this council has a primary function to share information?" and "what is

Table 8   Critical Functions and Focal Points

Critical Functions	*Focal Points*
Build a grassroots base	Guilford County
Share information	Community
Advocate for a specific group or issue	Local food
Conduct referrals as a group	Healthy
Move a policy agenda forward	Sustainable
Conduct research as a group	System
Form a joint messaging campaign	Access
	Food insecurity

Mission Statement: The Guilford Food Council (GFC) supports the development of a vibrant, sustainable, and healthy local food system for Guilford County and its cities, municipalities, and rural areas. Members of the GFC serve to examine the food system in Guilford County, bring together stakeholders from the many food-related sectors, and create a successful local food system that promotes *vibrant farms, thriving economies,* and *healthy neighborhoods.*

the system you want to create?" Table 8 summarizes the results of each workshop, as well as how they informed the construction of the Guilford Food Council mission statement.

The critical functions and focal point exercises helped refocus the task force. They gave us a clearer language to begin drafting our more formal documents, and they helped us work through some tensions that had slowed some of our previous work. In August 2014, we were ready to host a series of community listening sessions to get some feedback on these critical functions and focal points, as well as some early ideas for a charter. We held two events in Greensboro—one for the general public at a regional grocery store chain and the other at a local farmers market for growers and farmers in Guilford County. Then, we moved to High Point, where we hosted events at a local church for the general public and the High Point Health Department for health care providers. With the exception of the general public meeting in High Point, which we admittedly could have promoted more effectively, the turnout at each session was respectable. Each event attracted about twelve to fifteen participants, and they reinforced the need to focus not only on food insecurity, but also the larger food system. As one participant at the Greensboro public meeting explained, "This conversation appears to be largely about food access, but the part that I have been concerned about is how our food production is controlled by industry. If there are robust food councils, we might talk about things like that."

Using the collective wisdom of the task force alongside the feedback from the community listening sessions, we had enough information to finalize a draft of our charter and membership application, which we have included in the Resources section for this chapter. The Guilford Food Council charter highlighted priorities including vibrant farms, thriving economies, healthy neighborhoods, education and awareness, and policies and land use. The topic areas also provided the backbone for structuring the food council membership. The council would initially include eight positions and an advisory board. The eight positions comprised three at-large members, whose responsibilities involved organizing meetings and managing communication, as well as five cluster leaders for each of our priorities. Each cluster leader was responsible for building up the membership in their respective areas and identifying topics and policies that needed the council's attention.

We created the advisory board as a way to include membership from city and county offices. During the critical functions exercise, some representatives from city, county, and other taxpayer-funded offices suggested that their positions made it difficult for them to advocate. "I'm allowed to provide support and resources," said a task force member from the Cooperative Extension, "but I'm not supposed to advocate." Since the task force identified advocacy and activism as important critical functions of our food council, we designed the advisory board as a way to preserve the council's freedom to advocate while inviting participation from city and county offices. This move also helped us maintain our grassroots base as we defined our relationship with local governments.

Between January and March 2015, we turned our attention to recruiting members to fill the positions for the first Guilford Food Council. During an open membership call, we received applications from twelve people for eight seats on the council. We solicited an additional ten applications from community members, which resulted in three more submissions, for a total of fifteen applications. At our March 2015 meeting, the task force

assembled to select the council leaders. Our guiding principle in constructing the council was maximizing its diversity, which we defined in terms of
relationship to the food system and community representation. We wanted
to represent as many voices as possible, and we wanted to see how applicants fit alongside each other. Our final selections included a communication researcher from UNCG, an undergraduate student from Guilford
College, and a connection to faith-based organizations for our at-large
members. The Thriving Economies cluster was directed by a restaurant
owner, an urban horticulture professor from NCA&T guided the Education and Awareness cluster, and the Vibrant Farms cluster was led by two
farmers.[8] Although our leadership remained largely white (67%), the task
force did attempt to maximize diversity in many ways. New council members included three voices from communities of color, two immigrants, two
members of the LGBTQ community, five women, three people from High
Point, five people from Greensboro, and one from Gibsonville.

Just as the task force put the pieces in place to launch the Guilford
Food Council, we were again confronted by the precarious timing of our
organizing. Much of our early work had taken place before Greensboro/
High Point reached the top of the Food Research and Action Center's list
of communities with high rates of food hardship. When we ranked second
in 2014, many members of the task force saw reducing food hardship as a
natural extension of the Guilford Food Council's work. At the same time,
our focus had always been on taking a systems approach, as opposed to
concentrating specifically on hunger or food hardship, which is what we
chose to continue to emphasize. But conversations in communities across
Guilford County had begun to emerge in ways that changed how we talked
about food in Greensboro and High Point, and we would soon learn that
the best thing the Guilford Food Council could do was slowly step aside.

Maintaining a Conversation while Slowly Stepping Aside

In May 2015, the newly formed Guilford Food Council met for a potluck at
the Guilford County Cooperative Extension. Meetings were open to both
the council leaders, which we had started to call the steering committee,
and general community members who wanted to join a cluster. After sharing some food, we reviewed and approved the charter, which was adopted

one month later on June 3, 2015. The potluck would be the first and last time that the Guilford Food Council, as originally conceived and designed, would meet. Some of the reasons were natural parts of organizing. For example, not long after our first meeting, unexpected changes in life circumstances would require two of our members to leave the council. But the larger conversation involved the emergence of the Greater High Point Food Alliance (GHPFA) and the Greensboro Community Food Task Force (GCFTF).[9] These two groups started organizing in response to Greensboro/High Point's ranking on the FRAC food hardship list, with High Point mobilizing in 2014 and Greensboro the following year. With their specific focus on hunger and food access, these two organizations would change how the conversation unfolded in Guilford County around food justice advocacy and activism.

In late 2014, just as the Guilford Food Council Task Force had finished drafting a charter, we were visited by High Point pastor Carl Vierling and High Point University professor Joe Blosser, both with the GHPFA. The two men were interested in learning more about the Guilford Food Council, as well as sharing what they had been up to in High Point. Their work with the GHPFA had been inspired by a series of articles in the *High Point Enterprise* that focused on hunger and food hardship in their community.[10] With Greensboro/High Point's climb atop the FRAC list, they had formed the GHPFA with plans to host a hunger summit in High Point the following spring. Their growing network already included several churches, food pantries, and High Point University, and it would soon grow to include foundations, the United Way of Greater High Point, and High Point Medical Center.

Following the success of their 2015 hunger summit, which attracted over five hundred participants to a two-day series of presentations, meals, and workshops, the GHPFA would begin to move quickly to generate a concrete list of both short-term and long-term goals to alleviate hunger and increase food access in High Point.[11] They received financial support from the United Way of Greater High Point to hire Carl to manage GHPFA operations. They built community gardens and connected them to food banks in neighborhoods with some of the highest concentrations of poverty in Guilford County. They developed a smartphone app for people to find local and free food across the city. Simply put, the GHPFA moved very quickly from their initial organizing to creating new resources for their community.

Meanwhile, the Guilford Food Council struggled to make a similar transition. After adopting our charter in June 2015, we turned to our list of critical functions, which was generated by the task force. At-large members started work on a website and social media pages as a way to begin sharing information about local food events and activities in Guilford County. At the same time, members wanted a more tangible conversation than "let's build communication infrastructure." Much of the early activity in the Guilford Food Council had coalesced around the steering committee meetings and the Education and Awareness cluster. By far our most active group, the Education and Awareness cluster was hosted by Odile Huchette, an urban horticulture professor from NCA&T, and it had a growing email list and a semi-regular meeting schedule. Odile observed this gap in the discourse surrounding the food council at an October 2015 steering committee meeting:

> I have talked about the Guilford Food Council with some of my students and colleagues, and I've tried to get people interested in the Education and Awareness cluster. But everyone asks me the same thing. "What do you do?" People like the idea of a food council, but they need a theme or a topic or an issue to focus on—maybe something different every year—something that can bring us together.

Odile's comment speaks to another of the critical functions that the food council had identified in our task force days—advocate for a specific issue or group. Although we were building a communication platform to launch conversations around local food and vibrant food systems in Guilford County, we had not identified a specific issue to anchor our advocacy in the same way that the GHPFA had focused in on hunger and food insecurity. Concepts of food systems and communication infrastructure were too abstract for our audience, and we needed something more tangible to mobilize the 115 voices that were on our general mailing list. Moreover, we were losing momentum around our remaining clusters, particularly the Healthy Neighborhoods group, as potential members were drawn to the newly forming Greensboro Community Food Task Force.

Shortly after the Food Research and Action Center announced that Greensboro/High Point had topped their 2015 list of cities experiencing food hardship, Jamal Fox—the Greensboro city councilman for District 2 at the time—announced plans for a hunger task force.[12] Facing pressure because of the high rates of food insecurity and the number of food deserts in his district, Fox hastily pulled a task force together and charged the City's Planning and Parks and Recreation Departments with creating a community-based plan to end hunger in ten years. Although Fox was fully aware and ostensibly supportive of the Guilford Food Council, and a member of his Parks and Rec team also sat on our advisory board, he seemingly saw the need to start a third council-like group in Guilford County to focus on food and its related concepts of access, hunger, and food insecurity. Members of our fledgling food council were left wondering how all of these groups might work together.

Several Guilford Food Council members were invited to one of the first GCFTF meetings in June 2015, where the City's planners and organizers laid out the purpose of the task force—to focus on food access in Greensboro and develop a plan to end hunger in ten years. The conversation was ambitious, with more than twenty-five people from local food nonprofits, community organizations, funding agencies, school systems, city and county health agencies, agricultural extensions, and research universities taking a seat at the table to consider how the task force might work. For example, one of the first projects that the task force planned to undertake was developing a network of summer meal locations for K–12 students in Greensboro. Although the National School Lunch Program did operate through most of the summer, students still faced some gap weeks at the end of July and parts of August. Many nonprofit organizations and churches had stepped up to fill that gap, and the task force wanted to coordinate efforts between locations. These kinds of projects sounded similar to the type of work that the Guilford Food Council wanted to spearhead, leaving some of us in the room wondering about the need for both groups. Consider the following conversation, from Marianne's field notes, with Phil Fleischmann—who was chairing the GCFTF in his role with Greensboro Park and Rec and had a seat on the Guilford Food Council's advisory board:

About half of the attendees had left the conference room as I approached Phil to talk about the meeting. "So, what do you think this means for the food council?

"I knew you were going to ask me that," he replied as he laughed quietly at my candor.

"Well, I want to make sure that we're not doubling efforts. And that we don't get into a situation where we're meeting ourselves to death . . . and we don't get anything done . . . because all we're doing is planning meetings."

"Here's what I think. There's a need to focus on food systems and the Guilford Food Council does that. There's also a need to address hunger in Greensboro, and the task force does that. Maybe we merge together at some point, but I think it's best to keep both groups going."

Although Phil made an excellent ideological point about the need for both the Guilford Food Council and the Greensboro Community Food Task Force, the practical reality was that between the Food Council, the GCFTF, and the GHPFA, we were relying on participation, advocacy, and work from many of the same people.

Despite some concerns that we were reproducing efforts, the Guilford Food Council continued to meet throughout the rest of 2015 and parts of 2016. We picked an issue—food waste and its relationship to food insecurity—around which we could organize some advocacy and activism. Odile and the Education and Awareness cluster took on the topic and began meeting regularly to discuss it in 2016. However, participation in the steering committee meetings started to slow considerably. Some of our members with professional connections to the food system, namely those who worked with city and county health agencies, had been assigned to work with the GHPFA and/or the GCFTF, and they found it increasingly difficult to maintain a meeting schedule for each group. Marianne called attention to how meetings had started to fragment participation in the Food Council at a steering committee meeting in early 2016:

> We're going to burn ourselves out—this kind of participation isn't sustainable. It's too many meetings—we're completely overscheduled and we're not making the kind of progress we want to. I don't know if that means we dissolve the council and join the Greensboro task force. I don't want to do that, because Odile—you've got a lot of interest in the Education and Awareness group. Maybe we think differently about what we offer the community and the conversation.

It may have taken them another month or two, but the remaining council members eventually realized that something in our approach needed to change—and that we needed to work on sustaining the conversation, even if we couldn't sustain the council in the way we originally planned.

As we looked to our neighbors in High Point, and the early wins with their garden networks and food access app, alongside the growing momentum around the task force in Greensboro, the Guilford Food Council realized that the best way we could sustain a conversation around food security was to simply step aside. Our role might not have been to serve as an umbrella organization to bring all of the food groups in Guilford County together, but we did have other resources to offer the conversation. Taking a hint from our critical functions exercise during our task force days, we started to focus more on two of our strengths—providing referrals and creating a joint messaging campaign.

Rather than organizing a series of monthly meetings, we wanted to concentrate more on facilitating connections and providing social and professional support for the organizations and individuals working across Guilford County's food system. To start, we changed our approach to meetings. We stopped steering committee meetings altogether. While hosting monthly steering committee meetings was not our strength, we were good about assembling a group of advisors to help other groups solve problems and navigate systems. For example, in 2017, our partners from the GHPFA started working with Rock and Wrap It Up, a food reclamation nonprofit, to advocate changing some restrictive food donation policies. State health officials had made it more difficult to donate prepared food, and these partners wanted to change that. The Guilford Food Council helped organize a meeting to provide advice and strategy for these groups, and we helped facilitate some connections with the Guilford County Department of Public Health so they could take their next steps. In providing referrals and connections in this way, our steering committee started to operate as a sort of pop-up advisory board around local food.

In addition to our pop-up advising, the Guilford Food Council also helped the County Cooperative Extension and the GHPFA launch Guilford Local Foods Week in 2016. This messaging campaign, which the Cooperative Extension continues to host, showcases all things local in Guilford County's food system. The week highlights events, like restaurant

Figure 20. The Ugly Food Feast 2017. Students from NCA&T State University assist Food Council member Janet Mayer (pictured, top) in serving food they gleaned from local farms. Photo credit: Marianne LeGreco.

meetups and the GHPFA's annual food summit, organizes cash mobs at local food co-ops, arranges farm tours throughout Guilford County, promotes our various farmers markets, and routinely features a community meal. Local Foods Week also gave our Education and Awareness cluster, which had continued to meet around their food waste agenda, an opportunity to host an Ugly Food Feast. This event, hosted during the 2017 and 2018 Local Foods Week lineup, featured food that doesn't always make it to the grocery store as a way to encourage community members to think differently about food waste. Figure 20 gives a snapshot of the 2017 feast.

Although the Guilford Food Council looks very different from when it was originally designed, we have managed to adapt to the conversation in order to sustain some of our original work. Food councils can help communities disrupt and sustain conversations across our food systems. But organizing for change and communicating food justice activism, especially when working to build alliances and partnerships across existing organizations and groups, demands flexibility. Part of sustaining a conversation, as opposed to sustaining a project or intervention, means recognizing when environments and situations change, when new voices enter, and where the attention is needed most. When the early organizers started a conversation about food councils at the Come to the Table conference, we had no way of anticipating how the FRAC rankings would inspire other individuals and groups to start organizing alliances, councils, and task forces. Rather than focus on how we might compete for members, resources, and publicity, however, all three groups remained flexible about the potential for us to fit together.

The story of the Guilford Food Council also creates a unique occasion to consider what researchers, organizers, and activists might do when the immediate discourse changes, but the larger conversation remains desirable. Both the GHPFA and the GCFTF emerged in response to Greensboro/High Point's 2014 and 2015 FRAC rankings, while the Guilford Food Council always had its eye on the long game of organizing around food systems. Whenever the Food Council considered dissolving its charter or merging with the GCFTF, we were always encouraged by organizers from the other two groups that both conversations were necessary—both the immediate attention needed around food insecurity that the GHPFA and the GCFTF provided and the larger focus on food systems with the Food Council. Frequently, the same people are interested in both conversations, however, which requires us to think critically about our timing and whether it's best to press an issue or simply step back.

REFLECTIONS, RECOMMENDATIONS, AND RESOURCES

Local food councils possess great potential for food justice organizers to mobilize policy, economic, and practical changes in their communities. Social movement and community activism rely increasingly on organizing and networking people and institutions in order to move toward more equitable systems.[13] Through the Guilford Food Council, we recognized this potential for local food councils to mobilize change, but we learned more about the importance of sustaining a conversation and navigating the constraints of organizing with a little creativity. We offer reflections, recommendations, and resources that consider the design of the council and the process of stepping aside.

Reflections

Both Marianne and Niesha worked closely with the Guilford Food Council across its design and launch, and Marianne offers some specific reflections here:

If I could choose one project, intervention, or organized effort to do again—across all of the food partnerships I have pursued in Greensboro and Guilford County—I would want another try at the Guilford Food Council. If I knew then what I know now, I would say that we made a misstep when we chose to focus on Guilford County as opposed to Greensboro. It's easy to say that now—seven years later with the benefit of hindsight—and I sometimes wonder if it's even useful to think about what might have been different. But as organizational scholar Karl Weick frequently reminds me, sensemaking is an important exercise.[14] So here I am—reflecting on what we did, sifting through the various interpretations, and keeping what is useful for future conversations.

Let me be clear: like many of my colleagues, I believe that Guilford County needs a food council that focuses on a systems-level perspective on food security. I also believe that a county-level food council can operate alongside both the GHPFA and the GCFTF in productive and meaningful ways. But if I could go back and do it all again, I would have tried to grow the conversation differently. After our listening sessions in High Point in 2014 and our visit from Carl and Joe with the GHPFA later that year, it became clear that we were not sufficiently aware of the organizing going on in that community. By the time we learned about the GHPFA, they were already highly networked and moving much more quickly on identifying priorities within their scope. In this case, it was easy for us to step aside, because we didn't want to invade their space or disrupt the work they were doing.

Things were not as clear or easy in Greensboro. Our network had always been larger in Greensboro, which made it a little more difficult to navigate our relationship with the GCFTF. After an early acknowledgment that both the Food Council and the GCFTF were needed, partners made a concerted effort to maintain both groups. But the average person didn't always see the difference between the Food Council and the GCFTF, which would be easy to miss for anyone who isn't familiar with the nuances of food councils. This frequently led to confusion about the purpose and scope of each group. Moreover, we regularly attracted the same people to both meetings, which sometimes made our conversations insular and redundant—as if we were simply rehashing the same ideas between the two groups.

If we had chosen to focus on Greensboro and responded to the FRAC study more directly, that choice might have made two key differences. First, the Food Council could have either evolved into the City's task force or merged our efforts much more easily when the task force was commissioned. Had we done this, the GCFTF would likely be further along in their organizing, scope, and purpose. After an early win when partners quickly coordinated summer meal sites for K–12 students, the GCFTF struggled with the larger mandate from Councilman Fox—to create a plan to solve hunger in ten years. While GCFTF members recognized the need to have a plan, many of them also recognized that the councilman's goal was lofty and framed the conversation in way that missed key points about hunger and food insecurity. Specifically, hunger and food insecurity are reproduced across systems—systems that are also tied up in poverty and likely need more than ten years to sufficiently (and ethically) understand, critique, dismantle, and rebuild. Moreover, two years after issuing his directive, Councilman Fox resigned from his seat on the Greensboro City Council to move across the country and take a position in Portland, Oregon. Since his departure, the GCFTF has gone through some of the same organizing, identity, and leadership building conversations that the Food Council went through three to four years earlier. Although the GCFTF is beginning to clarify its voice in the conversation, particularly through a series of forum discussions organized in 2020, it's hard not to think about the creative potential we likely missed because we spent so much energy trying to maintain both groups.

Second, if the Guilford Food Council had started as the Greensboro Food Council, where our initial networks were strongest, we might have grown a county-level council more organically—out of an authentic relationship between Greensboro, High Point, and other communities in

Guilford County. Instead, we often strictly adhered to a model that suggested most food councils were organized at the county level. Additionally, many of our health and agriculture agents—who are crucial voices to have at the table—were employed through the County, meaning that it was easier for them to participate if we focused on Guilford County and not simply Greensboro. Perhaps we are biased, because we live in Greensboro, but at least Marianne has always felt like we made the choice to focus on Guilford County without sufficiently engaging communities *outside* of Greensboro. At the same time, we *had* sufficiently engaged multiple communities *within* Greensboro, and we didn't play to the strengths of the networks that were in the room. Had we focused more on Greensboro, we might have been more prepared to partner with High Point's food alliance when their work started mobilizing. And in doing so, we might have gradually built up our collective capacity to organize a more representative Guilford Food Council that could focus on countywide food systems issues.

Recommendations

The case study of the Guilford Food Council also helped us crystalize some ideas about sustaining conversations as part of food justice activism. We would like readers to consider the following recommendations about organizing food councils and the process of stepping aside:

1. Be appropriately critical of best practices. We started organizing the Guilford Food Council as many counties across North Carolina and the United States were beginning to do the same. Best practices and models for organizing emerged from numerous sources, including research centers and the counties themselves. At the same time, most councils were still refining their process and best practices were often changing overnight. This is not to say that best practices are not useful—quite the contrary, as they often provide excellent starting points. But our experiences organizing the Guilford Food Council have made us a little wary of practices that are labeled "best." The cultures and resources of each county, city, or township—especially in terms of local politics—are often unique, and those nuances need to be considered in organizing a council. So our best advice is to consult multiple resources before selecting an organizing strategy.

2. Look for the voices who aren't at the table. Most approaches to organizing food councils do an exemplary job of outlining different stakeholders across a food system who should be a part of the
   conversation—like farmers, restaurant owners, food distributors and
   retailers, and consumers. But not all councils are as savvy as the
   Detroit Black Community Food Security Network in advocating for
   equitable racial and economic representation on food councils. Black
   communities and other communities of color, and immigrant and refugee communities are frequently underrepresented in food council
   organizing. Not only must organizers and activists recognize when
   certain voices or groups are not at the table, we must also take intentional steps to invite them into the conversation—and, if we truly want
   those voices to be there, we must also recognize when the voices along
   the margins are the ones who need to bring the table to begin with.

3. Consider stepping aside as an option in sustaining conversations.
   Sometimes, conversations start and go in a completely different
   direction. Although we feel it would be premature to recommend a
   specific communication framework or process for individuals and
   groups to follow as they step aside, we can suggest some critical
   points of reflection that we gleaned from our experience:

   • Approach organizing with humility and consider your privilege. Be
     prepared to cede some ground, especially when voices from marginal-
     ized communities start to join the conversations and share experiences
     related to the inequity being addressed. These experiences may take
     conversations in unexpected directions, especially when groups are
     launched by largely privileged voices.

   • Acknowledge tensions. Be reflexive when organizers and community
     members recognize unnecessary contradictions, double binds, and
     paradoxes. Ask if meetings are leading to unnecessary fragmentation
     among partners.

   • Consider how other groups and voices might use resources. Sometimes
     one partnership starts a conversation, while another is meant to carry
     it—especially because of their ability to mobilize resources. Ask which
     partners are best positioned to use resources to serve the greatest need.

   • Recognize what's worth maintaining and the potential to return or
     reorganize. Again, most of the partners in conversation around the
     Guilford Food Council recognized the need for both the county-level
     Food Council and the city-level groups. The communities simply had
     more need to focus on the immediacy of the FRAC study.

Resources

Considering the growth in food councils over the last ten years, several excellent resources are available online. We recommend starting with the following list. We also provide a copy of the Guilford Food Council charter in appendix D.

> Community Food Strategies: Starting in 2012, this organization has built a wealth of resources for designing and supporting food councils. As they have refined their approach, their online resources are useful for councils both within North Carolina and across states.[15]

> The Detroit Food Policy Council and the Detroit Black Food Security Network: We strongly urge anyone doing work that resembles a food policy council or food security network to study the work of Malik Yakini and these two organizations out of Detroit.[16]

> Doing Food Policy Councils Right: Mark Winne has spearheaded food policy council development across the United States. His guide to policy and action provides an excellent starting point for organizing food councils.[17]

10 The Renaissance Community Co-op

With Casey Thomas and Alyzza May

Most organizers committed to food justice launch interventions with a goal of creating sustainable changes in our food system that can ensure equity. But despite those best hopes and intentions, even the most promising programs sometimes meet messy conclusions. Casey Thomas provides the following account of her experience shortly after the closing of the Renaissance Community Co-op (the RCC), a community-owned grocery store in a majority-Black neighborhood. A former board member, Casey is among the numerous community members currently making sense of the RCC's closure after several years of organizing and two years of operation. This story is written from her perspective.

Our store had closed. When I thought about the two short years since we opened the Renaissance Community Co-op, I realized just how much had happened. We had provided jobs for dozens of neighborhood residents, we had garnered national and even international press, and we had brought fresh, healthy, affordable food to a food desert. But a week before Christmas 2018, our loans would soon be in default.

Representatives from our business incubator and largest funder—the Fund 4 Democratic Communities (F4DC)—sent two staff members to our board letting us know that our store would need to close. It was a difficult moment for everyone, made harder by the fact that our board would be in breach of our confidentiality agreements if we leaked a word to the staff. As a board member myself, I was incensed—this was not how it was supposed to go.

For months, our board had been asking about our funding and how to proceed—how could we prepare for the future we envisioned for this necessary and important project?

Nothing had been easy. During a previous board meeting, when I asked if they were pulling our funding, one of the codirectors of F4DC laughed and asked why I would think that. Everyone loved the project of the RCC. It was a novel way to fill an important community need. So, when I learned that the board had been informed *after* our lenders, I took that very personally. To us, this was a community project, and the community needed to come first.

The cadre of people working on this project had become connected, and real relationships had been formed. This was a hurt. It seemed as if the decision to close was either made capriciously or truly at the last minute. In either case, we felt left out of the conversation that led up this point— even though we'd asked repeatedly if F4DC would continue to fund us. Did they not think we deserved the truth or the opportunity to prepare?

As I was feeling sorry for myself and betrayed, I was driving through the neighborhood where the store had been, and I saw a woman trying to cross the street. She stopped in front of my car and yelled, "You fucked us!" I thought she had me confused with someone else, and just stared at her, uncertain of what was happening. She continued, "You fucked us! You were with the store! You said we were going to get rich . . . and build community wealth! I bought a share. It was supposed to work like the stock market! Who's going to give me my $100 back?"

I now understood what was happening. I insisted to her that I had never told her anything of the sort—that wasn't the model we were using. I asked who she had purchased her membership from, and where she'd heard that. She informed me that she had heard this from the staff, while buying a membership in the store.

My face fell. I wanted to tell her that I felt that I had been played, too. That even though I was a board member, the board didn't even have enough power over most decisions—including those decisions that resulted in the staff not getting any real training on what cooperatives were, how they worked, and what owner shares were. But that wasn't the right response. Her accusation was correct.

We absolutely did a lot of things right, but there were also many missteps. I understood the outsized role our incubator had played in our co-op. We had allowed operational decisions to be funneled through one of our outside funders—who then pushed out seemingly uncooperative board members and undermined the board's autonomy and the membership's power. I was complicit. My silence in the final days of the RCC—in the face of all that was at stake for this woman's community—meant that even as the board's autonomy was being undermined, I was undermining the membership by not giving them what they needed to successfully govern their co-op.

The woman went on to say that I had a car. And here she was walking back from Food Lion, over a mile away from the intersection where we were talking, and that I wouldn't have to deal with what we had done. I wanted to justify my silence. I wanted to say, "I was protecting you! This funder has a history of quickly pulling out of projects, and that we felt like we walked a line between pleasing funders and serving the community. I wanted to say that we felt like any misstep on our part would have left you without a store!"

But it made no sense to say all this, because this woman and this neighborhood was left without a store anyway . . . and she was walking with her groceries again.

"Trust the people and they become trustworthy," adrienne maree brown said. I still think often about how that store started, and how it ended. There are relationships that have never been repaired. There are people I am still upset with. But in the end, I have to ask myself what parts did we participate in? We didn't trust the people.

·   ·   ·   ·   ·

A CASE STUDY OF MAKING AN EXIT

Exits can be messy, and not all partners and participants share the same perspective on what leads to disruptions in organizing. Certainly, not even the four coauthors of this chapter share the exact same viewpoint on what led to the RCC's closure. But making sense of how we exit interventions—even when they are perceived as failures—offers something worthwhile. Perhaps most challenging yet most crucial, the difficult and sometimes painful act of sensemaking amid a failed intervention can help food justice activists, organizers, researchers, and communities recognize—and possibly reconcile—the various paradoxes of structure and power that can keep social movements from becoming sustainable. As such, our goal with this chapter is not to identify root causes of failure; rather, we hope to create a space where multiple voices—including the uncomfortable and inconvenient ones—can make sense of what we learned from the RCC.

The RCC opened in November 2016 to much accolade and celebration across both the neighborhood and greater Greensboro.[1] Decades earlier, the neighborhood Winn Dixie had closed, and nothing had moved in to replace it. Since 1998, neighborhood residents were left to walk over a mile to another grocery store or take a bus to a Walmart north of the neighborhood—causing no small amount of hardship on the aging and poor residents, who often lacked transportation or resources for this sort of travel.

In 2011, residents started working with city agencies, local nonprofit organizations, and several community groups to create a neighborhood-driven, cooperative grocery store. The idea quickly gained traction. Not only could local residents have better access to food (and in particular fresh food), but they also could be decision-makers and own the store, creating much-needed community wealth.

When we first proposed this book, we had hoped to tell a different story about the RCC—one that recounted the resilience of a neighborhood with a history of community organizing, their persistence in sustaining a conversation to open a grocery store, and their unique approach to advocacy and activism that resulted in a community-owned, co-op. But just two short years after their celebratory opening, the RCC would face the unfortunate position of selling off their remaining assets, informing members about the details of the demise, and ultimately closing the doors on a once promising community-based food program. With the announcement of the RCC's closing in January 2019, the story we wanted to tell changed. And instead, we were presented with a unique opportunity to consider how partners engage in sensemaking when an intervention cannot be sustained.

Communicating food justice is not always neat and tidy, and with this chapter, we most directly address our fourth guiding question: how stakeholders manage tension in their pursuit of food justice. Chapter 10 draws from numerous voices and perspectives attached to the Renaissance Community Co-op in order to focus on sustaining conversations while making an exit. We traced local and academic articles on the RCC, interviews with RCC and F4DC organizers, as well as other publicly available documents regarding the co-op. We also offer perspectives as owners and shoppers—as Marianne was an owner in the co-op and attended several owner meetings, and Niesha lived briefly in the neighborhood and occasionally shopped at the RCC. Finally, we invite a former RCC board member, Casey Thomas, and a former F4DC staffer, Alyzza May, to discuss the challenges of sustaining community-based participation at the co-op.

A Cooperative Approach to Community Food Justice

Communicating food justice often requires densely connected partners working toward *both* food *and* economic justice. By many accounts, the Renaissance Community Co-op grew out of the convergence of three different conversations involving food and economic justice in Greensboro.[2] The first conversation stretches back to 1998, when the residents living in the northeast corner of the city formed the Concerned Citizens of Northeast Greensboro (CCNG) in response to the closing of the Winn-Dixie grocery store.[3] Although they were not able to prevent Winn-Dixie from closing, the CCNG continued to advocate for a grocery store in their neighborhood and expanded their advocacy and activism to include topics like reviving smaller neighborhood groups, neighborhood crime and safety, and advocating to close the White Street Landfill—the City's primary dump, which was located in their neighborhood and closed in 2006 as a result of their activism.

The second conversation surfaced several years later, as the City of Greensboro considered reopening the White Street Landfill in 2011. CCNG joined efforts with the newly-formed Citizens for Economic and Environmental Justice (CEEJ) to keep the landfill closed. The emerging partners engaged in some tactful organizing—including strategic partnerships with student coalitions across the city and the leadership of neighborhood advocates like Goldie Wells, who had represented the neighborhood for numerous terms on the Greensboro City Council. Through their combined activism, they stopped the landfill and gained some serious organizing credibility and respect across the city.

The third conversation also emerged in 2011, from the fading sparks of the Occupy Greensboro movement.[4] Organizers from the Fund for Democratic Communities (F4DC), a local foundation focused on economic democracy and cooperative ownership, had been leading discussions about economic development, cooperatives, and home foreclosures as part of Occupy Greensboro's work. F4DC leaders were committed to a concept of democratizing wealth, and organizers saw cooperatives as a way to disrupt economic systems that were reproducing inequity and keep more resources in local communities.

Those three conversations converged in June of 2011 on the steps of Greensboro's City Hall, as the CCNG and the CEEJ celebrated a victory in the White Street Landfill case. As former Greensboro food writer Eric Ginsburg noted:

> The day the landfill deal died, activists rallied outside city hall to celebrate. Seasoned leftists Marnie Thompson and Ed Whitfield were there, playing with radical drum corps Cakalak Thunder. As residents celebrated around them, the duo approached Goldie Wells. Northeast Greensboro had built some serious muscle in the landfill fight, Thompson remembers saying as she leaned over the huge drum strapped around her. Now that Wells' group could return its focus to a grocery store, why not flex that muscle and build their own?[5]

The CEEJ continued to hold meetings after the landfill victory, and alongside the CCNG and F4DC, their focus turned back to a neighborhood grocery store.

Early in the partnership, organizers with F4DC steered these merging conversations toward organizing a cooperative grocery store that the community could own. They arranged for members of the CCNG, CEEJ, and the larger Greensboro community to visit the nearby Company Shops Market in Burlington, North Carolina. This food co-op had opened the year before to fill a gap in grocery store access in downtown Burlington, and to establish cooperatively owned food businesses.[6] Those early meetings and co-op visits would create a space where the CCNG, CEEJ, and other community residents had positioned themselves as the voice of a neighborhood who wanted a grocery store, and F4DC had positioned themselves as the technical experts who could incubate a food cooperative. By the end of 2012, the partners had officially established the Renaissance Community Co-op. They describe their partnership on the RCC's Facebook page as: "A group of Northeast Greensboro residents and friends who have outlined a plan with the guidance of F4DC to open a cooperative grocery store in the old Bessemer Center. The vision is to create a community-driven, full-scale grocery store that meets the needs of the community."

Over the next four years, the RCC grew from three converging conversations to a fully functioning, cooperative grocery store with more than thirteen hundred owners and co-op supporters. For $100 a share, community members from northeast Greensboro to anywhere across the globe could buy in to the RCC. Together, the RCC partners designed extensive outreach and canvassing programs and public meeting schedules across the neighborhood to garner support for the co-op. With funding support from F4DC, partners created savvy media campaigns—including a two-and-a-half-minute video that featured neighborhood residents and community organizers talking about wanting a grocery store in their neighborhood, where "community health and wealth grow with every purchase," and that doesn't "pick up and leave."[7] Partners focused on identifying young leadership from within the Black community for membership on the RCC board. They navigated dramatic setbacks and negotiations with Greensboro City Council about community support for the co-op and the availability of the space in their proposed plan.

What took most communities ten years to organize, partners in northeast Greensboro were doing in half the time. With recurring themes of "We Want a Co-op" and "More Than a Grocery Store," the Renaissance Community Co-op was quickly being hailed as a model for community organizing.[8] Their message was inspiring—one of community resilience that grew into community organizing to open a grocery store that the community owned.

But the story of organizing and opening the Renaissance Community Co-op has already been told.[9] Our intent with this chapter had always been to focus on the stories that emerged after the doors opened, and although those stories certainly include some inspiring examples of community participation—like when the RCC plaza served as a staging ground for support after a tornado ripped through northeast Greensboro[10]—the most important contribution that the four of us can collectively make emphasizes how the RCC partners have made sense amid the store's closing. The following section outlines sensemaking as a communication practice for organizing and draws on examples from the RCC to generate a framework for making an exit to sustain a conversation.

MAKING SENSE AMID AN EXIT

"It is with a heavy heart that we inform you that we must close our grocery store," the email began. "Our goal from the beginning was to build a self-sustaining store that met the community's needs for good jobs and fresh, affordable food. Since the store opened, we have not been able to produce the sales we need to be sustainable." Owners of the Renaissance Community Co-op in northeast Greensboro received the news on January 9, 2019, that the grocery store their community had organized would close by the end of the month. The email extended an invitation to attend a co-op owner meeting the following week to begin making sense of the co-op's closing.

As an organizational communication practice, sensemaking is the process of taking a situation and turning it into words to serve as a launchpad for future action.[11] Sensemaking is "a way station on the road to a consensually constructed, coordinated system of action.[12] The relevance of sensemaking to communicating food justice is rooted in a practice of reflexive organizing, which means creating a space for community members to try and succeed *or* fail. And when we fail, organizers have just as much responsibility to commit to words their position on "what happened" as when we succeed. That's how organizers sustain conversations, even when that conversation goes in a direction we never intended. As a reflection on the closing of the RCC, we draw attention to the following four communication practices that may be considered the beginnings of a framework for making sense amid an exit: acknowledge the narrative, take sensemaking public, make space for uncomfortable and inconvenient interpretations, and confront tensions and paradoxes.

Acknowledge the Narrative

When a situation that requires sensemaking arises, especially during interventions in which multiple partners and stakeholders are involved, organizers must commit the story to words.[13] Acknowledging the narrative requires partners to recognize both the strengths and shortcomings of an intervention with a sense of humility. The purpose of acknowledging the narrative is not to assign blame, engage in gossip, or further fragment what is likely already a delicate situation—although partners should be prepared for when those sorts of conversations arise. Rather, making sense amid an exit requires partners to develop an account—a collective one, if possible—of both the points of pride and areas of tension around an intervention. The collective process of outlining how the work began and how the conversation might continue helps communities retain the useful pieces of failed interventions for future organizing, advocacy, and activism.[14]

In the case of the RCC, acknowledging the narrative played out in a series of emails to the co-op ownership, local news articles, and two final owner meetings held at the store in January and March 2019. The early signs that the RCC was struggling emerged in a series of emails from the RCC board starting in October 2018. The subject line read, "Attention OWNERS!" and a letterhead featuring a bright red box with white letters announced, "We NEED You Now." The email went on to describe a dire financial situation for the RCC. The store needed to begin increasing sales—substantially. Sales showed a $15,000 shortfall between projected sales and actual sales. Although the RCC had seen a 33.8 percent increase in third-quarter sales, the board reminded owners that "it is our responsibility to remind you that *if we do not increase our sales even faster, it is not guaranteed that the store can remain open.*"

In the January 9 email, the owners got the news that the store's last day of operation would be January 25. The RCC board also announced plans for a community meeting to apprise owners of the situation, celebrate its opening, and mourn its closing. Local media provided additional context to account for the closing of the store, mostly through interviews with RCC partners. The most frequently quoted partners were Goldie Wells, a former leader with CCNG and CEEJ and current city councilwoman representing the RCC's district, and Roodline Volcy, the sitting board president. Both women offered comparable interpretations for the store's closure. "For a community that didn't have a grocery store for over 16 years, I think people developed patterns. Overcoming those habits can be difficult," Volcy said.[15] Wells offered a similar sentiment, stating that "we were never able to get those sales up. I guess after 18 years, they'd found other means of getting their groceries."[16] These stories often remained hopeful, with several partners highlighting the importance of the organizing and community mobilization that went into opening the store.

The most substantial practices of acknowledging the narrative came at the first of two owner meetings on January 14, 2019. Close to one hundred owners, residents, board members, organizers, and employees packed into an empty storefront that had served as a makeshift meeting room adjacent to the grocery store. Board members, including Roodline and Casey, sat along the front wall of the long, narrow room, with everyone else seated in four long rows of chairs or tucked into corners of the standing-room-only meeting. The community heard first from Goldie Wells, who reminded residents:

> We fought the landfill twice. We have come a long way despite what we're facing. I want you all to encourage yourselves. We're not giving up. There will be a grocery store. African Americans, we can do it ourselves. Let's not give up and be proud of what we did accomplish.

We heard from F4DC organizers, board members like Casey, the store's bookkeeper and assistant manager, and finally from Roodline. The latter two women outlined some of the key reasons for the store's closure—namely, the store could not sustain sales at a level to keep up with the co-op's business model and mission.

Store employee's and RCC volunteers passed around handouts with the RCC's financial information and profit and loss statements. The total cost of goods sold between October 2016 and December 2018 was $1,562,149 and the total income from sales was $1,623,793. Although the gross profit

was $61,644 over that two-year period, the rent was $351,407 and personnel expenses were $1,185,453—and those were only the two largest
expenses after the cost of food. Many people in the room were drawn
immediately to the labor costs, with Guilford County Board of Education
member Byron Gladden asking why the personnel costs were so high. The
RCC had prided itself on working toward a living wage for employees.
Their goal was $15/hour and most employees ranged between $10 and
$12/hour. The RCC could have slashed their budget by almost a third if
they had paid their employees minimum wage—but that went against
their employment ethics and mission. "We could have cut wages," Casey
interjected from the row of board members, "but we weren't trying to
solve a problem created by poverty by creating poverty jobs."

Several owners and residents asked what efforts the board had pursued
to try to increase sales, and if they had reached out to the city council
or attempted to raise funds outside of grocery store sales. But organizers
brought it back to the simple point that the store's sales could not keep
up with the RCC's business model and mission. The RCC needed to average $100,000 per month in sales to remain solvent, and as of the Janu-
ary 2019 owner meeting, they were averaging $40,000 to $90,000 per
month. So the board had made the painful decision to close. The remainder of the meeting outlined how the board planned to close the store. That
plan included selling the remainder of the store's inventory by January 25,
preparing severance packages for all employees, holding a job fair to help
employees find new positions, and preserve as much of the RCC's physical
infrastructure as possible to attract a new grocery store to the space. The
owners would reconvene in March to take care of the final piece of co-op
business, which was to dissolve the RCC as a legal entity.

In the immediate weeks and months following the RCC's closing, community members and partners seemed to easily identify some consistent
strengths of the RCC—namely, the efforts to mobilize people in the community to advocate for a co-op. Organizers were equally praised for their
promotional materials and public campaign, which in addition to the two-
minute "We Want a Co-Op" video also included a booklet titled "More
Than a Grocery Store" to commemorate the Grand Opening of the store.
This booklet outlined a history of both northeast Greensboro and the RCC
and contained a two-page outline that answered the question "what is a

co-op?"[17] The Grand Opening, itself, was also consistently recognized as a source of pride, because of its celebratory tone and sense of community. Across the accounting of the RCC's narrative was a reminder that, even though the store had closed, the residents of northeast Greensboro now knew that they could advocate for what they wanted to see in their neighborhoods and organize resources to address their community's future needs.

Acknowledging the narrative of what led to the store's closure—and the RCC's inability to produce the sales that partners had anticipated—was much more challenging in the early stages of the RCC's exit. Partners and board members could articulate that the store's sales could not keep up with their model and mission, but they could not as easily identify why the community wasn't shopping at the store. In the months that followed the RCC's closing, ongoing sensemaking would help clarify some of their interpretations.

Take Sensemaking Public

Practices of sensemaking are often ongoing. Partners commit actions to words to make sense of a situation and create the foundation for future actions. We argue that an important part of making an exit in community-engaged and partnered interventions involves taking those processes of sensemaking and making them public. When the RCC owners and organizers collectively acknowledged the store's narrative, much of that work was done through email correspondence and two owner meetings with about a hundred people. If future organizers—especially those who are interested in opening food cooperatives—could learn from the strengths and shortcomings of the RCC, then partners needed to take the sensemaking into more public venues.

In December 2019, about a year after the board members learned that the RCC would be closing, F4DC organizers Marnie Thompson, Sohnie Black, and Ed Whitfield participated alongside former board president Roodline Volcy in two public accounts with *Non-Profit Quarterly*. The first was an article by Marnie, Sohnie, and Ed entitled "The Ballad of the RCC, or 'Nice Try. Now Try Again,'" which outlined the basic story of the RCC and some data on what the RCC did accomplish economically. For example, the authors wrote:

RCC had big dreams. Of course, we never reached anything close to profitability, but over our two-plus years of operation, we employed local people, paid more than $12,000 in city property taxes, and supported other local and regional businesses, including buying more than $1.6 million in goods from area distributors.

Perhaps the good jobs RCC provided were its biggest contribution. We had hoped to move over $2 million in wages and benefits into the neighborhood in the first three years. We fell short, as we closed before the three-year mark and cut staff as sales lagged. But we did provide $1.3 million in wages and benefits, and the vast majority of people earning those wages and benefits were from the immediate neighborhood.[18]

The second account was a webinar titled "The Anatomy of a Failed Co-op," where Sohnie, Ed, and Roodline dug much deeper into the reasons for the RCC's lack of sales and general failure. To open the conversation, Sohnie framed the use of failure as a way to make sense for future organizing: "I wanted to emphasize that we are using that word *failure*, not in a negative way. We don't think that failure is a negative thing. Very often, you have to have some failures and tries before you succeed, so we want to take the negative stigma away from that."[19] In both the article and the webinar, the organizers went on to identify what partners had begun to call the two C's and the three M's—which highlighted corporate competition and capacity, with its three related concepts of management, marketing, and movement building—as core reasons for the RCC's failure.

Corporate competition invoked images of Walmart and Dollar General as low-cost competitors where people had become used to shopping in the absence of a grocery store in the immediate neighborhood. Capacity challenges included underestimating three things: the training needed to close some of the skills gaps for the folks hired from within the neighborhood, the marketing required to reach potential shoppers because of the publicity the RCC had received, and the ongoing engagement and organizing within the community. As Sohnie clarified in the webinar:

Some of the marketing fallacies that we had coming into this is "If we build it, they will come." We thought because the community said to us, "We want this; we want this store; we need this," that if we opened a store people would come and shop there. Especially people in the community, in droves.

We also felt like, because this was the only full-service grocery store within a two-and-a-half-mile radius, that was our market area, people would come to the store because they had no other choice. We failed to take into account that people have been shopping other places and managing to get food for almost two decades. So they had already had these really deeply entrenched shopping habits. We had to recapture that market audience that we lost when the store closed two decades earlier.[20]

Sohnie also spoke about how the RCC and F4DC organizers had failed to maintain the level of organizing and activism that had helped them open the store in the first place. She continued, by focusing on the spirit of building a movement:

But with stores like the RCC there are two things you have to keep in mind: it *is* a business but *also* it's a movement. And again that's something that our competition can't do. They can't build a movement; that was our strong suit and we kind of lost sight of that. . . . The spirit of self-determination and the deep democracy that we had engendered by working together, thinking together, building this store together—we lost. So some of the lessons we learned [about the] keys to sustainability: organize, organize, organize, and never stop.[21]

Her comment alludes to the importance of sustaining communication and engagement practices across key turning points over the life of an intervention.

In taking their sensemaking public through the webinar, RCC and F4DC organizers were able to acknowledge another key factor in the failure of the co-op. Specifically, the three conversations that converged to launch the RCC were rooted in a general social and economic justice framework. The partners who initiated some of the earliest conversations that grew into the RCC focused their attention on social and economic justice, but not necessarily food justice. As Roodline explained:

What isn't covered in the slides that I think is important is that the board itself struggled to meet and face the external challenges that the RCC was having. We had done so much organizing around the store opening, as Sohnie said. We had been knocking on doors. We had phone banks. We were having community meetings. Just a lot of organizing had been happening prior to the opening of the store.

And now, we were faced with running it right. And this was a whole beast, in itself, that I don't think we were prepared for.[22]

The RCC and F4DC partners learned that it was one thing to rally people around drum circles, invite neighborhood residents to community meetings, and speak before the city council about the community's desire for a co-op. Running a grocery store *after* they got the doors open was something quite different.

Roodline's public sensemaking illustrated a challenge that RCC and F4DC organizers faced as they struggled to reconcile their roots in social and economic justice with the language and practice of food justice. This disconnect between social and economic justice and food justice is also evident in the very language used to name and promote the RCC. Throughout the initial organizing, the recurring slogans of "We Want a Co-op" and "More Than a Grocery Store" consistently prioritized the message about organizing a cooperative over understanding neighborhood food practices. The RCC's name itself—Renaissance Community Co-op—does not feature the words food, market, or grocery in the title, something that partners realized led to confusion after the store initially opened.[23] Although the RCC was *more* than a grocery store, it was also *still* a grocery store, and organizers did not adequately prepare to align their social and economic justice frameworks with their new need to emphasize food justice.

Make Space for Uncomfortable and Inconvenient Interpretations

Recognizing voices that speak dissent and disruption is a necessary practice when organizing with communities to direct social change.[24] Voices of dissent and disruption give communities the opportunity to reimagine organizing practices and the possibilities for social activism.[25] In the sensemaking that followed the closing of the RCC, partners were adept at identifying the strengths of the co-op as a way to reframe what future organizers could learn from their story. For example, Casey was quoted in the local *Carolina Peacemaker* newspaper as saying, "The take-away from this should be that we can do things for our communities and build community wealth."[26]

But it has taken more time to come to terms with the shortcomings of the RCC. Certainly, the article and webinar with *Non-Profit Quarterly* are good examples of how RCC and F4DC organizers used the first year following the RCC's closing to make sense of what needs to be done differently the next time partners launch interventions with communities that address both economic and food justice. At the same time, making an exit to sustain a conversation also demands that partners make space for uncomfortable or inconvenient interpretations as the sensemaking unfolds.

Simply because people live in the same neighborhood, or share common threads across a culture, or get routinely classified as a similar race doesn't mean that they share the same opinions, perspectives, or practices—when it comes to food or any other topic. But that's when dialogue, storytelling, and other forms of communication are perhaps most crucial to sustaining conversations in pursuit of equity and social justice.[27] Making space for uncomfortable and inconvenient conversations can be a source of productivity. Communication scholars Shiv Ganesh and Heather Zoller refer to this as an agonistic approach to dialogue.[28] Agonistic dialogue embraces conflicting interpretations as a way to discursively open conversations in ways that promote ethical and transparent change. As we make sense of a situation—like an intervention that fails—interpretations will be messy and unpredictable. But there is value in creating space to work through the uncomfortable and inconvenient threads of the larger narrative.

We included Casey's story as our opening narrative in an effort to make space for uncomfortable conversations. Without a doubt, the story infused this case study of the RCC with a particular feeling—but the truth is, from opening to close the RCC was a highly emotional and even personal feeling project for many. Casey's story brings up some difficult and inconvenient experiences around organizing the RCC after the store opened, the RCC's relationship with the residents in the neighborhood, and the RCC's partnership with F4DC. Our purpose in inviting Casey and Alyzza to contribute to this chapter is not to reframe their experience to align with dominant interpretations about what led to the RCC's failure. On the contrary, we recognize that many RCC partners and community members are in the midst of making sense of the RCC's closing. Aside from the owner meetings to close the co-op and the *Non-Profit Quarterly* accounts, however, there have been few opportunities for partners to engage in this kind of sensemaking from a dialogic perspective. So we look to storytelling as a way to do similar work in making sense of uncomfortable and inconvenient interpretations.[29] We continue that practice in the following section.

Confront Tensions and Paradoxes

If partners and community members create spaces for inconvenient and uncomfortable interpretations, we must also be prepared to confront the various tensions and paradoxes that will inevitably arise when multiple voices commit situations to words.[30] As partners and community members go through the practices of sensemaking, both publicly and within their partnerships, one of the most useful communication frameworks we can offer involves the paradoxes of participation.[31] When interventions add layers of community partnerships and economic justice, the work requires a greater attention to how paradoxes arise as a natural part of organizing. From an organizational communication perspective, paradoxes are defined as practical situations in which, during the pursuit of one goal, another goal enters the situation and undermines the first goal.[32] Paradoxes of participation do not suggest that both goals are not worthy—they are often seemingly compatible, and one goal tends to undermine the other unintentionally.

In the case of the RCC, this chapter has already laid out evidence to suggest that introducing the goal to open a cooperative unintentionally undermined the community's initial goal to have a grocery store in their neighborhood. RCC and F4DC organizers were not prepared for the amount of work that would be required to educate community members, potential owners, and the larger public about how cooperatives operate. It became a part of the promotional materials, the community outreach, and the rationale for why the neighborhood should become invested—to own the grocery store in their neighborhood. But organizers had not mobilized a similar conversation about what it would take for people to change their shopping habits, which is what the RCC ultimately needed in order to be successful. Without people who were going to change their food practices and start shopping at the RCC, the cooperative structure that gave the store its foundation also began to unravel.

Community-based and participatory approaches to organizing can be particularly susceptible to paradoxes of structure and power. Paradoxes of structure involve the architecture and design of democratic practices, like "mandating grassroots participation from the top," and paradoxes of power are concerned with how power is exercise as a part of organizing, like "failing to see the value of resistant or oppositional voices."[33] Paradoxes can arise when partners have unequal financial resources or racial privileges in a given context, when partners do not have clear expectations for how they share control, or when outside partners ask community members to organize collectively but assign tasks that are beyond those community members' capacities.[34] For example, partners likely encountered a paradox of structure when, as the business incubator for the RCC, F4DC organized the board, the owners, and the community to work as a cooperative toward opening the store, but underestimated the work that was needed to manage a food business once the doors opened.

As a way to confront tensions and manage paradoxes, which is a necessary part of making an exit so those tensions are not reproduced in future organizing, partners can always choose to ignore the paradoxes. But in doing so, they may waste a precious opportunity to capture the productive potential that lies within confronting tensions. Partners can also choose to reframe and reconcile goals—like food justice and economic justice—to consider how they might strengthen as opposed to undermine each other.

Here, in the spirit of confronting tensions as a way to make space for uncomfortable and inconvenient interpretations, we turn to Casey and Alyzza for an account of their experience managing paradoxes of structure and power around the organizing of the RCC:

The RCC didn't just set out to be a store. We set out to be a tool for people to build our local economy on our terms, using democracy and the principles of cooperation—including democratic control, autonomy, and education and training among cooperatives. While there were several areas in which we did live up to cooperative values—like concern for community by striving to pay more than minimum wage—there were also significant ways in which we came up short of these principles. Our most significant shortcoming was that we compromised our autonomy by failing to establish appropriate boundaries between ourselves, as a cooperative set of owners and their board, and our funders and advisors—namely, F4DC.

Although F4DC was helping us learn how to form and govern a co-op, they also led the conversations when it came to securing funds for the RCC, and they managed the bulk of the work when it came to opening and operating the store. Our failure in boundary setting was two-fold. F4DC didn't want to limit their power when it came to the co-op, and we didn't want to limit our access to their help. With no clear boundaries set between the two entities, an F4DC staffer was present during every RCC board meeting, and if the board held a closed session, F4DC staff would ask individual RCC board members what had transpired. For the majority of the co-op's existence, there was no contract or agreement between the RCC and F4DC that stipulated roles and rules of engagement. This often worked in the RCC's favor, allowing us to access F4DC resources or staff time when we needed it. However, it also meant that F4DC made numerous decisions about the community-run store.

The way the RCC closed illustrates how little control the board and membership really had, and it serves as a visceral reminder of the paradox of power we experienced. In early 2018, F4DC presented the RCC with an impressive and comprehensive ten-point plan for improvement to help us overcome our abysmal sales and to improve our performance. In addition to this plan, F4DC sent us their first formal agreement that outlined a relationship between F4DC and the board. In the agreement, they committed up to $1.17 million to the co-op as additional bridge funding. While we worked to become sustainable, these bridge funds would help support the RCC through February 2019, or until the funds were expended. The board voted to sign this agreement, but we asked if F4DC would offer no further funding if we did not meet the benchmarks. We were assured that it did not necessarily mean that they would not fund us, so long as the co-op was on an upward trajectory. The improvement plan did give some direction, but the board was not left with much clarity around which benchmarks we did need to meet or how we would know if we needed to prepare to close.

As the year went on, our co-op was not meeting expectations. We continued to seek clarity about our future funding from F4DC and if it would be prudent to seek other funding sources. Without guidance, it was unclear to our board if our efforts were best spent landing the benchmarks from the ten-point plan or seeking additional grant funding.

The co-op's fate, however, was clearly in question. One of the points of improvement involved proper board governance, but F4DC also insisted that the RCC board members sign nondisclosure agreements. By November, when F4DC's codirector attended an RCC board meeting, the board directly asked if F4DC was going to cease funding us. We still received no clear answer. It was not long before we received a letter from our largest lender informing us that our loans were in default, but not because we were behind on our payments. Instead, it was because F4DC would no longer be funding us. We were informed that we would need to shut down quickly.

It was a gutting realization that we had either been misled or that the co-op, our employees, and the board held so little weight with a champion of cooperative organizing and justice work. We felt unseen.

With the store's closing, F4DC's $1.17 million was used to offset losses and attempt to implement remedies. While the RCC board had the community connections to provide input into how best to use that money, the F4DC maintained control over the decisions about its allotment. There is no question that the RCC needed the F4DC—they were by leaps and bounds our largest funder and, in fact, largest champion. They also carried the expertise and connections that we lacked and offered those to us readily. However, although we had an elected board, a voting membership, and owner shares, and we had opened with the intention of building shared, democratic, and economic power, the relationship that gave us access to our funding and helped open our doors wound up being what kept us from succeeding as an economic democracy.

REFLECTIONS, RECOMMENDATIONS, AND RESOURCES

It would be irresponsible to suggest that the RCC would still be here if partners had established clearer boundaries and shared power more equitably. Even stores with the perfect synthesis of food justice and economic justice cannot guarantee that people will shop there.[35] The RCC is part of a growing narrative of struggle for cooperative ownership of food businesses. Just eight months before the RCC announced to owners that the store would close, the Company Shops Market in Burlington, North Carolina, closed after seven years in operation. In Detroit, where we have drawn many comparisons in conversations about food justice, partners in the Detroit Black Community Food Security Network (DBCFSN) are organizing to open a co-op as an extension of their work with the D-Town Farm and the Detroit Food Policy Council. They have taken a slower route toward opening their doors, including over fifteen years of organizing with the community to build wealth and resources through the D-Town Farm and a network of hyper-local produce and food businesses. But organizers have also encountered a variety of setbacks in launching their co-op, as the COVID-19 pandemic bolstered the demand for memberships but also slowed plans for construction.[36]

In the closing sections of this chapter, Marianne and Niesha offer some reflections about the importance of sensemaking and storytelling in building communication infrastructure, particularly in terms of local food organizing. Casey and Alyzza provide some recommendations about working in cooperative structures. And finally, we collectively suggest resources for information about the Renaissance Community Co-op.

Reflections

Routine is a powerful thing, especially when it comes to something as everyday as what to eat. RCC and F4DC organizers were not prepared for how the larger neighborhood had changed their everyday food habits in the eighteen years that the neighborhood had gone without a grocery store. Their underestimations were reflected in how partners stopped organizing after the store opened and consistently prioritized opening a co-op over more directly talking about food. Acknowledging the narrative and taking their sensemaking public, particularly through the *Non-Profit Quarterly* article and webinar, gave RCC and F4DC the opportunity to publicly account for the co-op's failure in ways that could be productive for future food and economic justice advocates. This practice of *publicly* committing a situation to words can help partners sustain conversations amid failed interventions. At the same time, centering communication and storytelling recognizes that many partners are still working through the uncomfortable and inconvenient interpretations of the RCC's demise and confronting the various paradoxes of participation that came into tension during the co-op's operation.

In this way, the story of the RCC reinforces both the need for sensemaking amid an exit, as well as the importance of community-communication infrastructure.[37] Including both storytelling networks and infrastructures of listening, community-communication infrastructure routinely centers voices, experiences, and expertise of the community members who are most affected by disparities like food insecurity. Even more, the strength of community-communication infrastructure lies in community ownership of both material and communication resources in the neighborhoods that anchor the organizing.[38] In other words, it's not enough to invite community members and voices at the margin to the table, food advocates and activists must begin to question who gets to bring the table. This sentiment was referenced across several reflections shared in this chapter—particularly in Sohnie and Roodline's comments about the failure to continue engaging the community after the store opened.

Communities with a strong communication infrastructure are also more likely to sustain conversations by navigating the tensions and paradoxes that will inevitably arise in any community-based and community-driven path toward food justice. The conversation to organize a co-op did not need to draw attention away from the conversations about food. In the case of the RCC, however, organizers repeatedly suggested that the communication infrastructure had not been sufficiently developed to encourage residents to change the way they shopped for food. Community members wanted to see resources developed for their neighborhood, and the RCC showed us that developing those resources was only the first part of that conversation.

We admit that this chapter is messy, but so is organizing for food justice. The way we have told the story of the RCC—focusing particularly on sensemaking amid an exit—suggests that sustaining the conversation is an ongoing and multifaceted process. Attention to how communities can sustain their activism and advocacy are crucial at this point, especially because of the fragility and volatility of food systems, as well as the unintended consequences of our discourse. From a communication perspective, we recognize that resources—particularly those related to food and community—will change over time; however, creating spaces for intentional dialogue, imagining new food and communication infrastructures, and constructing shared yet complex narratives can help communities sustain conversations while disrupting systems that reproduce inequity.

Recommendations

For groups who are working to organize grocery cooperatives in their own communities, Casey and Alyzza recommend the following:

1. Keep any incubators, funders, co-op developers or outside entities in an accountable relationship. The RCC did an excellent job of organizing to open the cooperative. Once the store opened, unfortunately, the board did not organize a clear relationship with F4DC to hold them accountable—both to the board and to the owners. Our organizing muscles were built around F4DC as the bones, and we did not treat F4DC as a discrete partner that we needed to be able to negotiate with, like any other organization. When individuals and groups partner to start any sort of food project, those partners should create a memorandum of understanding (MOU) that outlines who controls the funds, defines the scope of work, delineates responsibilities and decision-making power, and sets firm boundaries.

2. Educate your board. Ensure that boards are adequately trained on reading and interpreting financial statements and understanding finance as it relates to cooperatives. Boards need to know the right questions to ask and changes to request—of their owners, their managers, and their funders. Train board members on policy governance and have a tolerance for more hands-on governance early in the co-op's development. Learn as much as possible about the grocery industry and food distribution before opening a grocery store or joining a co-op board.

3. Make sure your co-op's membership is made up of the people you are trying to serve. Co-ops operate best when the majority of owners and members are people from the immediate neighborhood. They are often the most committed to using the co-op because they have the most direct need. It's tempting and easy to get solidarity ownerships— and the money is helpful—but you can get a better understanding of who is going to shop in your store if you focus on people down the street. The majority of the RCC's membership was from the neighborhood where we opened, but many of our members continued to shop

elsewhere. They were more interested in the store as a symbol of economic development and community pride than as a resource for buying food.

4. Explore numerous cooperative structures. During the co-op's tenure, more than one shopper asked us to clarify how the store was a "community store," when there was no free food to give away to the community. To me, this comment demonstrated that a lot of people had needs that weren't met through the RCC. Be willing to explore other structures of cooperative ownership—like creating a common-good cooperative. This kind of co-op is still governed by the people who use it, and they can accept donations and offset losses to provide food for people who cannot afford it.

Resources

Non-Profit Quarterly webinar: A link to the webinar mentioned in this chapter where RCC and F4DC engage in public sensemaking about the RCC's closing.[39]

More Than a Grocery Store: The booklet that F4DC created with the RCC in preparation for the co-op's Grand Opening celebration in November 2016.[40]

Cooperative Grocery Network: An excellent summary of key points related to opening the RCC.[41]

Conclusion

SECURING FOOD FOR A JUST FUTURE

With Gwen Frisbie-Fulton

Figure 21. Too good to pass up. A customer at the Mobile Oasis Farmers Market contemplates adding some rainbow swiss chard to her purchase. Photo credit: Marianne LeGreco.

Food (in)security, food hardship, and food justice are not always easy conversations to navigate—especially for communities that attempt to face poverty and access in order to build more equitable food systems. While we cannot isolate exactly how food justice organizing has changed the levels of food security in Greensboro and Guilford County, partners have started tracking improvements across our food system and neighborhoods. In June 2016, just one year after reaching the top of the Food Research and Action Center's list of communities experiencing food hardship, Greensboro/High Point dropped from first to ninth.[1] Our food hardship rate also improved, moving from 28.2 percent to 22.2 percent. Within two more years, Greensboro/High Point was out of the top ten—with a ranking of 14 and a food hardship rate of 19.2 percent.[2] These numbers mirror a nationwide trend in 2015 that showed a significant drop in food insecurity rates across the United States, from 15.4 percent to 13.4 percent.[3] Although the media coverage and public acknowledgment of Greensboro/High Point's improved food hardship rates did not get the same level of attention as when we reached the top of FRAC's list, many organizers, activists, and researchers quietly celebrated and got back to work.

And the strength of Greensboro's local food system alongside our food justice organizing has been put to the test since our FRAC numbers started to fall. In spring 2020, we completed the first draft of this manuscript two weeks before North Carolina, like many other states, began issuing stay-at-home orders due to COVID-19. Social distancing practices almost immediately changed the structures that people had typically used to get food, especially as people lost jobs, restaurants and schools closed, and food markets changed their hours. We do not yet have the FRAC data to demonstrate how COVID-19 has impacted our food hardship rates, but we can demonstrate how the strength of our local networks around food helped us respond to abrupt changes in how people eat. For example, within two days of Guilford County Schools closing, the school system partnered with local nonprofit agencies and food pantries to put up their summer meal network—a network of thirty-four locations where children and students could get grab-and-go meals while school cafeterias were closed.[4] Neighborhood farmers markets, including the Corner Market and the People's Market, launched advanced ordering and drive-thru pickup models before stay-at-home orders were even issued.[5] Marianne worked closely with public health, K–12 and university partners, local nonprofits, and local food businesses to create a shareable (and updateable) public document with local food resources including free meal locations, grocery store hours, and restaurants that were open for curbside pickup and delivery.[6] The changes in food accessibility around COVID-19 social distancing and stay-at-home orders tested the infrastructure and partnerships we had built over the previous ten years and show how we have worked to engage communities, mobilize resources, document process, and sustain conversations.

While Greensboro's story of working toward vibrant, equitable, and resilient food systems certainly demonstrates creativity in the face of hardship, our story is not necessarily unique. Throughout this book, we have referenced numerous programs, interventions, and organized food justice activism in communities like Detroit, Milwaukee, and Chicago. We could call attention to countless examples of food systems organizing in small, medium, and large cities across the United States—including Buffalo, Knoxville, Asheville, and Santa Fe. In his book, *The Town That Food Saved*, Ben Hewitt recounts the story of Hardwick, a 3,200-person community in Vermont that used their local food system to transform their local economy and networks. Hewitt further explains that communities like Hardwick are evidence "that a healthy agricultural system can be the basis of communal strength, economic vitality, food security, and general resilience in uncertain times."[7] Although it would be premature for us to suggest that food has saved Greensboro, partners and everyday people across our community are unquestionably more focused on mobilizing conversations around food than we have been in years past. If we continue to do the work and sustain those conversations, we have abundant creative potential to build the kind of equitable food systems that can ensure everybody eats.

For this conclusion to the book, we first draw some lessons from the threads about communicating food justice that we have woven across our case studies. In an effort to glean specific insights about transferring communication practices across different communities, we offer both constructive criticism and possible strategies for sustaining conversations about food. We also invite Gwen Frisbie-Fulton, a local writer with a history of community activism and professional experience with food banks, to help us consider some of the next conversations in food justice that deserve our attention.

REIMAGINING FOOD SYSTEMS
THROUGH COMMUNICATION

If we hope to unlock the creative potential of our communities around our local food systems, then communication must be at the center of our practices. Recognizing the pervasiveness of communication is a crucial component of organizing social change.[8] Across the case studies featured in this book, we have used various examples of food systems organizing and food justice activism to highlight communication practices including dialogue as a form of community needs assessment, policy talk around local food economies, the use of multimedia and face-to-face platforms to strengthen community networks, and the importance of community-based interactions to design, implement, and evaluate food systems interventions.

There is much to unpack, and part of our reason for framing this book as a series of case studies was to invite readers to draw their own conclusions about what the stories represented here teach us about communicating food justice and how they might transfer to other contexts and communities. At the same time, we can lift out some meaningful observations that help us reimagine food systems through a communication lens. These observations highlight various overlaps in our four-part perspective on engaging communities, mobilizing resources, documenting process, and sustaining conversation. These four practices work continuously and frequently reinforce each other, and in the case of Greensboro, the framework gave us insight into the need to include poverty alongside more conversations about food access, the difficulties in managing transitions across the life of an intervention, the ways in which we underestimate communication in food justice organizing, and the meaning of secure food systems.

Acknowledge Access and *Poverty*

At the beginning of this book, we made the case that three of our central concepts—food insecurity, food hardship, and food deserts—were defined in terms of the relationship between access and poverty. We measure these concepts by asking everyday people if they have enough money to buy food. These case studies illustrate that when they answer no, health agencies, community partners, and even many activists tend to focus organizing efforts on how to get folks food, as opposed to how to get them more money. Simply put, organizers in Greensboro were very adept at mobilizing a conversation around food access, but not always as effective at considering the relationship between access and poverty. Consider the following reflection from Marianne's perspective:

I remember sitting in a meeting in 2016—another citywide visioning session that was designed to bring people together to talk about Greensboro's food hardship rankings and the FRAC study. Before we broke into smaller groups to generate a list of important discussion topics, the organizers asked us each to talk about what brought us to the meeting. When it came to my turn, I told the room of about fifty people that I was here because it's time for us to start pushing the conversation in Greensboro beyond access. We have to start talking about poverty in more productive ways.

After about twenty minutes of small-group brainstorming, the event organizers brought us back to identify the most popular topics from each group. I was sitting next to Niesha—I looked at her and said, "They're gonna say access." One of the discussion leaders walked to the front of the room and told the large group that one topic rose to the top of discussions at almost every table. "Can you guess what it was?" She asked, with an oblivious smile on her face.

"*Access*," I quickly responded, with more than a hint of snark in my voice. The discussion leader fumbled her words a bit as the smile dropped from her face. "Yes," she said. "It was *access*, so what do we want to do about access?"

Our short answer to the discussion leader's question is that we have to reframe the conversation. Discourse and organizing in Greensboro, and other communities facing food insecurity, have emphasized food access over meaningful dialogues, policy initiatives, and interventions that get at the more insidious side of food hardship—poverty.

Access is easy to talk about. Partners can identify gaps in food distribution and convenient access to fresh food, and we've become pretty savvy at filling those gaps with free meals, food banks, food pantries, and food recovery programs. We can almost immediately see the return on the investment of our time and resources when people who otherwise couldn't afford food now have access to something to eat. Filling those gaps makes us feel good. But if communities and their partners continue to emphasize only one side of the equation, we risk reproducing food systems that are never quite secure.

This is not to say that organizers, activists, researchers, and community members in Greensboro did not contribute something substantial to conversations around food hardship and food security by focusing on access. On the contrary, the case studies featured in this book speak to great levels of creativity and ingenuity across our communities and neighborhoods. And as our framework suggests, these case studies provide useful insights about communicating food justice by engaging communities, mobilizing resources, documenting process, and sustaining conversations.

Reimagining food systems in ways that are secure, equitable, vibrant, and resilient will require us to confront the relationship between access and poverty more directly—which is one reason food justice activists need more advanced communication approaches to telling stories and developing strategies that directly address poverty as it relates to food access.[9] We consider this point further, when Gwen joins us later in this chapter.

Never Stop Organizing

Everybody has to eat—almost every day. Questions about organizing food systems to promote food security and alleviate food hardship are questions that communities will always have to answer as long as people keep eating.[10] As such, food justice activists and advocates must be prepared to never stop organizing. But what does that mean—never stop organizing? For us, it means that everyone who has a stake in our food systems, from local to national to global, should have an opportunity to advocate for the kinds of food they want to see in their communities. Never stop organizing means pursuing food sovereignty and sustaining conversations about the importance of food to our local economies, our organizations and communities, our relationships and families, and our everyday individual practices.

Even more so, never stop organizing is about the idea that intentional and strategic communication is necessary to maintain community engagement across the life of an intervention. Across the case studies, organizers, activists, and communities in Greensboro appeared to struggle most when managing the transitions and tensions that arise between the creativity and excitement of generating ideas and arriving at the outcomes of our work. With the Warnersville Community Food Task Force and the Warnersville Community Garden, the interventions struggled to keep organizing with the community after the death of Otis Hairston. Although the work of building a garden and farmers market continued, we were never able to recapture that same connection with Warnersville residents as we had when Otis was a leading voice. As a consequence, we learned about the need not only to engage the community, but also to continue engaging them and never stop organizing.

We also observed these complications in managing transitions with both the Mobile Oasis Farmers Market and the Renaissance Community

Co-op. When partners had to shift their focus from leveraging social capital to advocate for mobile markets and grocery stores to managing the financial capital of running a food business, the emphasis on organizing and engaging with the community faded or stopped altogether. Although we framed both the Mobile Oasis and the RCC as food systems interventions, they are also food businesses, and partners recognized being underprepared for managing that aspect of the programs—to the point where they lost touch with some of their communities. For the Mobile Oasis, we argued that their potential was underrealized, and the market has been able to regain some of this kind of organizing, by partnering with the Cottage Grove neighborhood and embedding community partnerships in their strategy for identifying new sites. But for the RCC and F4DC organizers, they lost their audience when they stopped organizing, and that cost them their grocery store.

Never stop organizing means that communities are given the resources and opportunity to engage in conversations around food security and the types of food we want to see in our communities, and that partners are enabled and prepared to implement the creative and innovative ideas that are feasible within local food systems. Perhaps most important, never stop organizing means that we recognize the value of social capital when building community infrastructure.[11] At some point, most partnerships will require some sort of external funding or business model in order to secure the resources needed to launch an intervention; however, we cannot let the demands of managing that enterprise detract from the relationships that we must maintain across our partnerships and communities.

Never Underestimate Communication

One way food justice advocates and activists can ensure that we never stop organizing is to never underestimate communication. In an innovative forum article for the *Journal of Applied Communication Research*, food and communication scholar Megan Schraedley organized a Facebook conversation between various food researchers and security scholars in our field. Several voices whom we have cited heavily in this book—including Mohan Dutta and Sarah Dempsey—participated in the conversation, which was used as a foundation for a collective article.[12] In the forum, a question was posed that asked us to consider if communities and partners undervalued communication as it relates to food insecurity. Marianne participated in the forum, and this was part of her response:

> The individuals and groups with whom I've worked value good communication practices—they certainly recognize when communication infrastructure is absent from our conversations about food insecurity. Yet, when it comes to developing programs and strategies for confronting food insecurity and food hardship, I have regularly seen communities focus almost exclusively on the technical side of communication as opposed to its more constitutive, dialogic, or discursive aspects. This kind of technical communication usually involves managing the social media pages, organizing email and meeting schedules, and developing advertising materials—where communication is viewed as a product. Although these sorts of communication are crucial in organizing efforts to address food insecurity, they operate from a narrow definition of what communication scholars can offer.[13]

Since making that comment, I've shared it with many of my community partners, and they all have an identical response. Their eyes shoot open, like two headlights staring back at me, and they nod their head yes . . . very slowly, with a keen awareness.

Our critique, then, raises the question, how can partners more robustly estimate the communication required to mobilize change around food systems? In addition to the technical aspects of communication outlined above, we can suggest some practical ways that communities might think about communication in their work:

- Start with humility: We first encountered the call to start with humility from food activist Malik Yakini, who encourages food advocates and activists to avoid taking a missionary-style approach to organizing around food.[14] We can't pretend to know everything about a community's relationships with food, especially if we are external partners from outside the neighborhood. Organizers must take the time to get to know the people, build interpersonal relationships, and learn what folks have already tried in the past.

- Followed by an environmental scan: the practice of identifying resources from within the community—both material and human—has long been a practice associated with organizing for health activism, and communication scholars have begun to recognize its importance in social justice organizing as well.[15] If our first step is to start with humility, one way to

"see" the community is to work with people in the neighborhood to identify their assets and strengths.

- Develop a solid memo of understanding (MOU): Although MOUs are
  most frequently associated with grant funding and other professional
  contracts, they are also useful documents for establishing relationships,
  expectations, and boundaries for communities and partners. In addition
  to developing an MOU between partners, revisit it regularly to ensure
  that expectations are being met.

- Visualize your process: although the partner wheel we introduced in
  chapter 3 might not work for every community project, the process of
  visualizing relationships, processes, goals, brainstorming sessions, and
  data has become increasingly useful for community organizing.[16] Visualizing the process gives partners more resources to clearly identify gaps
  that need attention and helps everyday people get familiar with more
  complex and abstract ideas.

- Create an exit strategy that includes both a succession plan and a plan for
  failure: early in the process of organizing, ask the partnership if they plan
  to be short term or long term, how roles and responsibilities will change
  when people join and leave the group, how the group will monitor, and
  what steps they will follow if they decide to dissolve the partnership.

- Commit actions to words: the process of sensemaking can be both
  therapeutic and cathartic.[17] When we commit words to action, we create
  a process for collectively identifying how our organizing is enabled and
  constrained by different structures across food systems. In doing so, this
  communication practice can help communities retain the most useful
  conclusions for future food justice activism.

Define Food Security at the Community Level

In the previously mentioned forum article for *JACR*, the contributors also
included communication scholars who focus on the organizational concept of security.[18] In that conversation, Hamilton Bean argued that communities often try to "securitize" things like food and the environment in
a way to make the system appear safe—even in the face of uncertainty.
Megan Schraedley also noted that there are gaps in how governments,
cities, neighborhoods, families, and individuals define the concept of food
"security." Both the forum article and the case studies featured in this
book demonstrate the need for communication scholars and food justice

advocates and activists to more thoroughly consider what it means for communities to have "secure" food systems.

From a food systems perspective, food security means—in a very basic sense—the availability, access, utilization, and stability framework that we outlined back in chapter 1.[19] However, in terms of food justice organizing, food security often means building food systems that are vibrant, equitable, and resilient, as well. The word *vibrant* elicits images of food systems that are diverse in terms of environment, physical systems, cultures, and people.[20] *Equitable* centers the conversation around both access to resources and equity in outcomes for all people who eat.[21] And *resilience* speaks to the ways in which individuals and communities "bounce back" after difficult situations.[22] These words add an intriguing layer to an already complicated language of food security, as communities must often construct the meaning of vibrancy, equity, and resilience in practice.

From a communication perspective, we argue that communities construct what it means to have vibrant, equitable, and resilient food systems at a very local level, and by centering these concepts in our communication about food, communities and partners can reimagine and reorganize their local food systems.[23] Moreover, we can unpack the meaning of secure food systems through sharing local food stories.[24] For example, communication scholar Kristen Okamoto coined the term *narrative resilience* as a way for individuals and communities to share stories about how they manage food resources—both in times of abundance and in times of hardship.[25]

Simply put, securing food systems requires communities to start with stories from people who eat. This book has largely focused on organizing for food justice activism, but we have seen the power of stories as a way to construct community—as in the case of Ethnosh, and how they used relationship building and trust to solicit stories from immigrant-owned restaurants. At the same time, several of the voices featured in this book come from people who live in food insecure and under-resourced neighborhoods, and although we haven't featured their stories of food hardship, we have featured their stories of communicating food justice.

As we imagine the possibilities for local food stories and their potential to open up conversations about building food systems that are vibrant, equitable, and secure, we recognize a need to establish more sophisticated forms of ethical storytelling in communities experiencing food hardship.

In chapter 6 on the Mobile Oasis Farmers Market and elsewhere we have advocated for the use of the culture-centered approach and pop-up forms of organizing as a way to start those conversations. In the following section, we expand our rationale to consider how not only Greensboro, but also many other communities facing similar circumstances might consider the value of local food storytelling and launch their next conversations.

THE NEXT CONVERSATIONS IN FOOD SECURITY AND FOOD JUSTICE

Food systems do not change overnight. Partners in Greensboro recognized the early signs of food hardship six years before we reached the top of the FRAC list, so even though our food hardship rates dropped significantly in the two years that immediately followed our peak, some of our success reaches back to organizing, advocacy, and activism that started mobilizing much earlier. If we take seriously the need to never stop organizing when it comes to food systems, we must also consider how to launch some of the next conversations in food security that Greensboro and many communities will face in the coming years.

In this final section of *Everybody Eats*, we look to local food storytelling as a way to engage communities, mobilize resources, document process, and sustain conversations about building secure food systems. For some of our final thoughts, Gwen Frisbie-Fulton joins us to outline how we can develop more culturally centered approaches to storytelling from a community and activist perspective. Although we write this next section with a collective voice, we highlight some specific stories from Gwen's work with various food systems interventions across Greensboro. We frame our approach to local food storytelling as creating space for intersectional, inconvenient, and disruptive narratives.

Intersectional Narratives

It is undeniable that breakdowns in our food systems are not about capacity, but about distribution and access. In Greensboro and Guilford County, we have become very good at developing ways to increase access in the material sense: mobile pantries, community grocery stores, and apps and printed guides for residents to locate food pantries and free meals. But we have been less successful in unpacking the underlying conversations about access: Why are so many people in our communities food insecure? Even as our language around food (in)security has developed, and a more justice-oriented analysis has emerged, organizers have failed to find a way of speaking about food that resonates outside of our small spaces and into the communities where it matters most.

When organizers, activists, researchers, and communities appreciate more fully that stories of food (in)security are often intersectional, we can begin to consider how food is implicated in conversations about race, poverty, and numerous other narrative threads.[26] For example, it turns out, rarely does one self-identify as living in a "food desert."[27] Most people just simply live too many bus transfers from the nearest grocery store to make it there on a Tuesday after work. Complex, academic language that describes common and age-old realities doesn't empower communities to grow their own narratives. But on the other hand, the over-simplified language of the anti-hunger, charitable sector often feels insincere or even trite. "Helping the needy," "the least of these," and other such phrases are phrases for the charitable, not for those facing food insecurity or organizing for foundational change. Consider the following story from Gwen's perspective:

I once went out with a local advocacy group to collect stories about food insecurity in a small rural town north of Greensboro and I found myself sitting at a sunny picnic table with eighty-four-year-old Betty. Betty was introduced to us by the director of a local mobile food pantry as being both a regular volunteer for the program and a weekly food recipient who might be willing to share her story. "How long have you been facing hunger?" the researcher asked Betty, gently prodding. "Hunger? I've never been hungry," Betty replied. "I guess some people are hungry and I feel sorry for them."

To the researcher Betty, of course, was hungry. When you are eighty-four years old and living off a few hundred dollars a month and waiting for a mobile food pantry to pull into your subsidized housing complex, to the researcher's thinking that's exactly what you are. But Betty never once self-identified as "hungry" or "food insecure." Instead, Betty explained the ways she purchases food, uses coupons, and helps pay for the neighbor's gas when they share rides to the Walmart clear across town. Betty described herself not as food insecure, but as resourceful and good at making her dollars stretch—tactics that include getting fresh produce from the mobile pantry.

Nonprofit organizations, task forces, civic leaders, and others continue to talk about food and food access in isolation from other issues. For most people, however, accessing food is just one struggle in the much larger, more complex struggle of poverty and insufficient incomes. Poverty, near-poverty, and even the contemporary instability that comes with being working class is a droning hum—its individual parts are sometimes indistinguishable in the day-to-day struggle to make ends meet. Paying bills—rent, co-pays, utility payments, gas money to get to work—are all part of a heavy rotation of making nothing short of financial magic happen. Paying for groceries is just one more of these daily feats. Gwen offers the following illustration:

I think often of friends of mine who lived in a motel in Greensboro for over a year with their infant son. They cooked in a crockpot and on a hot plate, living in one room all together. It was here that the baby learned to walk and say his first words, where he spent his first Christmas, and, later, his first birthday. It was a cheap, dingy motel where a room cost $46 a night, $52 if you wanted a minifridge. Every day, the father (Jimmy) would do odd jobs in an attempt to come up with $46. He frequently did repairs for the motel itself, but also found work through the day labor center. "Always chasing that $46" I remember him saying to me, like it had become his mantra that year.

The hard reality is that the room could have been cheaper: It was only $225 for the week. Jimmy could never save up that kind of money if he was paying for the room each night. Spending that $46 a day came at the expense of new clothing for the growing baby, diapers, and fresh food. But Jimmy and his family didn't describe themselves as "housing unstable" or "food insecure." They were broke.

For many groups organizing to address food insecurity in Greensboro, their mission limits them to the singular focus of food and food access, which leaves them unable to address the full scope of Jimmy's family situation. While it may benefit an organization to identify a clear mission or vision, especially when it comes to developing actual resources and solutions, the conversations we are having around food access should not be limited to food. Instead, our discourse about food and access must include larger conversations about poverty or they won't make sense. Larger conversations about poverty will and should include discussions about affordable housing, transportation, health care, and childcare—and it is unlikely that conversations around these issues will stop there. We must also expand the topics at the table to include more thoughtful discourse about wages and inequality. Opening up these spaces will ultimately lead to discussions of contemporary and historical discrimination, namely issues of race, class, gender, and identity. Organizers must be ready to embrace these kinds of intersectional stories. Many groups will wish to avoid these kinds of conversations—mostly to avoid alienating supporters, or to prevent a perceived sense of mission creep. But these intersectional stories already make up the social fabric of so many communities, and we would be grossly remiss not to recognize and encourage their telling.

In the last decade, communication researchers and organizers who examine food (in)security and poverty have increasingly centered the voices of those with lived experiences.[28] This has mostly taken the form of recognizing storytelling networks and listening infrastructures as an important tool in our movements. The emphasis on storytelling enables communities and organizers to shift public will toward action and change. As a larger strategy for communicating food justice, however, much of our local storytelling has often been constrained, as many stories are commonly used for fundraising or to sell the importance of the work. These stories frequently evoke compassion and sympathy, but they also reproduce one-dimensional tales of poverty with a prescribed solution and an ask for donations at the end. This type of writing misses the more difficult and substantive stories that require more complex and intersectional responses. From a fundraiser's point of view, there is a difference between an elderly widow living on a fixed income who would benefit from a hot meal and a young man with a criminal record barring him from viable employment who has run out his time limits on SNAP. But in a community, both are equally food insecure, and both need solutions.

Finding . . . *and hearing* . . . these intersectional narratives takes time, but solutions to this can be found. From West Bengal, India, to Tippecanoe County, Indiana, organizers have been using a culture-centered approach to address food insecurity, using methods such as co-constructive data gathering and analysis, community conversations, community-driven white papers, media, advocacy and town hall meetings.[29] For example, in 2017, Marianne organized a series of focus groups with a diverse set of people connected to our local food system. The purpose of these conversations was to identify how communities might think differently about "data" as we define, track, and monitor food (in)security in Greensboro. The conversations quickly turned to stories as a necessary component of understanding food (in)security, but the participants just as quickly realized that as communities, we often lacked the mechanisms to solicit those stories.

One of the participants, Lavinia Jackson, suggested a very simple solution to the complex problem of gathering stories and community input. Her suggestion was, in essence, that we do what we have culturally been doing forever—gather around food. Sharing food has always been a way to build trust, perhaps especially in the South.

To create a space conducive and inviting for gathering, Lavinia suggested, "it has to be in a restaurant. It has to be someplace that is strategically designed to do so but is comfortable." She also stressed the need to build relationships and trust around sharing food resources:

> Say we're going to give you some free food, or we want to open up this restaurant that gathers food that's almost "expired." And we fix it, and we show you how we fix it, and we serve everybody a great wholesome meal for like five dollars . . . which you can afford, and we'll take your SNAP. . . . Like if we're not doing that, then we can't get the data we need.

Lavinia captures our point so succinctly—if the goal is to collect intersectional stories about food (in)security, we need to share food and build community.

Inconvenient Narratives

If developing the communication infrastructures that are necessary to gather more intersectional and authentic stories from communities is the first hurdle, listening to them and truly hearing them may well be the second. Local food stories, especially those that deal with food hardship and food insecurity, are often inconvenient. They give us insight into inconvenient features of a food system that seemingly works for most people. They are inconvenient to tell, in that they often ask the storyteller to talk about difficult times about being poor and not having food. They are also inconvenient to collect, as they involve establishing trust between the person telling the story and the person soliciting it.

For example, in the previously mentioned focus groups, one nonprofit food organizer expressed concerns about the toll of asking people to tell stories of hardship without folding those folks into the work more deeply:

> I think it's completing the circle. Not just grabbing people to tell their "terrible" stories . . . and then [saying] goodbye, and you never hear about it. It's like the headlines, you know, you hear a story and then it disappears. . . . I just think you have to complete the circle and don't invite people unless you're going to do that.

Lavinia reiterated this concern with the trend of story capturing, suggesting it can feel exploitative and damaging. She asked, "Do you have support there for them? They go through telling their stories, and [if] somebody invalidates them, then they have to go back to those spaces and say, 'Well I tried, but they're not really hearing me.'"

One way to avoid these hurtful repercussions is to embrace the full potential of stories beyond their utility in fundraising and compassion-building. The real promise of storytelling is not singular, but threefold. Yes, stories can help win hearts and minds to our causes, but stories can also help researchers obtain a deeper understanding of food insecurity as well as contain useful solutions to the problems we hope to address. Moving community voices beyond "sharing stories" and into roles where they can have real impact and make decisions can truly shift our work.[30] Consider another story from Gwen's work in food pantries:

A pastor in High Point whose church operates a food pantry once told me the story of putting aside a large turkey for a family of eight that had been coming to his pantry for months. He knew that there were eight family members from the intake sheets the pantry kept on each client. He explained that while he was not in the habit of "saving" food for specific clients, he thought that it was a kind and useful gesture to do so in this case given the size of the family. When the family came, however, the mother said she could not take it. As it turns out, the family did not have electricity in their home so they could not safely store it. When he offered for the church to help pay an electric bill, he learned that it was actually a wiring problem and the family was hesitant to report the landlord's neglect due to their immigration status. The pastor remarked that he realized how little he knew about this family he had been serving for so many months and, after this, he recommitted to engaging in longer, fuller conversations with those coming to his pantry to better understand the conditions surrounding their food insecurity.

It's a huge leap for researchers, non-profits, charities, and even community groups to go "into the weeds" around food (in)security and embrace stories that are both intersectional and inconvenient. After all, it's not a process for the risk averse. But it is a process for the long-term thinkers: gardeners know that you have to tend the soil in the winter to produce a bounty in the summer. We know that seeking out and embracing authentic narratives will open doors to new topics and could be messy, but that is not the only risk. Listening to and truly hearing people living in food-insecure communities—especially when they share with us narratives that are inconvenient—will also likely disrupt the way many organizers, health agencies, and nonprofits have been doing things—things that we thought were right.

Ambitious and confident groups frequently create solutions before fully understanding a problem. Funding is more easily found for results-driven programs than for taking the time to deeply understand an issue. Sometimes organizers use outside narratives to shape responses to food insecurity instead of seeking out stories and solutions from within the community. The result is a collection of convenient stories and interventions that don't move the needle.

One place where organizers may be missing inconvenient narratives is around cooking. A popular response to addressing food insecurity is to introduce cooking classes, recipes, and fresh, raw ingredients into local programming. This shift is a response to the need for healthier and more nutritious food options for low-income families who frequently choose calories over quality when trying to stretch their food dollars. The idea is that cooking from scratch and using fresh, raw ingredients is healthier and more economical, but that's not always true. Nor is it realistic. As it turns out, research backs what we continually hear from community members—no one really likes to cook.

Across all incomes in the United States, eating out or consuming prepared food is becoming the norm. Trends indicate that only 10 percent of Americans like to cook and that cooking itself is becoming a niche activity, used for socializing but not for day-to-day sustenance.[31] Consider the following story from Marianne's work with the Warnersville Farmers Market:

Every week, without fail, Beatty and Mabel Petty would visit the market. They had been married for decades and were dedicated members at Prince of Peace Lutheran Church (POPLC). That summer, the market was held in POPLC's parking lot, and many church members would attend the market just to socialize and maybe pick up a few vegetables.

I was seated under a white pop-up tent with a table full of squash that were not too big and not too small, the first tomatoes of the season, and onions from a garden bed that just kept on giving. I stood up as Brother Petty came over to look over the vegetables. "Well, Doc, it looks like you've got some mighty fine things here. Oh, wow!" he said, as he picked up a zucchini. "This one looks just about perfect. And I've got to have some of these tomatoes."

As Brother Petty continued to pick up random pieces of produce, Sister Mabel sauntered over. He handed her an armful of vegetables, and quickly trotted away to visit with some other members of POPLC. Sister Mabel promptly put every squash, tomato, and onion back on the table. She looked at me and said with a laugh, "He thinks he wants to eat all of these things, but that means I'm gonna have to cook 'em. And I really don't have the energy to cook anymore."

Much of the advice coming out of the USDA regarding food and nutrition practices and the majority of research studies about healthy eating reinforce norms of cooking at home. For many people who eat, however, especially in our elderly communities, providing advice and resources that encourage cooking might not be filling the right kind of gaps. And for families with working parents—which is the bulk of low-income families—cooking at home, using fresh and local produce, is often not an option, especially if they are working shifts or pulling doubles. Why are we insistent that low-income families need to learn to cook, when there is strong evidence that most American families are abandoning cookbooks, cutting boards, pots, and pans?

Besides the health benefits of using fresh, raw ingredients, there may be certain moralism at play when we demand that low-income families learn to cook while people of other income brackets are rapidly abandoning the practice. Inherent in many charity-driven narratives is the idea that poor people should work and struggle in exchange for help, perhaps somehow proving their need. The most enduring critics of the SNAP reflect these judgments, namely the insistence that people receiving SNAP work and use their benefits to purchase only healthy food. As a result of these moralistic narratives, most prepared food cannot be purchased with SNAP, even as the demand for prepared foods nationally has increased by 11 percent just in the last two years, with 66 percent of consumers purchasing prepared foods at least three times a month compared to 55 percent in 2017.[32]

Home cooking enthusiasts insist that cooking from scratch is cheaper than eating out—this is likely the case if one is only calculating the expense of ingredients. But for poor and working-class families who have sometimes long commutes on public transportation, childcare responsibilities, and household chores, as well as second jobs in the gig economy, the precious few hours they have off-the-clock do not afford the time and effort needed to cook at home. When cooking a meal takes time away from repairing a broken lawn mower or helping a child with homework, what began as frugal quickly becomes a very expensive meal.

Hearing these stories and narratives from community members is inconvenient and will require those who address food issues to rethink their approaches. It may also require that we reengage our funders and explain that we need their money for things that may not fit into their commonly funded categories and grant guidelines. Future conversations must include the uncomfortable narrative about how some of our downstream solutions (e.g., opening a grocery store in a food desert) might not be keeping the water healthy upstream (e.g., creating more part-time jobs without living wages, creating more food-insecure families). Not all pro-food solutions are good anti-poverty solutions, and without listening carefully to the right people, we might not hear this.

Disruptive Narratives

As communities begin to share stories that are both intersectional and inconvenient, food systems and food security organizers must also prepare for stories that disrupt both language and structural practices around food. The disruptive potential of narratives as a source of productive social change has gained traction in communication research and practice. In a 2017 special issue of *Management Communication Quarterly*, communication scholar Lynn Harter organized a series of articles that emphasize how "scholars and community partners can leverage narrative theory and practice to shake up habitual ways of organizing and envision more fulfilling and just social orders."[33] As part of that special issue, Marianne and Niesha were invited to make a contribution about organizing to address food (in)security, where Niesha offered the following disruptive narrative:

> In 2009, I began my journey to understand poverty as it relates to food. After working with key stakeholders and city officials, I realized I grew up in a food desert and was currently living in one. Even though my family had never gone to sleep without a good meal, we were labeled as being "food insecure." How could that be? Every night we had two vegetables, a starch, and a protein on our plates for dinner. On Sundays and holidays, we fed more people! How could my family acquire this label with so little evidence that identified us as such?
>
> Numbers lead to labels, and narratives can disrupt some of those assumptions. Metaphors like "desert" often conjure images of more than "no food." They also paint a picture of no resources of any kind. As scholars and individuals committed to food justice, we have to disrupt these emerging narratives around food deserts and food insecurity, instead putting the focus on individual stories and not neighborhood plights.[34]

Stories can disrupt the language of how we talk about food security. Similar to Betty's story earlier in this section, Niesha called attention to how the labels that many organizers and researchers use to talk about food insecurity are often meaningless to the community they are used to describe. Even more so, perhaps it is time for food justice activists to disrupt the language around terms like "food desert" to reimagine new possibilities and more hopeful metaphors within our communities.

Stories can also carve out space for communities to disrupt specific practices and structures across our food systems. So many of the conversations that have been happening in Greensboro have focused around one important question: How do we get healthy food to the people and communities that need it? The local solutions have been creative, and we should be proud of them—even when they have struggled. As projects wane and new challenges arise, we will likely never stop asking this question.

But we cannot settle on that one question, when we know there are so many more to ask. For example, Gwen offers the following account from a meeting about food insecurity in a neighboring county:

I sat at a table with a few local nonprofit leaders and a couple community representatives from a low-income neighborhood. We were asked to do an exercise called "The Five Whys," where a problem or quandary was given to us, and we were supposed to ask "Why?" It took five times to peel back the layers of the problem to its core. Our group was given the question as to why a grocery store didn't exist in the neighborhood.

When we asked "why?" the first time, the entire table quickly agreed; it was because the City was having trouble attracting a grocery store into a low-income neighborhood. We asked "why?" again, and the group agreed that it was because profit margins were low. The response on the third "why?" slowed down the group, but we agreed that it was because the neighborhood didn't have as much money to spend as other neighborhoods might. But the fourth "why?" stopped us in our tracks: While half the table debated the competitive nature of the contemporary retail economy, the other half simply said: "Racism." There was no question in their minds.

The process of asking "why?" is the action of moving up the chain or toward a core. Asking "why?" will move us off the ground, away from our local food spaces, and into an examination of food systems on a larger—even global—scale. We might worry we will lose our footing, but this, too, is important work.

Being honest in these conversations will disrupt the ways we talk about things. Locally, we have been discussing food waste through events like the Ugly Food Feast during Guilford Local Foods Week, as well as a grassroots initiative to relax restrictive policies about reclaiming wasted food. Local food banks rescue food as one of their primary sources of product, diverting literal tons of food daily from local landfills. Food banks highlight this activity as part of their contribution—as they well should; they are making a significant environmental impact by salvaging perfectly good food while rerouting it to families in need. *Win-win.*

But moving up the chain, we need to ask why there is so much waste at the distribution, manufacturing, and agricultural level in the United States. Why is there so much food in need of being rescued? Asking this "why?" points to a serious problem in our food system. Food waste is, largely, not a problem solvable by home composting. In the United States, an estimated 30 to 40 percent of the food supply goes to waste.[35] Thirty-one percent of food is wasted at the retail and consumer level, meaning the vast majority of that waste is taking place up the chain.

Asking why there is so much waste is a disruptive narrative, and not every food advocate will be able to ask it. Food distribution centers operate on such a large scale that food waste appears to be part of the business model. Many local organizations rely heavily on donations and support from large companies and feel they must remain grateful to the relationship. However, those interested in food justice do have to ask these important questions: Why is wasting food economically strategic, and is that ethical in a world where families are still struggling to eat?

We only mention food waste here as one potentially disruptive conversation. Recent food shortages at grocery stores and food pantries, due to COVID-19 reorganizing, coupled with images of farmers disposing of produce and milk because of disrupted distribution networks have only amplified these kinds of questions. That's because food insecurity is not an issue of moving food or creative on-the-ground solutions, although it's impossible to stress enough how important these activities are. Food insecurity and food hardship are a systems issue, and we, as a community, have to start talking about what is happening upstream from our actions. As organizers, activists, researchers, and community members, we have a responsibility to disrupt narratives that suggest food security is an isolated problem and illustrate its connections to much larger issues—like economic inequality driven by low wages.

Over the last few decades, economic inequality driven by stagnating wages has surged. At the same time, the charitable food sector has become ever more institutionalized and complicit with neoliberalism. By failing to organize around wages and jobs, and perpetuating dependency on free food and food stamps, many local food efforts have pretended that the problem is hunger and not poverty. We've pretended that the solution to hunger is charity, as opposed to ensuring the right to food or increasing the political power of the poor. We've pretended that corporations are not to blame—at least in part—for the economic inequality that leads to insecure food systems.

Food justice organizers have gained traction and wins in the last two decades, for important programs like SNAP, school meals, and other federal food programs. Thanks to this lobbying, these programs stayed largely intact, while other welfare programs were gutted. But these programs don't get at the heart of food insecurity: they do not ensure the right to food, address the conditions leading to poverty and inequality, or increase the political power of the poor. Advocating for anti-poverty policies and legislation that increase wages and decrease inequality moves the conversation up the stream, so less food needs to be moved down here.

Storytelling around local food creates a space for intersecting and inconvenient narratives, and furthering our conversations around the disruptive potential of narratives can give organizers, activists, partners, and communities needed resources to reimagine the potential within and across local food systems. Communication scholar Rebecca de Souza explains that "telling a more complex story means moving beyond the poles of depicting people as 'victimized' or 'resilient' and writing in a way that recognizes the courage and limits of individual acts of resistance."[36]

As we look toward the next topics in food security, our conversations will only get bigger. Food systems are always and often changing, and disruptions in environment and climate, policies and trade, and countless other relationships across food systems mean that we must always keep organizing to ensure people eat. But even in the most centralized food systems—that coordinate food distribution across large populations at local, regional, national, and global scales—we see the potential for diversity, embraced at the local level, to build more equitable systems.

WE ALL HAVE TO EAT: THE FUTURE, REGARDLESS . . .

When Greensboro was at the peak of its climb on FRAC's food hardship list, Marianne was invited to give talks at the 2014 and 2015 TEDxGreensboro events. The theme for the 2014 talks was "The Future, Regardless . . ." Although some of the speakers struggled to relate their talks to that theme, I knew exactly how to handle it. In the opening minutes of my talk, I said, "If there's one thing I've learned from my research, it's that we all have to eat. And that's not going to change in the future, regardless of how everything else changes. We all have to eat." When we remind ourselves that food is one of the few things that unites all of us, we unlock so much creative potential within our communities. Throughout this book, we have made several references to food justice activist Malik Yakini. He begins each of his presentations about food by thanking his ancestors, and he concludes each talk with a reminder that everybody eats. Yakini pushes the conversation further, however, suggesting that food justice activism can be a gateway to other forms of social organizing and activism. Talking about food can help us open up conversations about structural and systemic racism, poverty, immigration, and community and economic development. We share a similar hope.

Greensboro's story of communicating food justice is a story that is intersectional, sometimes inconvenient, and with any luck a little disruptive. It is also a story that is community-driven, occasionally provocative, and above all—hopeful. By focusing on the value of engaging communities, mobilizing resources, documenting process, and sustaining the conversation, our goal has been to leave you with a range of communication, food, and other practical resources that can organize further conversations along the various paths to food justice. These are conversations we all hope to continue, so if you ever make it to Greensboro, stop by and share some food. Marianne will make you some pierogi, and Niesha will make you some peach ice cream.

Warnersville Community
Food Task Force
Project Concept

WARNERSVILLE HEALTHY
COMMUNITY PROJECT PROPOSAL

Please Note: *This Project Proposal represents a statement of the Warnersville Community Action Plan based on input from the Warnersville Health Task Force and the Healthy Carolinians Healthy Lifestyles Learning Cluster. Specific elements of the plan may change as the proposal is refined and developed.*

Project Concept: Improving community health through increasing access to healthy food choices and increasing physical activity

Goals and Objectives
- Reduce rates of chronic disease and risk factors high blood pressure and obesity in the Warnersville Community (census tract 11400)
- Increase rates of physical activity
- Increase consumption of fresh fruit and vegetables and other healthy foods

Project Principles
- Holistic project development
  - Promote community
  - Promote economic development
  - Promote employment
  - Promote education

- Healthiest standards for food projects
  - ○ Sustainable food cultivation methods
  - ○ Natural and organic value-added prepared foods
  - ○ Whole grain bakery products
- Community Engagement
  - ○ Programs reflect needs of the community
  - ○ Warnersville Health Task Force will be involved in planning and implementation

MOBILE FARMERS MARKET

The Mobile Farmers Market will carry fresh produce to community sites such as churches, worksites, and community centers on a regular schedule.

- The mobile unit will accept EBT cards and WIC vouchers.
- In addition to fresh produce, will sell milk, eggs, cheese
- Sell produce from the Urban Farm and from other local and regional small farms
- Sell value-added food products—cheese, bakery products—from local and regional small producers
- Deliver food to under-served populations at nursing homes, public housing
- Disseminate cooking instructions and recipes
- Based at the JC Price school annex or other Warnersville area site

Lead Organization: UNC-G Communication Studies Department

Funding
- Robert Wood Johnson Foundation Rapid Response Grant
- USDA Farmers Market Marketing Grant
- HHS Community Economic Development Grant

Partners
- Urban Harvest
- Warnersville Community Coalition
- Cooperative Extension
- Department of Public Health

- Greensboro College
- NC A&T State University
- Prince of Peace Lutheran Church
- Healthy Carolinians

Opportunities for Employment
- Mobile Market driver
- Support for local farmers, value-added food producers

WARNERSVILLE COMMUNITY MARKET

- Base of operations for the Mobile Farmers Market
- Located at JC Price school annex building or other Warnersville area location
- Sell food items sold on the Mobile Farmers Market
  - Fresh produce
  - Eggs, cheese, and milk
  - Bakery products
- Accepts EBT and WIC
- Members receive discounts on food
- Membership provided entry into other health and wellness programs
  - Health screenings
  - Cooking classes

Lead Organization: Warnersville Community Coalition

Possible Funding
- USDA Farmers Market Marketing grant
- HHS Community Economic Development Grant
- Local foundation grants

Partners
- Warnersville Community Coalition
- Cooperative Extension
- Department of Public Health
- Healthy Carolinians
- NC A&T State University

- Prince of Peace Lutheran Church
- Urban Harvest
- UNC-G Communication Studies

Opportunities for Employment
- Farmers Market manager
- Support for local farmers and value-added food produce

COMMUNITY GARDEN AND FARM

The land at Prince of Peace Lutheran Church will be used by Warnersville neighbors and Greensboro residents to grow food. The space will provide physical activity and access to healthy foods for the residents of the Warnersville area and wider community while providing opportunities for social and spiritual growth. The structure (business model) and physical design of the garden/farm will be determined by the stakeholders of the gardens.

Using a democratic process, the garden/farm will grow food to be distributed to participating neighbors and through local markets, including the Mobile Farmers Market and Warnersville Farmers Market. Food will be grown year-round using sustainable and Permaculture growing methods. The garden/farm will include educational programs for youth and adults on sustainability, health, and wellness. The garden/farm can be accessed from the SE Greenway Trail and will provide recreation through gardening and physical activities in the garden; social and community activities; enjoying nature and experiencing wildlife; and meditation. The Farm will provide long-term and full-time employment, summer employment, job-training for youth, and volunteer opportunities for everyone.

Lead Organizations: Urban Harvest, Prince of Peace Lutheran Church

Possible Funding
- Local foundation and community development grants
- GrantsPlus Lutheran Church grant (with Prince of Peace Community Gardens proposal)
- Greensboro Neighborhood Congress Fruit Tree Foundation

Partners
- Warnersville Community Coalition
- Cooperative Extension
- Department of Public Health

• NC A&T State University
• UNC-G Communication Studies

WARNERSVILLE HEALTH AND WELLNESS PROGRAM

Warnersville Health and Wellness Program will provide individual-level interventions to residents of the Warnersville Community and SE Greensboro target area:

- Obesity screening and counseling;
  - This program will offer screening and health assessments for diabetes, high blood pressure and obesity, providing health plans and referrals for community residents.
  - Health assessment participants will receive incentives (discounts) to the Mobile Farmers Market.
- Walking programs
  - This program may include walkability assessments of Warnersville neighborhoods and organized group walking activities.
  - Walking will be encouraged to participate in the Community Garden and Farmers Market.
- Healthy cooking classes
  - Through train-the-trainer efforts, local residents will be educated on healthier methods of cooking traditional cultural foods and will then educate others in the community through cooking demonstrations, classes, and online (YouTube) videos.
  - Project partners will develop culturally appropriate healthy recipes that will be disseminated through the Mobile Farmers Market and Community Farmers Market.
- Exercise classes

Lead Organization: Guilford County Department of Public Health

Funding
- The Aetna Foundation health grant
- Translational Research and Clinical Sciences Institute (TRACS) Robert Wood Johnson Foundation
- Local foundations

Setting
- Warnersville Community Center
- The Community Farmers Market

- Hampton Homes
- Smith Homes
- Community churches

Partners
- Warnersville Community Center
- Warnersville Community Coalition
- Greensboro Housing Authority
- UNC-G/NCA&T School of Nursing

APPENDIX B   Blank Model Partner Wheel

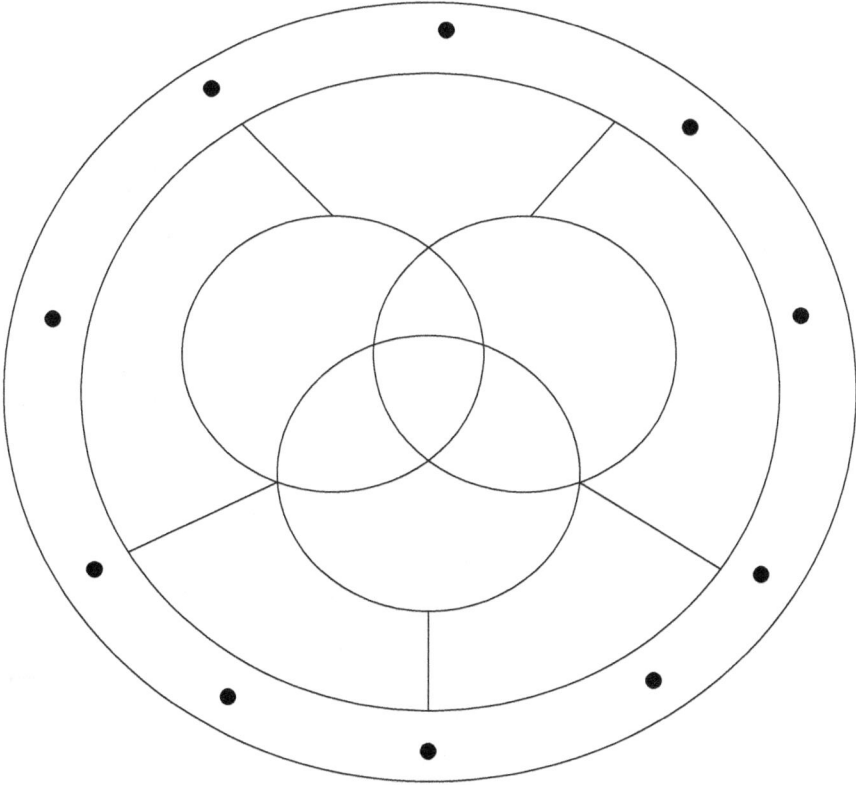

Mobile Oasis Recipes

RECIPES BY ANITA CUNNINGHAM

Summer Squash Mac & Cheese

Mobile Oasis
BRINGING THE FARM TO YOU

What TOOLS do you need?

- 1 large pot (to cook the noodles and the sauce)
- 1 grater or vegetable peeler (to shred the squash and cheese)
- 1 wooden spoon
- 1 strainer (to drain the water from the noodles)
- 1 medium bowl (to hold the pasta after you drain it)
- Measuring cup
- Measuring spoon
- Blender or food processor

Prep Time
10 mins
Cook Time
20 mins

Makes 4-6 servings

What INGREDIENTS do you need?

- 2 cups of dry macaroni noodles, shells, or any size of small pasta
- 3 medium yellow squash (shredded)
- 2 Tablespoons butter
- 1 Tablespoon flour
- 2 cups milk
- 2 cups medium cheddar cheese (you can shred it yourself or buy cheese that's already shredded)
- Pinch of salt

What STEPS do you follow?

1. Make sure that the squash and the cheese are shredded before you get started. You'll probably have to shred the squash yourself using a grater or a vegetable peeler. You can find shredded cheese, but it's cheaper to buy a big block of cheese and shred it yourself.
2. Fill your large pot about 2/3 full of water.
3. Place the pot on your stovetop and turn on the burner to medium-high heat.
4. Add a generous pinch of salt to the water and heat it up until it starts boiling.
5. Add the pasta to the pot of boiling water and cook it according to the directions on the package (usually about 9-11 minutes).
6. Drain the pasta and set it aside in a medium bowl.
7. Put the pot back on the stovetop and get ready to make the sauce.
8. Add 2 Tablespoons of butter to the same pot you just used to cook the macaroni. Let it melt.
9. Add the shredded yellow squash and a pinch of salt to the melted butter and cook over medium heat for about 4-5 minutes.
10. Add the flour to the squash, stir it around, and cook for another minute or so.
11. Reduce the burner heat to medium-low, pour in the 2 cups of milk slowly, and stir until the sauce starts to steam and thicken up.
12. Add the sauce to a blender or food processor, blend it until smooth, and return to the stovetop pot.
13. Remove the pot from the heat and add the shredded cheese.
14. Keep stirring until the cheese has melted.
15. Then you're ready to add the noodles back to the pot & enjoy your Summer Squash Mac & Cheese!!

Adapted by our own Anita C. from the Warnersville neighborhood via eating-made-easy.com

Chocolate Chip Zucchini Cookies

Mobile Oasis

What TOOLS do you need?

- Oven
- Baking sheet (and non-stick spray)
- 2 Mixing bowls
- Wooden spoon (or other mixing spoon)
- Measuring cup
- Measuring spoon
- Grater or food processor (to shred the zucchini)

Prep Time
20-30 minutes
Bake Time
10-13 minutes

**Makes about
3 dozen cookies**

What INGREDIENTS do you need?

- 2 cups all-purpose flour
- 1 cup whole wheat flour
- ½ cup wheat germ
- ½ teaspoon salt
- 1 teaspoon baking soda
- 1 teaspoon cinnamon
- ¼ teaspoon cloves
- ¼ teaspoon allspice
- ½ cup baking cocoa

- 1 cup vegetable or canola oil
- 2 cups brown sugar
- 2 eggs
- 1 tablespoon vanilla
- 2 cups shredded zucchini
- 1 cup chocolate chips
- 1 cup sunflower or pumpkin seeds
- 1 cup coconut (optional)

What STEPS do you follow?

1. Pre-heat your oven to 350 degrees F.
2. In a medium-sized mixing bowl, mix together the all-purpose and whole wheat flours with the wheat germ, salt, baking soda, baking cocoa, and spices.
3. Set the flour mixture to the side.
4. In a large-sized mixing bowl, beat together the vegetable oil and brown sugar until smooth.
5. Add ¼ cup of the flour mixture to the large mixing bowl with the oil and sugar. Mix it together until all of the ingredients are evenly combined.
6. Add the eggs and vanilla to the large bowl and mix it together until the eggs are evenly combined.
7. If you haven't shredded the zucchini yet, go ahead and do that. Make the shreds as large or small as you like.
8. Add the zucchini, chocolate chips, and sunflower or pumpkin seeds to the large mixing bowl.
9. Slowly add the rest of the flour mixture to the large mixing bowl. Add it one cup at a time, mostly so you don't end up with a big cloud of flour. Mix together until all ingredients are well combined.
10. Spray a baking sheet with some non-stick spray.
11. Use a teaspoon or small scoop to drop individual cookies onto the baking sheet.
12. Bake the cookies for 10-13 minutes. Cool them on a wire rack, if you have one.
13. Once the cookies have cooled, you can store them in a plastic container or storage bag – just make sure you enjoy a few first!!

Developed by our own Anita C. from the Warnersville neighborhood

Guilford Food
Council Charter

GUILFORD FOOD COUNCIL – OUR PURPOSE

The Guilford Food Council (GFC) supports the development of a vibrant, sustainable, and healthy local food system for Guilford County and its cities, municipalities, and rural areas. Members of the GFC serve to examine the food system in Guilford County, bring together stakeholders from the many food-related sectors, and create a successful local food system that promotes *vibrant farms, thriving economies,* and *healthy neighborhoods.*

The Guilford Food Council is dedicated to:

- Promoting food security for all individuals and families living in Guilford County
- Pursuing an evidence-based policy agenda that encourages the development of a robust local food system and a healthy population
- Fostering collaboration throughout our local food system, including active and healthy relationships with other food-related groups, civic organizations, municipalities, and government agencies
- Ensuring the responsible use of our county's natural resources, including farmland and other agricultural assets
- Respecting and recognizing ethnic, family, socio-economic, and cultural diversity among its membership

Focus of the Food Council

In order to encourage the development of a vibrant local food system and healthier communities across Guilford County, the GFC will focus on:

- sharing information, resources, and expertise among the diverse stakeholders of the community
- educating local and state policymakers, key stakeholders and community members regarding the needs and assets of Guilford County's local food system
- recommending specific regulatory and policy actions to ensure the agricultural, economic, and environmental sustainability of Guilford County's local food system

Structure of the Guilford Food Council

The GFC will follow a dynamic governance model in order to allow maximum participation from the individuals and groups who are a part of Guilford County's food system. The model includes a *steering committee* which will help in administrating and coordinating the council, as well as *cluster members* who address key topic areas across the Guilford County local food system.

These topic areas include, but are not limited to:

- **Vibrant Farms**: Supporting food production and local farmers and growers
- **Thriving Economies**: Encouraging local economic development and food businesses
- **Healthy Neighborhoods**: Promoting wide access to healthy food across our communities
- **Education and Awareness**: Educating the community and key stakeholders to ensure the future of our local food system
- **Policies and Land Use**: Improving the Guilford County local food system through sustainable policies and practices

Notes

CHAPTER 1. NAVIGATING THE LANGUAGE
OF FOOD SYSTEMS

1. Food and Agriculture Organization of the United Nations, et al., *The State of Food Security and Nutrition in the World 2017: Building Resilience for Peace and Food Security* (Geneva: World Health Organization, 2017), http://www.who .int/nutrition/publications/foodsecurity/state-food-security-nutrition-2017/en/.

2. Feeding America, "Hunger and Poverty Fact Sheet," 2017, http://www .feedingamerica.org/assets/pdfs/fact-sheets/poverty-and-hunger-fact-sheet .pdf.

3. Diane Alarcon et al., "Global Food Security Index 2017: Measuring Food Security Resource Risks," Global Food Security Index, 2017, https:// foodsecurityindex.eiu.com/.

4. Michael Pollan, "The Food Movement, Rising," *New York Review of Books*, 2010, http://www.nybooks.com/articles/2010/06/10/food-movement-rising/; Michael Pollan, *Cooked: A Natural History of Transformation* (London: Penguin, 2014); Joel Salatin, *Everything I Want to Do Is Illegal: War Stories from the Local Food Front* (Swoope, VA: Polyface Incorporated, 2007); Malik Yakini, "Food Justice: Challenges and Opportunities," video, 2017, https://www.youtube .com/watch?v=duVsOuaPHPk.

5. Via Campesina, "Via Campesina Declaration for Food Sovereignty of November 1996," World Food Summit, Rome Italy, November 13–17, 1996.

6. Martin Levine, " A Sad and Avoidable Story of a High-Profile Failure in Leadership Succession," *Nonprofit Quarterly*, December 6, 2017, https://nonprofitquarterly.org/2017/12/06/sad-avoidable-story-high-profile-failure-leadership-succession/; Stephen Satterfield, "Behind the Rise and Fall of Growing Power," *Civil Eats*, March 18, 2018, https://civileats.com/2018/03/13/behind-the-rise-and-fall-of-growing-power/.

7. United States Department of Agriculture, "Ag and Food Statistics: Charting the Essentials," April 2017, https://www.ers.usda.gov/webdocs/publications/83344/ap-075.pdf?v=42853.

8. Ron Wolford and Drusilla Banks, "Apples and More," University of Illinois Extension, 2017, https://extension.illinois.edu/apples/applemap.cfm.

9. Edward Evans and Freddy Ballen, "Banana Market," *EDIS University of Florida IFAS Extension*, 2015, http://edis.ifas.ufl.edu/fe901.

10. United States Department of Agriculture, "Official USDA Food Plan: Costs of Food at Home at Four Levels U.S. Average, April 2018," 2018, https://www.cnpp.usda.gov/sites/default/files/CostofFoodApr2018.pdf.

11. United States Department of Agriculture, "Food Consumption and Nutrient Intakes," 2016, https://www.ers.usda.gov/Data/FoodConsumption/.

12. Marcia Eames-Sheavly et al., *Discovering Our Food System: Experiential Learning and Action for Youth and Their Communities* (Ithaca, NY: Cornell University Department of Horticulture, 2011), 5, https://ecommons.cornell.edu/handle/1813/41244.

13. Eames-Sheavly et al., *Discovering Our Food System.*

14. Anthony Giddens, *The Constitution of Society: Outline of the Theory of Structuration* (Berkeley, CA: University of California Press, 1984).

15. Lynn Harter, "Masculinity(s), the Agrarian Frontier Myth, and Cooperative Ways of Organizing: Contradictions and Tensions in the Experience and Enactment of Democracy," *Journal of Applied Communication Research* 32 (2004), 89–118, doi: 10.1080/0090988042000210016; Marianne LeGreco, "Working with Policy: Restructuring Healthy Eating Practices and the Circuit of Policy Communication," *Journal of Applied Communication Research* 40 (2012), 44–64.

16. Cynthia Stohl and George Cheney, "Participatory Processes/Paradoxical Practices: Communication and the Dilemmas of Organizational Democracy," *Management Communication Quarterly* 14 (2001), 349–407.

17. Karl Weick, *The Social Psychology of Organizing* (Reading, MA: Addison-Wesley, 1979); see also Michael Elmes, Karla Mendoza-Abarca, and Robert Hersh, "Food Banking, Ethical Sensemaking, and Social Innovation in an Era of Growing Hunger in the United States," *Journal of Management Inquiry* 25 (2015), 122–38.

18. Mohan Dutta, Aguptus Anaele, and Christina Jones, "Voices of Hunger: Addressing Health Disparities through the Culture-Centered Approach," *Journal of Communication* 63 (2013), 159–80.

19. Marion Nestle, *Food Politics: How the Food Industry Influences Nutrition and Health, Revised and Expanded Edition* (Berkeley: University of California Press, 2002).

20. Kathleen Riley and Amy Paugh, *Food and Language: Discourses and Foodways across Cultures* (New York: Routledge, 2018); see also Janet Cramer, Carinita Greene, and Lynn Walters, eds., *Food as Communication, Communication as Food* (New York: Peter Lang, 2011).

21. Food and Agriculture Organization of the United Nations, "Rome Declaration on World Security," *World Food Summit*, (1996), 2, http://www.fao.org /docrep/003/w3613e/w3613e00.HTM.

22. United States Department of Agriculture, "Official USDA Food Plan: Costs of Food at Home at Four Levels U.S. Average April 2007," 2007, https:// www.cnpp.usda.gov/sites/default/files/CostofFoodApr07.pdf; United States Department of Agriculture, "Official USDA Food Plan." 2018.

23. Social Security Administration, "Measures of the Central Tendency of Wage Data," 2018, https://www.ssa.gov/oact/cola/central.html.

24. United States Department of Agriculture, "Definitions of Food Security," 2017, https://www.ers.usda.gov/topics/food-nutrition-assistance/food-security -in-the-us/definitions-of-food-security/#ranges.

25. Food and Agriculture Organization of the United Nations et al., *The State of Food Security*, 1.

26. United States Department of Agriculture, "The U.S. Household Food Security Module," 2017, https://www.ers.usda.gov/topics/food-nutrition -assistance/food-security-in-the-us/survey-tools/#household. The questionnaire can be tailored to different audiences at shorter and longer lengths.

27. Feeding America measures food insecurity in terms of poverty, employment, and homeownership and combines that number with food budget short-fall, cost-of-food index, and average meal costs. Details are available on their website at http://www.feedingamerica.org/research/map-the-meal-gap/how-we -got-the-map-data.html.

28. Alarcon et al., "Global Food Security Index 2017."

29. Food Research and Action Center, *"How Hungry Is America?"* (Washington, DC: Food Research and Action Center, June 2016), 2, http://www.frac.org /research/resource-library/hungry-america-fracs-national-state-local-index -food-hardship-june-2016.

30. Marianne LeGreco, "How Deep Is Our 'Food Insecurity'? More Data Would Help," *Greensboro News and Record,* May 29, 2016, https://www

.greensboro.com/opinion/columns/marianne-legreco-how-deep-is-our-food
-insecurity-more-data/article_9c966354-52f1-586b-87bb-bfbe77c26c53.html.

31. Ann Wright, "Interactive Web Tool Maps Food Deserts, Provides Key
Data," *United States Department of Agriculture*, 2011, https://www.usda.gov
/media/blog/2011/05/3/interactive-web-tool-maps-food-deserts-provides-key
-data.

32. Steven Cummins and Sally Macintyre, "'Food Deserts'—Evidence and
Assumption in Health Policy Making," *British Medical Journal* 325 (2002),
436–38, doi: 10.1136/bmj.325.7361.436.

33. J. Beaumont, T. Lang, S. Leather, and C. Mucklow, *Report from the Policy
Sub-Group to the Nutrition Task Force Low Income Project Team of the Department of Health* (Radlett, UK: Institute of Grocery Distribution, 1995).

34. Jonathan Fielding and Paul Simon, "Food Desert or Food Swamp?"
Archives of Internal Medicine, 171 (2011), 1171–72.

35. Jon Bare, "Get Rid of the 'Food Desert' Label," *CNN*, November 6, 2013,
https://www.cnn.com/2013/11/06/opinion/bare-food-desert/index.html.

36. Jacqueline Bediako, "Food Apartheid: The Silent Killer in the Black
Community," *Atlanta Black Star*, June 16, 2015, http://atlantablackstar.com
/2015/06/16/food-apartheid-the-silent-killer-in-the-black-community/; Anna
Brones, "Food Apartheid: The Root of the Problem with America's Groceries,"
The Guardian, May 15, 2018, https://www.theguardian.com/society/2018/may
/15/food-apartheid-food-deserts-racism-inequality-america-karen-washington
-interview.

37. Jason Block and S. V. Subramanian, "Moving Beyond 'Food Deserts':
Reorienting United States Policies to Reduce Disparities in Diet Quality," *PLoS
Medicine* 12 (2015), http://journals.plos.org/plosmedicine/article?id=10.1371
/journal.pmed.1001914; Steven Cummins, Ellen Flint, and Stephen Matthews,
"New Neighborhood Grocery Store Increased Awareness of Food Access but Did
Not Alter Diet Habits or Obesity," *Health Affairs* 33 (2014), 283–91; Paul Whit-
acre, Peggy Tsai, and Janet Mulligan, *The Public Health Effects of Food Deserts:
Workshop Summary*, 2009, https://www.nap.edu/catalog/12623/the-public
-health-effects-of-food-deserts-workshop-summary.

38. Amber Johnson, "Practicing Radical Forgiveness in the Political Now: A
Justice Fleet Exhibit Fostering Healing Through Art, Dialogue and Play," *Jour-
nal of Art for Life* 10 (2019), 8; Tim Huffman, "Imagining Social Justice within a
Communicative Framework," *Journal of Social Justice* 4 (2014), 1–14.

39. Mohan Jyoti Dutta and Jagadish Thaker. "'Communication Sovereignty'
as Resistance: Strategies Adopted by Women Farmers Amid the Agrarian Crisis in India." *Journal of Applied Communication Research* 47 (2019), 24–46;
Megan K. Schraedley, Hamilton Bean, Sarah E. Dempsey, Mohan J. Dutta,
Kathleen P. Hunt, Sonia R. Ivancic, Marianne LeGreco, Kristen Okamoto, and

Tim Sellnow. "Food (In) security Communication: A Journal of Applied Communication Research Forum Addressing Current Challenges and Future Possibilities." *Journal of Applied Communication Research* 48 (2020), 166–85.

40. Food First, *Food First Backgrounder*, 2010, https://foodfirst.org/wp -content/uploads/2013/12/BK16_4-2010-Winter_Food_Movements_bckgrndr -.pdf; Constance Gordon and Kathleen Hunt, "Reform, Justice, and Sovereignty: A Food Systems Agenda for Environmental Communication," *Environmental Communication* 13 (2019), 9–22.

CHAPTER 2. DISCOURSES OF FOOD (IN)SECURITY

1. Rahim Kanani, "The World According to Anthony Bourdain," *Food & Wine*, May 4, 2016, 1, https://www.foodandwine.com/news/world-according-anthony -bourdain.

2. Mohan Jyoti Dutta et al., "Narratives of Food Insecurity in Tippecanoe County, Indiana: Economic Constraints in Local Meanings of Hunger," *Health Communication* 31 (2016), 647–58; Mohan Jyoti Dutta and Jagadish Thaker. "'Communication Sovereignty' as Resistance: Strategies Adopted by Women Farmers Amid the Agrarian Crisis in India." *Journal of Applied Communication Research* 47 (2019), 24–46.

3. Garrett Broad, *More Than Just Food: Food Justice and Community Change* (Berkeley: University of California Press, 2016); Sarah E. Dempsey, "Critiquing Community Engagement," *Management Communication Quarterly* 24 (2010), 359–90.

4. Sonia Raines Ivancic, "Gluttony for a Cause or Feeding the Food Insecure? Contradictions in Combating Food Insecurity through Private Philanthropy," *Health Communication* 32 (2017), 1441–44; Adam Marc Pine and Rebecca de Souza, "Including the Voices of Communities in Food Insecurity Research: An Empowerment-Based Agenda for Food Scholarship," *Journal of Agriculture, Food Systems, and Community Development* 3, no. 4 (2013), 71–79.

5. Janet Cramer et al., eds., *Food as Communication, Communication as Food* (New York: Peter Lang, 2011).

6. Lawrence R. Frey et al., "Looking for Justice in all the Wrong Places: On a Communication Approach to Social Justice," *Communication Studies* 47, nos. 1–2 (1996), 110.

7. Megan K. Schraedley, Hamilton Bean, Sarah E. Dempsey, Mohan J. Dutta, Kathleen P. Hunt, Sonia R. Ivancic, Marianne LeGreco, Kristen Okamoto, and Tim Sellnow. "Food (In) security Communication: A Journal of Applied Communication Research Forum Addressing Current Challenges and Future Possibilities." *Journal of Applied Communication Research* 48 (2020), 166–185.

8. As quoted in Carole Counihan and Penny Van Esterik, eds., *Food and Culture: A Reader,* 3rd ed. (New York: Routledge, 2012), 24.

9. Dempsey, "Critiquing Community Engagement;" Dutta and Thaker, "'Communication Sovereignty' as Resistance." Robert Gottlieb and Anupama Joshi, "Food Justice," *Dissent,* October 25, 2010, https://www.dissentmagazine.org /online_articles/food-justice; Joshua Sbicca, "Growing Food Justice by Planting an Anti-Oppression Foundation: Opportunities and Obstacles for a Budding Social Movement," *Agriculture and Human Values* 29 (2012), 455–66; Dutta and Thaker, "'Communication Sovereignty' as Resistance."

10. Gerda Wekerle, "Food Justice Movements: Policy, Planning, and Networks," *Journal of Planning Education and Research* 23 (2004), 378–86.

11. Charles Z. Levkoe, "Learning Democracy through Food Justice Movements," *Agriculture and Human Values* 23 (2006), 89–98.

12. The term *local* has been used to describe a variety of geographic and community boundaries—particularly in community food programming. For the purposes of this project, we frame local interventions as those occurring at the county, city, or neighborhood level.

13. See, for example, Caitlin Caspi et al., "The Local Food Environment and Diet: A Systematic Review," *Health & Place* 18 (2012), 1172–87; Laura K. Cobb et al., "Baltimore City Stores Increased the Availability of Healthy Food after WIC Policy Change," *Health Affairs* 34 (2015), 1849–57.

14. Dutta and Thaker, "'Communication Sovereignty' as Resistance;" David H. Holben and Michelle Berger Marshall, "Position of the Academy of Nutrition and Dietetics: Food Insecurity in the United States," *Journal of the Academy of Nutrition and Dietetics* 117 (2017), 1991–2002; Christine McCullum et al., "Evidence-Based Strategies to Build Community Food Security," *Journal of the American Dietetic Association* 105 (2005), 278–83.

15. Dempsey, "Critiquing Community Engagement;" Dutta and Thaker, "'Communication Sovereignty' as Resistance;" Schraedley et al., "Food (In) security Communication.

16. Dempsey, "Critiquing Community Engagement;" Sarah E. Dempsey and Kevin Barge, "Engaged Scholarship and Democracy," In *The SAGE Handbook of Organizational Communication: Advances in Theory, Research, and Methods,* 3rd ed., eds. Linda L. Putnam and Dennis K. Mumby, 665–88 (Thousand Oaks, CA: SAGE, 2014); Shiv Ganesh and Cynthia Stohl, "Community Organizing, Social Movements, and Collective Action," In *The SAGE Handbook of Organizational Discourse,* eds. David Grant et al., 743–66 (Thousand Oaks, CA: SAGE, 2014).

17. See, for example, Kevin M. Carragree and Lawrence R. Frey, "Communication Activism Research: Engaged Communication Scholarship for Social Justice," *International Journal of Communication* 10 (2016), 3975–99; Dempsey, "Critiquing Community Engagement."

18. Alan H. Bloomgarden and KerryAnne O'Meara, "Faculty Role Integration and Community Engagement: Harmony or Cacophony?" *Michigan Journal of Community Service Learning* 13, no. 2 (2007), 5–18; Marie Sandy and Barbara A. Holland, "Different Worlds and Common Ground: Community Partner Perspectives on Campus-Community Partnerships," *Michigan Journal of Community Service Learning* 13 (2006), 30–43.

19. McCullum et al., "Evidence-Based Strategies."

20. Broad, *More Than Just Food*; Dempsey, "Critiquing Community Engagement."

21. Kristian Larsen and Jason Gilliland, "A Farmers' Market in a Food Desert: Evaluating Impacts on the Price and Availability of Healthy Food," *Health & Place* 15 (2009), 1158–62.

22. Alison M. Sheppard, "Curbside Eating: Mobilizing Food Trucks to Activate Public Space," (Master's thesis, Massachusetts Institute of Technology, 2013).

23. Daniel Block et al., "Food Sovereignty, Urban Food Access, and Food Activism: Contemplating the Connections through Examples from Chicago," *Agriculture and Human Values* 29 (2012), 203–15; Dutta et al., "Narratives of Food Insecurity."

24. Dutta and Thaker, "'Communication Sovereignty' as Resistance"; Lynn M. Harter et al., "Storytelling and Social Activism in Health Organizing," *Management Communication Quarterly* 31 (2017), 314–20; Yong-Cham Kim and Sandra J. Ball-Rokeach, "Civic Engagement from a Communication Infrastructure Perspective," *Communication Theory* 16 (2006), 173–97; Dan H. O'Hair, Katherine M. Kelley, and Kathy L Williams, "Managing Community Risks through a Community-Communication Infrastructure Approach," In *Communication and Organizational Knowledge*, eds. Heather E. Canary and Robert D. McPhee, 223–43 (New York: Routledge, 2010).

25. Tamar Ginossar and Sara Nelson, "Reducing the Health and Digital Divides: A Model for Using Community-Based Participatory Research Approach to E-Health Interventions in Low-Income Hispanic Communities," *Journal of Computer-Mediated Communication* 15, no. 4 (2010), 530–51; Hernando Rojas and Eulalia Puig-i-Abril, "Mobilizers Mobilized: Information, Expression, Mobilization and Participation in the Digital Age," *Journal of Computer-Mediated Communication* 14 (2009), 902–27.

26. Marianne LeGreco, Michelle Ferrier, and Dawn Leonard, "Further Down the Virtual Vines: Managing Community-Based Work in Virtual Public Spaces," In *Management and Participation in the Public Sphere*, ed. Mika Merviö, 147–69 (Hershey, PA: IGI Global, 2015).

27. Angela Trethewey and Steve Corman, "Anticipating K-Commerce: E-Commerce, Knowledge Management, and Organizational Communication," *Management Communication Quarterly* 14 (2001), 619–28.

28. Jeffrey T. Child and Michelle Shumate, "The Impact of Communal Knowledge Repositories and People-Based Knowledge Management on Perceptions of Team Effectiveness," *Management Communication Quarterly* 21 (2007), 29–54.

29. Barbara Holland, Geoff Scott, and Leonid Grebennikov, "Rationale and Model for an Online System for Tracking and Assessing Community Engagement," In *2010 AUCEA National Conference: Communities, Participation & Partnership, 5–7 July 2010, University of Tasmania, Launceston Campus: Conference Proceedings*, 262–75, 2010, http://www.academia.edu/download /30251586/proceedings_of_aucea_2010.pdf#page=267.

30. Paul M. Leonardi, "Social Media, Knowledge Sharing, and Innovation: Toward a Theory of Communication Visibility," *Information Systems Research* 25 (2014), 796–816; Heather M. Zoller, "Health Activism Targeting Corporations: A Critical Health Communication Perspective," *Health Communication* 32 (2017), 219–29.

31. Michelle Shumate, Rahinah Ibrahim, and Raymond Levitt, "Dynamic Information Retrieval and Allocation Flows in Project Teams with Discontinuous Membership," *European Journal of International Management* 4 (2010), 556–75.

32. Julia Kotlarsky, Bart van den Hooff, and Leonie Houtman, "Are We on the Same Page? Knowledge Boundaries and Transactive Memory System Development in Cross-Functional Teams," *Communication Research* 42 (2015), 319–44; Dorit Nevo and Yair Wand, "Organizational Memory Information Systems: A Transactive Memory Approach," *Decision Support Systems* 39, no. 4 (2005), 549–62.

33. Claire Lamine, "Sustainability and Resilience in Agrifood Systems: Reconnecting Agriculture, Food and the Environment," *Sociologia Ruralis* 55 (2015), 41–61; Stephen Whitfield et al., "Sustainability Spaces for Complex Agri-Food Systems," *Food Security* 7 (2015), 1291–97.

34. Spoma Jovanovic, *Democracy, Dialogue, and Community Action: Truth and Reconciliation in Greensboro* (Fayetteville: University of Arkansas Press, 2012).

35. Marianne LeGreco and Niesha Douglas, "Everybody Eats: Carrying and Disrupting Narratives of Food (In) Security," *Management Communication Quarterly* 31 (2017), 307–13.

36. Lynn M. Harter, "Engaging Narrative Theory to Disrupt and Reimagine Organizing Processes," *Management Communication Quarterly* 31 (2017), 297–99.

37. Lawrence R. Frey and Kevin M. Carragee, eds., *Communication Activism, Vol. 3: Struggling for Social Justice Amidst Difference* (New York: Hampton Press, 2012); Shiv Ganesh and Heather M. Zoller, "Dialogue, Activism, and Democratic Social Change," *Communication Theory* 22, no. 1 (2012), DOI:10.1111/j.1468-2885.2011.01396; Harter, "Engaging Narrative;" Harter et

al., "Storytelling and Social Justice;" Nina M. Lozano-Reich and Dana L. Cloud, "The Uncivil Tongue: Invitational Rhetoric and the Problem of Inequality," *Western Journal of Communication* 73 (2009), 220–26.

38. Cindy M. Spurlock, "Performing and Sustaining (Agri) Culture and Place: The Cultivation of Environmental Subjectivity on the Piedmont Farm Tour," *Text and Performance Quarterly* 29 (2009), 5.

39. LeGreco and Douglas, "Everybody Eats."

40. Anju Aggarwal et al., "Importance of Taste, Nutrition, Cost and Convenience in Relation to Diet Quality: Evidence of Nutrition Resilience Among US Adults Using National Health and Nutrition Examination Survey (NHANES) 2007–2010," *Preventive Medicine* 90 (2016), 184–92; Patrice M. Buzzannell, "Resilience: Talking, Resisting, and Imagining New Normalcies into Being," *Journal of Communication* 60 (2010), 1–14; Ziyu Long et al., "Global Communication for Organizing Sustainability and Resilience," *China Media Research* 11 (2015), 67–77.

41. Elizabeth Kneebone, "The Growth and Spread of Concentrated Poverty, 2000 to 2008–2012," *Brookings,* July 31, 2014, https://www.brookings.edu /interactives/the-growth-and-spread-of-concentrated-poverty-2000-to-2008 -2012/.

42. Using a program called Tiki-Toki—not to be confused with TikTok—this timeline allowed us to anchor key events in Greensboro's food security history, including Greensboro's first appearance on the FRAC rankings in 2010 and the emergence of several nonprofit organizations and community groups. Marianne LeGreco, "Food Security in the Piedmont Triad," Tiki-Toki, 2017, https://www .tiki-toki.com/timeline/entry/842615/Food-Security-in-the-Piedmont-Triad/.

43. For references, see Tina Firesheets, "Quick Bites: Food Council, Farewell, Eggnog and More," *1808 Magazine,* November 25, 2014, https://www.greensboro .com/1808greensboro/food_drink/quick-bites-food-council-farewell-eggnog -and-more/article_5d8590c4-742c-11e4-a1f3-b7ac5385ad64.html; Eric Ginsburg, "Hungry for Change: Ideas for Tackling Food Insecurity," *Triad City Beat,* May 27, 2015, https://triad-city-beat.com/hungry-for-change-ideas-for -tackling-food-insecurity/3; Jordan Green, "Food Alliance Addresses Immediate Need and Long-Term Development," *Triad City Beat,* March 25, 2015, https:// triad-city-beat.com/food-alliance-addresses-immediate-need-and-long-term -development/; Jeff Sykes, "Crossing the Food Desert," *YES!Weekly,* March 4, 2015, https://yesweekly.com/CROSSING-THE-FOOD-DESERT-a22669/.

44. See https://www.tiki-toki.com/timeline/entry/842615/Food-Security-in -the-Piedmont-Triad/. We invite readers to visit the timeline, as a way to learn more about both food security in Greensboro and the many conversations, interventions, and communities that were mobilized across this ten-year period.

45. Marianne LeGreco and Sarah J. Tracy, "Discourse Tracing as Qualitative Practice," *Qualitative Inquiry* 15 (2009), 1516–43.

46. For a more thorough description of how discourse tracing operates, as well as a step-by-step process for using the methodology, applied in a food context, please see LeGreco and Tracy, "Discourse Tracing."

47. Our "Cast of Voices" was inspired somewhat by Dr. Omi Osun Joni L. Jones's performance anthology on gentrification in Austin, Texas.

PART II. ENGAGING COMMUNITIES

1. Tim Huffman, "Imagining Social Justice within a Communicative Framework," *Journal of Social Justice* 4 (2014), 1–14; Amber Johnson, "Practicing Radical Forgiveness in the Political Now: A Justice Fleet Exhibit Fostering Healing through Art, Dialogue and Play," *Journal of Art for Life* 10 (2019), 1–8.

2. Johnson, "Practicing Radical Forgiveness," 2.

3. See, for example, Mohan Dutta, Aguptus Anaele, and Christina Jones, "Voices of Hunger: Addressing Health Disparities through the Culture-Centered Approach," *Journal of Communication* 63 (2016), 159–80; Lawrence R. Frey and Kevin M. Carragee, eds., *Communication Activism, Vol. 3: Struggling for Social Justice amidst Difference* (New York: Hampton Press, 2012); Spoma Jovanovic, *Democracy, Dialogue, and Community Action: Truth and Reconciliation in Greensboro* (Fayetteville: University of Arkansas Press, 2012).

4. Mohan J. Dutta, "Communicating about Culture and Health: Theorizing Culture-Centered and Cultural Sensitivity Approaches," *Journal of Communication* 63 (2007), 304–28.

5. Kevin M. Carragee and Lawrence R. Frey, "Communication Activism Research: Engaged Communication Scholarship for Social Justice," *International Journal of Communication* 10 (2016), 3975–99.

CHAPTER 3. WARNERSVILLE COMMUNITY FOOD TASK FORCE

1. Mohan J. Dutta, "Theory and Practice in Health Communication Campaigns: A Critical Interrogation," *Health Communication* 18 (2005), 103–22; Mohan J. Dutta, Aguptus Anaele, and Christine Jones, "Voices of Hunger: Addressing Health Disparities through the Culture-Centered Approach," *Journal of Communication* 63 (2013), 159–80; Charlotte Ryan, Kevin M. Carragee, and Cassie Schwerner, "Media, Movements, and the Quest for Social Justice," *Journal of Applied Communication Research* 26 (1998), 165–81.

2. Greensboro History Museum, *Warnersville: Our Home, Our Neighborhood, Our Stories,* 2014, https://greensborohistory.org/exhibits/warnersville.

3. Teresa Prout, "In the Neigh-Boro-Hood: Warnersville Founded by Free Slaves," *1808 Magazine*, December 28, 2018, https://www.greensboro.com /1808greensboro/in-the-neigh-boro-hood-warnersville-founded-by-freed -slaves/article_b58c7dbd-9c76-5881-b86a-5feb7c7ea913.html.

4. Katherine Schwab, "The Racist Roots of Urban Renewal and How It Made Cities Less Equal," *Fast Company*, January 4, 2018, https://www.fastcompany .com/90155955/the-racist-roots-of-urban-renewal-and-how-it-made-cities-less -equal; Robert K. Nelson, "Mapping Inequality," *Digital Scholarship Lab*, 2018, http://dsl.richmond.edu/.

5. Digital Scholarship Lab, "Renewing Inequality," 2018, https://dsl.richmond .edu/panorama/renewal/#view=0/0/1&viz=cartogram.

6. Preservation Greensboro, "Future-Perfect-In-Past-Tense: Reclaiming the Historic Warnersville Neighborhood," 2008, para. 6, https://preservation greensboro.org/future-perfect/.

7. James Griffin, "Warnersville Celebrates 150 Years," *Carolina Peacemaker*, September 4, 2015, http://www.peacemakeronline.com/warnersville-celebrates -150-years/.

8. YMCA, "Community Healthy Living Index," https://www.ymca.net /communityhealthylivingindex; Soowon Kim et al., "Development of the Community Healthy Living Index: A Tool to Foster Healthy Environments for the Prevention of Obesity and Chronic Disease," *Preventive Medicine* 50 (2010), S80–S85, https://doi.org/10.1016/j.ypmed.2009.07.025.

9. Lawrence R. Frey et al., *Communication Activism: Volume 1 Communication for Social Change* (Cresskill, NJ: Hampton, 2006).

10. After additional research, the task force chose to focus on the garden and market. The community store was deemed too cost-prohibitive, and other groups in the community had started to focus on physical activity.

11. Kim et al., "Development of the CHLI."

12. Collaborative Cottage Grove, "Cottage Grove Community Marketplace," 2019, https://www.collaborativecottagegrove.org/.

13. Garrett Broad, *More Than Just Food: Food Justice and Community Change* (Berkeley: University of California Press, 2016); Frey et al., *Communication Activism*.

14. Megan Schraedley, et al., "Food (In)Security Communication: Addressing Current Challenges and Future Possibilities," *Journal of Applied Communication Research* (2020), https://doi.org/10.1080/00909882.2020.1735648.

15. Yong-Cham Kim and Sandra J. Ball-Rokeach, "Civic Engagement from a Communication Infrastructure Perspective," *Communication Theory* 16 (2006), 173–97.

16. Malik Yakini, "Keynote: Come to the Table Conference," video, 2013, https://www.youtube.com/watch?v=m59OgburT3Y.

17. Broad, *More Than Just Food*; Dutta, Anaele, and Jones, "Voices of Hunger."

18. Via Campesina, *Via Campesina Declaration for Food Sovereignty of November 1996*, World Food Summit, Rome Italy, November 13–17, 1996.

19. Center for Community Health and Development, "Community Toolbox," University of Kansas, 2020, https://ctb.ku.edu/en.

20. YMCA, "Community Healthy Living Index."

21. Barbara Cohen, Margaret Andrews, and Linda Scott Kantor, "Community Food Security Assessment Toolkit," United States Department of Agriculture, July 2002, https://www.ers.usda.gov/publications/pub-details/?pubid=43179.

CHAPTER 4. DOWNTOWN GREENSBORO FOOD TRUCK

1. Heather Canary, "Constructing Policy Knowledge: Contradictions, Communication, and Knowledge Frames," *Communication Monographs* 77 (2010), 181–206; Marianne LeGreco, "Working with Policy: Restructuring Healthy Eating Practices and the Circuit of Policy Communication," *Journal of Applied Communication Research* 40 (2012), 44–64.

2. Nurit Guttman, "Bringing the Mountain to the Public: Dilemmas and Contradictions in the Procedures of Public Deliberation Initiatives That Aim to Get 'Ordinary Citizens' to Deliberate Policy Issues," *Communication Theory* 17 (2007), 411–38, https://doi.org/10.1111/j.1468-2885.2007.00305.x.

3. Sarah E. Dempsey, "Critiquing Community Engagement," *Management Communication Quarterly* 24 (2010), 359–90; Virginia M. McDermott, John G. Oetzel, and Kalvin White, "Ethical Paradoxes in Community-Based Participatory Research," in *Emerging Perspectives in Health Communication: Meaning, Culture, and Power*, eds. Mohan J. Dutta and Heather Zoller (New York: Routledge, 2008), 182–202.

4. Canary, *Constructing Policy Knowledge*; Heather Canary, "Structurating Activity Theory: An Integrative Approach to Policy Knowledge," *Communication Theory* 20 (2010), 21–49; Heather E. Canary, Sarah E. Riforgiate, and Yvonne J. Montoya, "The Policy Communication Index: A Theoretically Based Measure of Organizational Policy Communication Practices," *Management Communication Quarterly* 27 (2013), 471–502.

5. LeGreco, "Working with Policy."

6. Tim Huffman, "Imagining Social Justice within a Communicative Framework," *Journal of Social Justice* 4 (2014), 8, 12–13.

7. Daniel Engber, "Who Made That Food Truck?" *The New York Times*, May 2, 2014, https://www.nytimes.com/2014/05/04/magazine/who-made-that-food-truck.html.

8. Richard Myrick, *Mobile Cuisine*, 2018, https://mobile-cuisine.com/.

9. modmealsonmendenhall, "Let's Roll 'em in," *Let's Roll Food Trucks into Downtown Greensboro* blog, August 9, 2012, para. 1–2, https://downtowngsofood trucks.wordpress.com/2012/08/09/hello-world/.

10. modmealsonmendenhall, "N&R Editorial: Downtown Diners Deserve Full Menu," *Let's Roll Food Trucks into Downtown Greensboro*, blog, August 15, 2012. https://downtowngsofoodtrucks.wordpress.com/2012/08/21/in-response -health-official-to-monitor-food-truck-issue/.

11. modmealsonmendenhall, "In Response: Health Officials to Monitor Food Truck Issue," *Let's Roll Food Trucks into Downtown Greensboro*, blog, August 15, 2012, para. 6.

12. modmealsonmendenhall, "Downtown Diners Deserve Full Menu," *Let's Roll Food Trucks into Downtown Greensboro*, blog, August 15, 2012, para. 15.

13. City of Greensboro, City Council Meeting, video, September 4, 2012, http://greensboro.granicus.com/player/clip/1571?view_id=2.

14. Downtown Greensboro Incorporated (DGI), 2012.

15. Personal Interview, October 2, 2012.

16. DGI, 2012.

17. Personal Interview, October 15, 2012.

18. DGI, 2012.

19. DGI, 2012.

20. Personal Interview, October 23, 2012.

21. Carter Coyle, "Downtown Greensboro Restaurants Say Business is Being Hurt by Food Trucks," *FOX8 WGHP*, November 9, 2012, https://www.journalnow .com/news/state/downtown-greensboro-restaurants-say-business-is-being-hurt -by-food/article_546928b8-2a6c-11e2-928b-001a4bcf6878.html.

22. DGI, 2012.

23. LeGreco, "Working with Policy."

24. DGI, 2012.

25. Travis Fain, "Health Officials to Monitor Food Truck Issue," *Greensboro News & Record*, August 20, 2012, para. 9–12, https://www.greensboro.com/news /political/health-officials-to-monitor-food-truck-issue/article_03e6c6be-8204 -528c-a819-99c04545803a.html.

26. modmealsonmendenhall, "In Response," para. 4.

27. LeGreco, "Working with Policy."

28. City of Greensboro, City Council Meeting, video, November 7, 2012, http:// greensboro.granicus.com/player/clip/1614?view_id=2.

29. Michael Spears, "Food Truck Businesses Double in Time for Summer," FOX8 WGHP, April 22, 2014, https://myfox8.com/news/greensboro-food-truck -businesses-double-in-time-for-summer/.

30. John Newsom, "Suspected Tornado Kills 1 in Greensboro; Damage Extensive on City's East Side," *Greensboro News & Record*, April 16, 2018, https://

www.greensboro.com/news/local_news/suspected-tornado-kills-in-greensboro
-damage-extensive-on-city-s/article_3fa1e99a-5bed-57d8-8f2f-010f944a75ec
.html.

31. Fox8 WGHP, "Free, Hot Meals Lifts Community Spirit After Disaster in Greensboro," April 19, 2018, para. 4, https://myfox8.com/news/free-hot-meals -lifts-community-spirit-after-disaster-in-greensboro/.

32. Lawrence Frey et al., "Looking for Justice in all the Wrong Places: On a Communication Approach to Social Justice," *Communication Studies* 47, nos. 1–2 (1996), 110–27; Huffman, "Imagining Social Justice."

33. Guttman, "Bringing the Mountain;" Spoma Jovanovic, *Democracy, Dialogue, and Community Action: Truth and Reconciliation in Greensboro* (Fayetteville: University of Arkansas Press, 2012).

34. McDermott et al., "Ethical Paradoxes."

35. Let's Roll Food Trucks Into Downtown Greensboro! https://downtowngso foodtrucks.wordpress.com.

36. City of Greensboro, City Council Meeting, video, September 4, 2012, http://greensboro.granicus.com/player/clip/1571?view_id=2.

37. City of Greensboro, City Council Meeting, video, November 7, 2012, http:// greensboro.granicus.com/player/clip/1614?view_id=2.

PART III. MOBILIZING RESOURCES

1. William Gamson and David Stuart, "Media Discourse as a Symbolic Contest: The Bomb in Political Cartoons," *Sociological Forum* 7 (1992), 55–86; Luther P. Gerlach and Virginia H. Hine, *People, Power, Change: Movements of Social Transformation* (Indianapolis, IN: Bobbs-Merrill, 1970); Charlotte Ryan, Kevin M. Carragee, and Cassie Schwerner, "Media, Movements, and the Quest for Social Justice," *Journal of Applied Communication Research* 26 (1998), 165–81.

2. Mohan J. Dutta, "Culture-Centered Approach in Addressing Health Disparities: Communication Infrastructures for Subaltern Voices," *Communication Methods and Measures* 12, no. 4 (2018), 239–59; Mohan J. Dutta and Jagadish Thaker, "'Communication Sovereignty' as Resistance: Strategies Adopted by Women Farmers amid the Agrarian Crisis in India," *Journal of Applied Communication Research* 47 (2019), 24–46; Yong-Cham Kim and Sandra J. Ball-Rokeach, "Civic Engagement from a Communication Infrastructure Perspective," *Communication Theory* 16 (2006), 173–97.

3. Kim and Ball-Rokeach, "Civic Engagement;" Robert J. Sampson, Jeffrey D. Morenoff, and Felton Earles, "Beyond Social Capital: Spatial Dynamics of Collective Efficacy for Children," *American Sociological Review* 64 (1999), 633–60.

4. Tamar Ginossar and Sara Nelson, "Reducing the Health and Digital Divides: A Model for Using Community-Based Participatory Research Approach

to E-Health Interventions in Low-Income Hispanic Communities," *Journal of Computer-Mediated Communication* 15, no. 4 (2010), 530–51.

5. Nurit Guttman and William Harris Ressler, "On Being Responsible: Ethical Issues in Appeals to Personal Responsibility in Health Campaigns," *Journal of Health Communication* 6, no. 2 (2010), 117–36; Ryan, Carragee, and Schwerner, "Media, Movements."

6. Heather J. Carmack, "'What Happens on the Van, Stays on the Van': The (Re) Structuring of Privacy and Disclosure Scripts on an Appalachian Mobile Health Clinic," *Qualitative Health Research* 20, no. 10 (2010), 1393–405; Amber Johnson, "Practicing Radical Forgiveness in the Political Now: A Justice Fleet Exhibit Fostering Healing through Art, Dialogue and Play," *Journal of Art for Life* 10 (2019), 1–8.

CHAPTER 5. THE WARNERSVILLE COMMUNITY GARDEN

1. United States Department of Agriculture, "North Carolina Field Office," National Agriculture Statistics Service, 2017, https://www.nass.usda.gov/Statistics_by_State/North_Carolina/index.php.

2. North Carolina Department of Commerce, "Key industries in North Carolina," 2019, https://www.nccommerce.com/business/key-industries-north-carolina.

3. Christopher Gergen and Stephen Martin, "If NC Wants to Feed Itself—and the World—It Needs to Save Its Farms," *News & Observer*, March 24, 2017, https://www.newsobserver.com/news/business/article140522363.html).

4. United States Department of Agriculture, "Urban Agriculture," National Agriculture Library, 2019, para. 1, https://www.nal.usda.gov/afsic/urban-agriculture.

5. Quina Weber-Shirk, "Community Gardens Locations," March 2020, https://guilford.ces.ncsu.edu/community-and-school-garden-network/community-gardens-locations/.

6. Dan Charles, "At the Community Garden, It's the Community That's the Hard Part," NPR, March 20, 2012, https://www.npr.org/sections/thesalt/2012/03/20/148999066/at-the-community-garden-its-community-thats-the-hard-part.

7. Elizabeth Gamble, "How to Organize a Community Garden," NC State Extension, June 17, 2019, https://content.ces.ncsu.edu/how-to-organize-a-community-garden.

8. Leah Penniman, *Farming While Black: Soul Fire Farm's Practical Guide to Liberation on the Land* (White River Junction, VT: Chelsea Green Publishing, 2018).

9. Virginia M. McDermott, John G. Oetzel, and Kalvin White, "Ethical Paradoxes in Community-Based Participatory Research," in *Emerging Perspectives in Health Communication: Meaning, Culture, and Power,* eds. Mohan J. Dutta and Heather Zoller (New York: Routledge, 2008), 182–202.

10. Susan Ladd, "Oasis Project: The Goal Is to Create an Urban Farm at a Church," *Greensboro News & Record,* October 27, 2013, A1, para. 6, https://greensboro.com/news/oasis-project-the-goal-is-to-create-an-urban-farm-at-a-church/article_400cc6be-a54d-5806-b53a-ecbf5e5419dd.html.

11. Ladd, "Oasis Project," A1, para. 1–5.

12. Growing Home, 2020, http://growinghomeinc.org/.

13. D-Town Farm, 2020, https://www.d-townfarm.com.

14. Conetoe Family Life Center, 2020, https://conetoelife.org.

15. American Community Gardening Association, "Growing Communities Across the U.S. and Canada," 2020, https://www.communitygarden.org.

16. Urban Teaching Farm, 2020, https://outofthegardenproject.org/programs/urban-teaching-farm/.

CHAPTER 6. THE MOBILE OASIS FARMERS MARKET

1. Kate Elizabeth Queram, "Guilford's Mobile Farmers Market Gets National Recognition," *Greensboro News & Record,* June 10, 2015, https://www.greensboro.com/news/guilford-s-mobile-farmers-market-gets-national-recognition/article_4522c8a0-0f11-11e5-ab04-13da58612e7d.html; Robert C. Lopez, "Rising Star: Marianne LeGreco Says Building Trust Helps Battle Food Insecurity," *Greensboro News & Record,* October 17, 2018, https://www.greensboro.com/entertainment/dining/rising-star-marianne-legreco-says-building-trust-helps-battle-food/article_4f1ad62f-d2b1-59ae-897b-ef629a3efc53.html.

2. Heather J. Carmack, "'What Happens on the Van, Stays on the Van': The (Re) Structuring of Privacy and Disclosure Scripts on an Appalachian Mobile Health Clinic," *Qualitative Health Research* 20, no. 10 (2010), 1393–405; Amber Johnson, "Practicing Radical Forgiveness in the Political Now: A Justice Fleet Exhibit Fostering Healing through Art, Dialogue and Play," *Journal of Art for Life* 10 (2019), 1–8.

3. Lynn M. Harter, "Engaging Narrative Theory to Disrupt and Reimagine Organizing Processes," *Management Communication Quarterly* 31 (2017), 297–99; Marianne LeGreco and Niesha Douglas, "Everybody Eats: Carrying and Disrupting Narratives of Food (In) Security," *Management Communication Quarterly* 31 (2017), 307–13.

4. Nancy McLaughlin, "Farmer's Market to Visit Warnersville," *Greensboro News & Record,* August 2, 2011, https://www.greensboro.com/news/farmers

-market-to-visit-warnersville/article_ea4a8008-a78a-5308-9ec7-f6a5c7aad25c
.html.

5. At the time, SNAP/EBT eligibility was more restrictive, and the application required a more permanent address to move forward. Only in 2013 did SNAP/EBT expand to include wide-scale mobile transactions at pop-up and test locations. United States Department of Agriculture, "A Short History of SNAP." 2013, https://www.fns.usda.gov/snap/short-history-snap.

6. For a description of the Prescriptions for Produce model, see Erika Trapl et al., "Dietary Impact of Produce Prescriptions for Patients with Hypertension," *Preventing Chronic Disease* 15 (2018), http://dx.doi.org/10.5888/pcd15.180301.

7. City of Greensboro, *Fresh Food Access,* August 18, 2015, https://www
.greensboro-nc.gov/home/showdocument?id=28019.

8. Daniel Wirtheim, "The Dinner," *Triad City Beat,* December 9, 2015, https://
triad-city-beat.com/the-dinner/.

9. Peter Block, *Community: The Structure of Belonging* (San Francisco: Berrett-Koehler, 2018).

10. Collaborative Cottage Grove, "Cottage Grove Community Marketplace," 2019, https://www.collaborativecottagegrove.org/.

11. David J. Hill, "Veggie Van Study Awards Funding to Nine Partner Mobile Markets," School of Public Health and Health Professions University at Buffalo, July 22, 2019, http://sphhp.buffalo.edu/home/news-events/news-archive/latest-news.host.html/content/shared/university/news/news-center-releases/2019/07/022.detail.html.

12. Mohan Dutta, "Communicating about Culture and Health: Theorizing Culture-Centered and Cultural Sensitivity Approaches," *Communication Theory* 17, no. 3 (2007), 304–28.

13. Lucia A. Leone, Lindsey Haynes-Maslow, and Alice S. Ammerman, "Veggie Van Pilot Study: Impact of a Mobile Produce Market for Underserved Communities on Fruit and Vegetable Access and Intake," *Journal of Hunger & Environmental Nutrition 12* (2017): 89–100, DOI: 10.1080/19320248.2016.1175399.

14. Dutta, "Communicating about Culture and Health."

15. See, for example, Johnson, "Practicing Radical Forgiveness."

16. University at Buffalo, "The Veggie Van Study," Veggie Van Mobile Market, https://www.myveggievan.org/current-research.html.

17. About Fresh, 2020, https://www.aboutfresh.org.

18. Market Umbrella, 2020, https://www.marketumbrella.org.

19. Harvie, "Welcome to Harvie: Your Local Farmer," 2020, https://www
.harvie.farm.

20. Justice Fleet, 2020, https://www.thejusticefleet.com/.

21. Eventbrite, "The Pop-Up Playbook," 2020, https://www.eventbrite.com/l/how-to-organize-a-pop-up-event/.

PART IV. DOCUMENTING PROCESS

1. Kevin M. Carragee and Lawrence R. Frey, "Communication Activism Research: Engaged Communication Scholarship for Social Justice," *International Journal of Communication* 10 (2016), 3975–99.

2. Barbara A. Holland, "Analyzing Institutional Commitment to Service: A Model of Key Organizational Factors," *Michigan Journal of Community Service Learning* 4, no. 1 (1997), 30–41; Barbara A. Holland, "A Comprehensive Model for Assessing Service-Learning and Community-University Partnerships," *New Directions for Higher Education* 114 (2001), 51–60.; see also Barbara R. Holland, Geoff Scott, and Leonid Grebennikov, "Rationale and Model for an Online System for Tracking and Assessing Community Engagement," in *2010 AUCEA National Conference: Communities, Participation & Partnership, 5–7 July 2010, University of Tasmania, Launceston Campus: Conference Proceedings* (2010), 262–75, http://www.academia.edu/download/30251586/proceedings_of_aucea_2010.pdf#page=267.

CHAPTER 7. ETHNOSH

1. Marianne wrote this story as part of an Ethnosh event to celebrate Local Foods Week. She and Donovan largely wrote this chapter together—Marianne took the lead in writing the body of the chapter, and Donovan provided reflections throughout.

2. Center for New North Carolinians, "Research," 2019, https://cnnc.uncg.edu/research/.

3. Caroline Wang and Mary Ann Burris, "Photovoice: Concept, Methodology, and Use for Participatory Needs Assessment," *Health Education & Behavior* 24 (1997), 369–87; see also Debbie Dougherty et al., "A Photovoice Study of Food (In) Security, Unemployment, and the Discursive-Material Dialectic," *Communication Monographs* 85, no. 4 (2018), 443–66, https://doi.org/10.1080/03637751.2018.1500700.

4. Mohan J. Dutta, "Communicating about Culture and Health: Theorizing Culture-Centered and Cultural Sensitivity Approaches," *Communication Theory* 17, no. 3 (2007), 304–28.

5. Osei Appiah, "Cultural Voyeurism: A New Framework for Understanding Race, Ethnicity, and Mediated Intergroup Interaction," *Journal of Communication* 68 (2018), 233–42.

6. Wang and Burris, "Photovoice."

7. Lavanya Ramanathan, "Why Everyone Should Stop Calling Immigrant Food 'Ethnic,'" *Washington Post*, July 21, 2015, https://www.washingtonpost

.com/lifestyle/food/why-everyone-should-stop-calling-immigrant-food-ethnic
/2015/07/20/07927100-266f-11e5-b77f-eb13a215f593_story.html.

8. https://www.thedailymeal.com/travel/poll-should-term-ethnic-food
-still-be-used, https://everydayfeminism.com/2016/07/stop-using-ethnic-to
-describe-poc/, https://www.nytimes.com/2017/04/02/us/racial-terms-that
-make-you-cringe.html, https://mabelkwong.com/2013/06/27/what-exactly-is
-ethnic-is-the-word-ethnic-relevant-anymore-today/.

9. Appiah, "Cultural Voyeurism."

10. Saru Jayaraman, *Behind the Kitchen Door* (Ithaca, NY: Cornell University
Press, 2013).

11. Wang and Burris, "Photovoice."

12. Center for New North Carolinians, "Research," 2019, https://cnnc.uncg
.edu/research/; Montagnard Dega Association, Montagnardda, 2020, https://
www.montagnardda.org.

13. Welcoming America, "Creating Home Together," 2020, https://welcoming
america.org.

14. Ethnosh, "Cuisine. Culture. Community," 2020, www.ethnosh.org.

15. Center for Community Health and Development, "Implementing Photovoice in Your Community," Community Toolbox, 2020, ctb.ku.edu/en/table-of
-contents/assessment/assessing-community-needs-and-resources/photovoice
/main; PhotoVoice, 2020, https://photovoice.org/.

CHAPTER 8. KITCHEN CONNECTS GSO

1. Barbara R. Holland, Geoff Scott, and Leonid Grebennikov, "Rationale and
Model for an Online System for Tracking and Assessing Community Engage-
ment," in *2010 AUCEA National Conference: Communities, Participation &
Partnership, 5–7 July 2010, University of Tasmania, Launceston Campus:
Conference Proceedings* (2010), 262–75, http://www.academia.edu/download
/30251586/proceedings_of_aucea_2010.pdf#page=267.

2. City of Greensboro, Fresh Food Access Plan, 2015, https://www.greensboro
-nc.gov/home/showdocument?id=28019.

3. Robert D. McPhee, "Agency and the Four Flows," *Management Communication Quarterly* 29 (2015), 487–92.

4. CHCS focused on the first five cohorts for the exit interviews, as these interviews helped inform a formative assessment of Kitchen Connects to help partners improve the program as it developed. As we moved to cohorts 6–8, the focus
shifted to capturing as many participants as possible for the six-month surveys.

5. Holland, Scott, and Grebennikov, "Rationale and Model;" Barbara A.
Holland, "A Comprehensive Model for Assessing Service-Learning and

Community-University Partnerships," *New Directions for Higher Education* 114 (2001), 51–60.

6. Center for Community Health and Development, "Community Toolbox," University of Kansas, 2020, https://ctb.ku.edu/en.

7. Daniel Gaines, "Food and Drug Protection Division: I Want to Start My Own Business. Now What," North Carolina Department of Agriculture and Consumer Services, 2020, www.ncagr.gov/fooddrug/food/foodbiz.htm.

PART V. SUSTAINING CONVERSATIONS

1. Garrett Broad, *More Than Just Food: Food Justice and Community Change* (Oakland: University of California Press, 2016).

2. Cindy M. Spurlock, "Performing and Sustaining (Agri) Culture and Place: The Cultivation of Environmental Subjectivity on the Piedmont Farm Tour," *Text and Performance Quarterly* 29 (2009), 5–21.

3. Spoma Jovanovic, *Democracy, Dialogue, and Community Action: Truth and Reconciliation in Greensboro* (Fayetteville: University of Arkansas Press, 2012); Marianne LeGreco and Niesha Douglas, "Everybody Eats: Carrying and Disrupting Narratives of Food (In) Security," *Management Communication Quarterly* 31 (2017), 307–13; Marianne LeGreco and Dawn Leonard, "Building Sustainable Community-Based Food Programs: Cautionary Tales from the Garden," *Environmental Community: A Journal of Nature and Culture* 5, no. 3 (2011), 356–62.

4. Lynn M. Harter, "Engaging Narrative Theory to Disrupt and Reimagine Organizing Processes," *Management Communication Quarterly* 31 (2017), 297–99.

CHAPTER 9. THE GUILFORD FOOD COUNCIL

1. Michael Burgan and Mark Winne, "Doing Food Councils Right: A Guide to Development and Action," *Mark Winne Associates,* September 2012, https://www.markwinne.com/wp-content/uploads/2012/09/FPC-manual.pdf; Malik Yakini, "Malik Yakini of Detroit Black Community Food Security Network Talks of the Challenges the Population of Detroit Faces," YouTube, video, January 16, 2014, https://www.youtube.com/watch?time_continue=4&v=f2pcCKGzXLQ&feature=emb_logo.

2. Community Food Strategies, "Resources," 2019, https://communityfood strategies.org/resource/.

3. Community Food Strategies, "Resources."

4. Karen Tracy and Aaron Dimock, "Meetings: Discursive Sites for Building and Fragmenting Community," *Annals of the International Communication Association* 28 (2004), 127–65.

5. United States Census Bureau, "Guilford County Quick Facts," 2019, https://www.census.gov/quickfacts/guilfordcountynorthcarolina.

6. Center for New North Carolinians, "Research," 2019, https://cnnc.uncg.edu/research/.

7. Chuck McShane, "Cabarrus' Lomax Farm Faces Uncertainty," UNC Charlotte, July 14, 2014, https://ui.uncc.edu/story/cabarrus-lomax-farm-faces-uncertain-future.

8. And this brought our final total of council members to nine.

9. The Greensboro task force was originally called the Greensboro Hunger Task Force but changed its name in 2017 to the Community Food Task Force. To limit confusion, we refer to the group by their current name.

10. Jimmy Tomlin, "Hunger in High Point Ranked 2nd in Nation." *High Point Enterprise*, November 16, 2014.

11. For an excellent summary of the GHFPA, please visit Heather Hunt and Gene Nichol, "'Surviving Through Together': Hunger, Poverty and Persistence in High Point, North Carolina," N.C. Poverty Research Fund, Fall 2019, https://law.unc.edu/wp-content/uploads/2019/12/HighPointHungerReport2019.pdf.

12. Carter Coyle, "Feeding Children during the Summer Months in Greensboro," FOX8 WGHP, June 5, 2015, https://myfox8.com/news/feeding-children-during-the-summer-months-in-greensboro/.

13. Christoph Haug, "Organizing Spaces: Meeting Arenas as a Social Movement Infrastructure between Organization, Network, and Institution," *Organization Studies* 34 (2013), 705–32.

14. Karl E. Weick, Kathleen M. Sutcliffe, and David Obstfeld, "Organizing and the Process of Sensemaking," *Organizational Science* 16 (2005), 409–21.

15. Community Food Strategies, "Cultivating Community," 2020, https://communityfoodstrategies.org.

16. Detroit Food Policy Council, 2020, https://www.detroitfoodpc.org; Detroit Black Food Security Network, 2020, https://www.dbcfsn.org.

17. Burgan and Winne, "Doing Food Councils Right."

CHAPTER 10. THE RENAISSANCE COMMUNITY CO-OP

1. Eric Ginsburg, "Renaissance Community Co-op Opens, Filling Considerable Void," *Triad City Beat,* November 1, 2016, https://triad-city-beat.com/renaissance-co-op-opens-filling-considerable-void/.

2. Michael Joseph Roberto, "Crisis, Recovery, and the Transitional Economy: The Struggle for Cooperative Ownership in Greensboro, North Carolina," *Monthly Review*, May 1, 2014, https://monthlyreview.org/2014/05/01/crisis -recovery-transitional-economy/.

3. Marty Schladen, "Concerned Citizens of Northeast Greensboro is Raising Its Profile as a Civic Player Since It Formed Nearly Two Years Ago," *Greensboro News & Record*, January 25, 2015, https://www.greensboro.com/citizens-broup -draws-residents-officials-notice-concerned-citizens-of-northeast/article _b87966e2-da84-592c-8049-609db4626376.html.

4. Roberto, "Crisis, Recovery."

5. Eric Ginsburg, "Supermarket Chains Ignore This Black Community, so Residents Opened a Co-Op," *Vice*, September 14, 2018, para. 9, https://www.vice .com/en_us/article/3keqnb/renaissance-community-co-op-greensboro.

6. At the time, Greensboro was home to one other food cooperative—Deep Roots Market—but they catered largely to natural and organic foods. The Company Shops Market was attractive, because they sold natural and organic foods alongside grocery items that folks were used to seeing in a conventional store. One of the organizers with F4DC was also a financial supporter of the Company Shops, which had given her a good working relationship with its founders.

7. Kevin Smith, "We Want a Co-Op!" video, September 15, 2014, https://www .youtube.com/watch?v=xM1YX_BEEZ4&t=2s.

8. Ginsburg, "Renaissance Community."

9. For excellent summaries of organizing and opening the RCC, please read Michael Roberto's account in *Monthly Review* and Eric Ginsburg's articles in both *Triad City Beat* and *Vice*. Both authors are cited at the end of this chapter.

10. Brian Clarey, "In Greensboro Tornado, the Finger of God," *Triad City Beat*, April 19, 2018, https://triad-city-beat.com/greensboro-tornado-the-finger -of-god/.

11. Karl E. Weick, Kathleen M. Sutcliffe, and David Obstfeld, "Organizing and the Process of Sensemaking," *Organizational Science* 16 (2005), 409–21.

12. James Taylor and Elizabeth J. Van Every, *The Emergent Organization: Communication as Its Site and Surface* (Mahwah, NJ: Erlbaum, 2000), 275.

13. Weick, Sutcliffe, and Obstfeld, "Organizing."

14. Amber Johnson, "Practicing Radical Forgiveness in the Political Now: A Justice Fleet Exhibit Fostering Healing Through Art, Dialogue and Play," *Journal of Art for Life* 10 (2019), 1–8; Spoma Jovanovic, *Democracy, Dialogue, and Community Action: Truth and Reconciliation in Greensboro* (Fayetteville: University of Arkansas Press, 2012).

15. Carol Wilson, "Food Desert Rescuer Renaissance Co-op in Greensboro is Closing," *Greensboro News & Record*, January 9, 2019, para. 23, https://www

.greensboro.com/news/local_news/food-desert-rescuer-renaissance-co-op-in
-greensboro-is-closing/article_35545715-1392-5258-abdd-1d317545fb4d.html.

16. Wilson, "Food Desert," para. 25.

17. Renaissance Community Co-Op, *More Than a Grocery Store* (Greensboro, NC: Fund for Democratic Communities, 2016), https://f4dc.org/wp-content /uploads/2019/04/More-than-a-grocery-store.pdf.

18. Marnie Thompson, Sohnie Black, and Ed Whitfield, "The Ballad of the RCC, or 'Nice Try, Now Try Again,'" *Non-Profit Quarterly*, December 17, 2019, https:// nonprofitquarterly.org/the-ballad-of-the-rcc-or-nice-try-now-try-again/.

19. Sohnie Black et al., "The Anatomy of a Failed Co-Op," *Non-Profit Quarterly*, YouTube webinar, December 17, 2019, https://www.youtube.com/watch?v =8IYJNLpCQ7M&feature=emb_imp_woyt.

20. Black et al., "The Anatomy."

21. Black et al., "The Anatomy."

22. Black et al., "The Anatomy."

23. Eric Ginsburg, "Supermarket Chains."

24. Peter Block, *Community: The Structure of Belonging* (San Francisco: Berrett-Koehler, 2018); Marianne LeGreco and Niesha Douglas, "Everybody Eats: Carrying and Disrupting Narratives of Food (In) Security," *Management Communication Quarterly* 31 (2017), 307–13.

25. Lynn Harter et al., "Storytelling and Social Activism in Health Organizing," *Management Communication Quarterly* 31 (2017), 314–20.

26. Regester, "Renaissance Community."

27. Shiv Ganesh and Heather M. Zoller, "Dialogue, Activism, and Democratic Social Change," *Communication Theory* 22, no. 1 (2012), DOI:10.1111/j.1468 -2885.2011.01396.x; Harter et al., "Storytelling;" Johnson, "Practicing Radical Forgiveness;" Jovanovic, *Democracy, Dialogue*.

28. Ganesh and Zoller, "Dialogue, Activism," 77.

29. Mohan Dutta, Aguptus Anaele, and Christine Jones, "Voices of Hunger: Addressing Health Disparities through the Culture-Centered Approach," *Journal of Communication* 63 (2013), 159–80; Harter et al., "Storytelling.

30. Sarah E. Dempsey, "Critiquing Community Engagement," *Management Communication Quarterly* 24 (2010), 359–90; Lynn Harter, "Masculinity(s), the Agrarian Frontier Myth, and Cooperative Ways of Organizing: Contradictions and Tensions in the Experience and Enactment of Democracy," *Journal of Applied Communication Research* 32 (2004), 89–118, DOI: 10.1080/009098804 2000210016.

31. Cynthia Stohl and George Cheney, "Participatory Processes/Paradoxical Practices: Communication and the Dilemmas of Organizational Democracy," *Management Communication Quarterly* 14 (2010), 349–407; Virginia M.

McDermott, John G. Oetzel, and Kalvin White, "Ethical Paradoxes in Community-Based Participatory Research," In *Emerging Perspectives in Health Communication: Meaning, Culture, and Power,* eds. Mohan J. Dutta and Heather Zoller (New York: Routledge, 2008), 182–202; Marianne LeGreco, "Working with Policy: Restructuring Healthy Eating Practices and the Circuit of Policy Communication," *Journal of Applied Communication Research* 40 (2012), 44–64.

32. Stohl and Cheney, "Participatory Processes," 354.

33. Stohl and Cheney, "Participatory Processes," 360.

34. McDermott, Oetzel, and White, "Ethical Paradoxes."

35. Stephanie Parker, "Can Food Co-Ops Survive the New Retail Reality?" *Civil Eats,* February 28, 2018, https://civileats.com/2018/02/28/can-food-coops -survive-the-new-retail-reality/.

36. Melinda Clynes, "A Co-Op for the People: The Rocky Process of Developing the Detroit People's Co-Op," *Model D,* January 15, 2018, https://www .modeldmedia.com/features/peoples-food-coop-north-end-011518.aspx; Detroit Black Community Food Security Network, 2019, https://www.dbcfsn.org/.

37. Mohan J. Dutta and Jadagish Thaker, "'Communication Sovereignty' as Resistance: Strategies Adopted by Women Farmers amid the Agrarian Crisis in India," *Journal of Applied Communication Research* 47 (2019), 24–46; Yong-Cham Kim and Sandra J. Ball-Rokeach, "Civic Engagement from a Communication Infrastructure Perspective," *Communication Theory* 16 (2006), 173–97.

38. Dutta and Thaker, "Communication Sovereignty."

39. Black et al., "The Anatomy."

40. Renaissance Community Co-Op, *More Than a Grocery Store.*

41. Cooperative Grocer Network, "Renaissance Community Co-Op," https:// www.grocer.coop/renaissance-community-co-op.

CONCLUSION

1. Food Research and Action Center, "How Hungry Is America," June 2016, http://www.frac.org/research/resource-library/hungry-america-fracs-national -state-local-index-food-hardship-june-2016.

2. Food Research and Action Center, "How Hungry Is America," August 2018, https://frac.org/wp-content/uploads/food-hardship-july-2018.pdf.

3. Emily Pickren, "Number of U.S. Households Experiencing Food Insecurity Drops Significantly," Food Research and Action Center, 2016, https://frac .org/news/number-u-s-households-experiencing-food-insecurity-declines -significantly-2015.

4. Jessica Winters, "Guilford County Schools Open Grab-and-Go Meal Sites amid Shutdown," WFMY News 2, March 18, 2020, https://www

.wfmynews2.com/article/news/local/guilford-county-schools-open-grab-and
-go-meal-sites-school-shut-down-for-two-weeks/83-d2dfad84-ffdf-45bb-b0d1
-d94dcc9b0e17.

5. Dan Bayer, "Corner Farmers Market Maintains Neighborhood Connections during Pandemic," NCA Center for Communication, Community, Collaboration, and Change, 2020, https://cccc.uncg.edu/projects/growing-green-for
-greens/corner-farmers-market-maintains-neighborhood-connections-during
-pandemic/.

6. Matthew Bryant, "Food Resources for Greensboro and High Point during COVID-19," *UNCG News*, March 20, 2020, https://news.uncg.edu/food
-resources-for-greensboro-and-high-point-during-covid-19/.

7. Ben Hewitt, *The Town That Food Saved: How One Community Found Vitality in Local Food* (Emmaus, PA: Rodale Books, 2010), 2.

8. Shiv Ganesh and Heather M. Zoller, "Dialogue, Activism, and Democratic Social Change," *Communication Theory* 22, no. 1 (2012), DOI:10.1111/j.1468-2885.2011.01396.x.

9. Mohan J. Dutta, Aguptus Anaele, and Christine Jones, "Voices of Hunger: Addressing Health Disparities through the Culture-Centered Approach," *Journal of Communication* 63 (2013), 159–80; Marianne LeGreco and Niesha Douglas, "Everybody Eats: Carrying and Disrupting Narratives of Food (In)Security," *Management Communication Quarterly* 31 (2017), 307–13.

10. Janet Cramer, Carinita Greene, and Lynn Walters, eds., *Food as Communication, Communication as Food,* (New York: Peter Lang, 2011); Megan K. Schraedley et al., "Food (In)Security Communication: Addressing Current Challenges and Future Possibilities," *Journal of Applied Communication Research* (2020), https://doi.org/10.1080/00909882.2020.1735648.

11. Peter Block, *Community: The Structure of Belonging* (San Francisco: Berrett-Koehler, 2018).

12. Schraedley et al., "Food (In)Security."

13. Schraedley et al., "Food (In)Security," 11.

14. Malik Yakini, "Working in Community as Partners, not Missionaries," *Johns Hopkins Center for a Livable Future,* YouTube, video, May 3, 2013, https://www.youtube.com/watch?v=qO9_dgcxdj4.

15. Amber Johnson, "Practicing Radical Forgiveness in the Political Now: A Justice Fleet Exhibit Fostering Healing through Art, Dialogue and Play," *Journal of Art for Life* 10 (2019), 1–8.

16. Stephen Sills, "Visualizing Data Leads to Better Local Decisions," TEDxGreensboro, YouTube, video, June 5, 2018, https://www.youtube.com/watch?v=oaBrAOlEyRc.

17. Karl E. Weick, Kathleen M. Sutcliffe, and David Obstfeld, "Organizing and the Process of Sensemaking," *Organization Science* 16 (2005), 409–21.

18. Schraedley et al., "Food (In)Security."

19. Food and Agriculture Organization of the United Nations, "Rome Declaration on World Food Security," World Food Summit, 1996, 2, http://www.fao.org/docrep/003/w3613e/w3613e00.HTM.

20. Marianne LeGreco, "Building Vibrant Food Systems," TEDxGreensboro, YouTube, video, June 18, 2014, https://www.youtube.com/watch?v=MOOk5YD3IcA&t=249s.

21. E. Melanie Dupuis, Jill Lindsey Harrison, and David Goodman, "Just Food?," In *Cultivating Food Justice: Race, Class, and Sustainability*, eds. Alison Hope Alkon and Julian Egyeman (Cambridge, MA: MIT Press, 2011), 283–308.

22. Patrice Buzzannell, "Resilience: Talking, Resisting, and Imagining New Normalcies into Being," *Journal of Communication* 60 (2010), 1–14.

23. Buzzannell, "Resilience"; Lynn M. Harter, "Engaging Narrative Theory to Disrupt and Reimagine Organizing Processes," *Management Communication Quarterly* 31 (2017), 297–99.

24. Dutta, Anaele, and Jones, "Voices of Hunger."

25. Kristen E. Okamoto, " 'It's Like Moving the Titanic': Community Organizing to Address Food (In)Security." *Health Communication* 32, no. 8 (2017): 1047–50; Schraedley, et al., "Food (In)Security."

26. Kimberle Crenshaw, "Demarginalizing the Intersection of Race and Sex: A Black Feminist Critique of Antidiscrimination Doctrine, Feminist Theory and Antiracist Politics," *University of Chicago Legal Forum* 1989, no. 1 (1989): 139-167; we use the term *intersectional* very intentionally here, to speak to the contributions of Black feminists in arguing that experience is not universal and is often influenced by intersections between race, class, gender, sexuality, and myriad other identity, material, and social markers.

27. LeGreco and Douglas, "Everybody Eats."

28. Dutta, Anaele, and Jones, "Voices of Hunger."

29. Dutta, Anaele, and Jones, "Voices of Hunger."

30. Mohan J. Dutta and Jagadish Thaker. " 'Communication Sovereignty' as Resistance: Strategies Adopted by Women Farmers amid the Agrarian Crisis in India." *Journal of Applied Communication Research* 47 (2019): 24–46.

31. Eddi Yoon, "The Grocery Industry Confronts a New Problem: Only 10% of Americans Love Cooking," *Harvard Business Review*, September 22, 2017, https://hbr.org/2017/09/the-grocery-industry-confronts-a-new-problem-only-10-of-americans-love-cooking.

32. Lauren Stine, "Demand for Prepared Food Jumped 11%, Report Says" *Grocery Dive*, January 7, 2020, https://www.grocerydive.com/news/demand-for-prepared-foods-jumped-11-report-says/569823/.

33. Harter, "Engaging Narrative Theory," 298.

34. Marianne LeGreco and Niesha Douglas, "Everybody Eats: Carrying and Disrupting Narratives of Food Insecurity," *Management Communication Quarterly* 31, no. 2 (2017): 310.

35. "Food Waste," National Resource Defense Council 2020, https://www.nrdc.org/issues/food-waste.

36. Rebecca de Souza and Lynn Harter, "Reimagining Food Pantries as Activist Spaces," *Defining Moments Podcast: Conversations about Health and Healing*. WOUB Public Media, June 15, 2020, 90 min., https://www.stitcher.com/podcast/woub-public-media-2/defining-moments-conversations-about-health-and-healing/e/71095146.

Selected Bibliography

Aggarwal, Anju, Colin D. Rehm, Pablo Monsivais, and Adam Drewnowski. "Importance of Taste, Nutrition, Cost and Convenience in Relation to Diet Quality: Evidence of Nutrition Resilience Among US Adults Using National Health and Nutrition Examination Survey (NHANES) 2007–2010." *Preventive Medicine* 90 (2016): 184–92.

Appiah, Osei. "Cultural Voyeurism: A New Framework for Understanding Race, Ethnicity, and Mediated Intergroup Interaction." *Journal of Communication* 68 (2018): 233–42.

Bediako, Jacqueline. "Food Apartheid: The Silent Killer in the Black Community." *Atlanta Black Star*, June 16, 2015. http://atlantablackstar.com/2015/06/16/food-apartheid-the-silent-killer-in-the-black-community/.

Block, Daniel R., Noel Chávez, Erika Allen, and Dinah Ramirez. "Food Sovereignty, Urban Food Access, and Food Activism: Contemplating the Connections through Examples from Chicago." *Agriculture and Human Values* 29 (2012): 203–15.

Block, Jason, and S. V. Subramanian. "Moving Beyond 'Food Deserts': Reorienting United States Policies to Reduce Disparities in Diet Quality." *PLoS Medicine* 12 (2015). http://journals.plos.org/plosmedicine/article?id=10.1371/journal.pmed.1001914.

Block, Peter. *Community: The Structure of Belonging*. San Francisco: Berrett-Koehler, 2018.

Bloomgarden, Alan H., and KerryAnne O'Meara, "Faculty Role Integration and Community Engagement: Harmony or Cacophony?" *Michigan Journal of Community Service Learning* 13, no. 2 (2007), 5–18.

Broad, Garrett. *More Than Just Food: Food Justice and Community Change.* Berkeley: University of California Press, 2016.

Burgan, Michael, and Mark Winne. "Doing Food Councils Right: A Guide to Development and Action." *Mark Winne Associates,* September 2012. https://www.markwinne.com/wp-content/uploads/2012/09/FPC-manual.pdf.

Buzzanell, Patrice M. "Resilience: Talking, Resisting, and Imagining New Normalcies into Being." *Journal of Communication* 60 (2010): 1–14.

Canary, Heather. "Constructing Policy Knowledge: Contradictions, Communication, and Knowledge Frames." *Communication Monographs* 77 (2010): 181–206.

Carmack, Heather J. "'What Happens on the Van, Stays on the Van': The (Re) Structuring of Privacy and Disclosure Scripts on an Appalachian Mobile Health Clinic." *Qualitative Health Research* 20, no. 10 (2010): 1393–405.

Carragee, Kevin M., and Lawrence R. Frey. "Communication Activism Research: Engaged Communication Scholarship for Social Justice." *International Journal of Communication* 10 (2016): 3975–99.

Caspi, Caitlin E., Glorian Sorensen, S. V. Subramanian, and Ichiro Kawachi. "The Local Food Environment and Diet: A Systematic Review." *Health & Place* 18 (2012): 1172–87.

Center for Community Health and Development. "Community Toolbox." *University of Kansas,* 2020. https://ctb.ku.edu/en.

———. "Implementing Photovoice in Your Community." *Community Toolbox,* 2020. ctb.ku.edu/en/table-of-contents/assessment/assessing-community -needs-and-resources/photovoice/main.

Child, Jeffrey T., and Michelle Shumate. "The Impact of Communal Knowledge Repositories and People-Based Knowledge Management on Perceptions of Team Effectiveness." *Management Communication Quarterly* 21 (2007): 29–54.

Cobb, Laura K. et al., "Baltimore City Stores Increased the Availability of Healthy Food after WIC Policy Change." *Health Affairs* 34 (2015), 1849–57.

Cohen, Barbara, Margaret Andrews, and Linda Scott Kantor. "Community Food Security Assessment Toolkit." *United States Department of Agriculture,* July 2002. https://www.ers.usda.gov/publications/pub-details/?pubid =43179.

Counihan, Carole, and Penny Van Esterik, eds. *Food and Culture: A Reader.* 3rd ed. New York, NY: Routledge, 2012.

Cramer, Janet, Carinita Greene, and Lynn Walters, eds. *Food as Communication, Communication as Food.* New York: Peter Lang, 2011.

Cummins, Steven, Ellen Flint, and Stephen Matthews. "New Neighborhood Grocery Store Increased Awareness of Food Access but Did Not Alter Diet Habits or Obesity." *Health Affairs* 33 (2014): 283–91.

de Souza, Rebecca, and Lynn Harter. "Reimagining Food Pantries as Activist Spaces." *Defining Moments Podcast: Conversations about Health and Healing,* WOUB Public Media, June 15, 2020, 90 min. https://www.stitcher .com/podcast/woub-public-media-2/defining-moments-conversations-about -health-and-healing/e/71095146.

Dempsey, Sarah E. "Critiquing Community Engagement." *Management Communication Quarterly* 24 (2010): 359–90.

Dempsey, Sarah E., and Kevin Barge. "Engaged Scholarship and Democracy." In *The SAGE Handbook of Organizational Communication: Advances in Theory, Research, and Methods,* 3rd ed., edited by Linda L. Putnam and Dennis K. Mumby, 665–88. Thousand Oaks, CA: SAGE, 2014.

Dougherty, Debbie S., Megan A. Schraedley, Angela N. Gist-Mackey, and Jonathan Wickert. "A Photovoice Study of Food (In) Security, Unemployment, and the Discursive-Material Dialectic." *Communication Monographs* 85, no. 4 (2018): 443–66. https://doi.org/10.1080/03637751.2018.1500700.

Dupuis, E. Melanie, Jill Lindsey Harrison, and David Goodman, "Just Food?" In *Cultivating Food Justice: Race, Class, and Sustainability,* edited by Alison Hope Alkon and Julian Egyeman, 283–308. Cambridge, MA: MIT Press, 2011.

Dutta, Mohan J. "Communicating about Culture and Health: Theorizing Culture-Centered and Cultural Sensitivity Approaches." *Communication Theory* 17, no. 3 (2007): 304–28.

———. "Culture-Centered Approach in Addressing Health Disparities: Communication Infrastructures for Subaltern Voices." *Communication Methods and Measures* 12, no. 4 (2018): 239–59.

———. "Theory and Practice in Health Communication Campaigns: A Critical Interrogation." *Health Communication* 18 (2005): 103–22.

Dutta, Mohan, Aguptus Anaele, and Christine Jones. "Voices of Hunger: Addressing Health Disparities through the Culture-Centered Approach." *Journal of Communication* 63 (2013): 159–80.

Dutta, Mohan Jyoti, Lareina Hingson, Agaptus Anaele, Soumitro Sen, and Kyle Jones. "Narratives of Food Insecurity in Tippecanoe County, Indiana: Economic Constraints in Local Meanings of Hunger." *Health Communication* 31 (2016): 647–58.

Dutta, Mohan J., and Jagadish Thaker. (2019). "'Communication Sovereignty' as Resistance: Strategies Adopted by Women Farmers amid the Agrarian Crisis in India." *Journal of Applied Communication Research* 47 (2019): 24–46.

Elmes, Michael, Karen Mendoza-Abarca, and Rober Hersh. "Food Banking, Ethical Sensemaking, and Social Innovation in an Era of Growing Hunger in the United States." *Journal of Management Inquiry* 25 (2016): 122–38.

Fielding, Jonathan, and Paul Simon. "Food Desert or Food Swamp?" *Archives of Internal Medicine* 171 (2011): 1171–72.

Food and Agriculture Organization of the United Nations. "Rome Declaration on World Food Security." *World Food Summit*, 1996. http://www.fao.org /docrep/003/w3613e/w3613e00.HTM.

Food First. *Food First Backgrounder*, 2010. https://foodfirst.org/wpcontent /uploads/2013/12/BK16_4-2010-Winter_Food_Movements_bckgrndr-.pdf.

Food Research and Action Center. *How Hungry Is America?* Washington, DC: Food Research and Action Center, June 2016. http://www.frac.org/research /resource-library/hungry-america-fracs-national-state-local-index-food -hardship-june-2016.

———. "How Hungry Is America?" August 2018. https://frac.org/wp-content /uploads/food-hardship-july-2018.pdf.

Frey, Lawrence. R., and Kevin M. Carragee, eds. *Communication Activism, Vol. 3: Struggling for Social Justice Amidst Difference*. New York: Hampton Press, 2012.

Frey, Lawrence R., Kevin M. Carragee, Robin D. Crabtree, and Leigh A. Ford. *Communication Activism: Volume 1 Communication for Social Change*. Cresskill, NJ: Hampton, 2006.

Frey, Lawrence R., W. Barnett Pearce, Mark A. Pollock, Lee Artz, and Bren A. O. Murphy. "Looking for Justice in all the Wrong Places: On a Communication Approach to Social Justice." *Communication Studies* 47, nos. 1–2 (1996): 110–27.

Ganesh, Shiv, and Cynthia Stohl. "Community Organizing, Social Movements, and Collective Action." In *The SAGE Handbook of Organizational Discourse*, edited by David Grant, C. Hardy, Cliff Oswich, and L. L. Putnam, 743–66. Thousand Oaks, CA: SAGE, 2014.

Ganesh, Shiv, and Heather M. Zoller. "Dialogue, Activism, and Democratic Social Change." *Communication Theory* 22, no. 1 (2012): DOI:10.1111/j.1468 -2885.2011.01396.x.

Gerlach, Luther P., and Virginia H. Hine. *People, Power, Change: Movements of Social Transformation*. Indianapolis, IN: Bobbs-Merrill, 1970.

Giddens, Anthony. *The Constitution of Society: Outline of the Theory of Structuration*. Berkeley: University of California Press, 1984.

Ginossar, Tamar, and Sara Nelson. "Reducing the Health and Digital Divides: A Model for Using Community-Based Participatory Research Approach to E-Health Interventions in Low-Income Hispanic Communities." *Journal of Computer-Mediated Communication* 15, no. 4 (2010): 530–51.

Gordon, Constance, and Kathleen Hunt. "Reform, Justice, and Sovereignty: A Food Systems Agenda for Environmental Communication." *Environmental Communication* 13, no. 1 (2019): 9–22.

Gottlieb, Robert, and Anupama Joshi. "Food Justice." *Dissent*, October 25, 2010. https://www.dissentmagazine.org/online_articles/food-justice.

Guttman, Nurit. "Bringing the Mountain to the Public: Dilemmas and Contradictions in the Procedures of Public Deliberation Initiatives That Aim to Get 'Ordinary Citizens' to Deliberate Policy Issues." *Communication Theory* 17 (2007): 411–38. https://doi.org/10.1111/j.1468-2885.2007.00305.x.

Guttman, Nurit, and William Harris Ressler. "On Being Responsible: Ethical Issues in Appeals to Personal Responsibility in Health Campaigns." *Journal of Health Communication* 6, no. 2 (2010): 117–36.

Harter, Lynn M. "Engaging Narrative Theory to Disrupt and Reimagine Organizing Processes." *Management Communication Quarterly* 31 (2017): 297–99.

———. "Masculinity(s), the Agrarian Frontier Myth, and Cooperative Ways of Organizing: Contradictions and Tensions in the Experience and Enactment of Democracy." *Journal of Applied Communication Research* 32 (2004): 89–118. DOI: 10.1080/0090988042000210016.

Harter, Lynn M., Stephanie M. Pangborn, Sonia Ivancic, and Margaret M. Quinlan. "Storytelling and Social Activism in Health Organizing." *Management Communication Quarterly* 31 (2017): 314–20.

Haug, Christoph. "Organizing Spaces: Meeting Arenas as a Social Movement Infrastructure between Organization, Network, and Institution," *Organization Studies* 34 (2013), 705–32.

Hewitt, Ben. *The Town That Food Saved: How One Community Found Vitality in Local Food.* Emmaus, PA: Rodale Books, 2010.

Holland, Barbara A. "Analyzing Institutional Commitment to Service: A Model of Key Organizational Factors." *Michigan Journal of Community Service Learning* 4, no. 1 (1997): 30–41.

———. "A Comprehensive Model for Assessing Service-Learning and Community-University Partnerships." *New Directions for Higher Education* 114 (2001): 51–60.

Huffman, Tim. "Imagining Social Justice within a Communicative Framework." *Journal of Social Justice* 4 (2014): 1–14.

Hunt, Heather, and Gene Nichol. "'Surviving Through Together': Hunger, Poverty and Persistence in High Point, North Carolina." *N.C. Poverty Research Fund*, Fall 2019. https://law.unc.edu/wp-content/uploads/2019/12/HighPointHungerReport2019.pdf.

Ivancic, Sonia Raines. "Gluttony for a Cause or Feeding the Food Insecure? Contradictions in Combating Food Insecurity through Private Philanthropy." *Health Communication* 32 (2017): 1441–44.

Jayaraman, Saru. *Behind the Kitchen Door*. Ithaca, NY: Cornell University Press, 2013.

Johnson, Amber. "Practicing Radical Forgiveness in the Political Now: A Justice Fleet Exhibit Fostering Healing through Art, Dialogue and Play." *Journal of Art for Life* 10 (2019): 1–8.

Jovanovic, Spoma. *Democracy, Dialogue, and Community Action: Truth and Reconciliation in Greensboro*. Fayetteville: University of Arkansas Press, 2012.

Kim, Yong-Cham, and Sandra J. Ball-Rokeach. "Civic Engagement from a Communication Infrastructure Perspective." *Communication Theory* 16 (2006): 173–97.

Kotlarsky, Julia, Bart van den Hooff, and Leonie Houtman, "Are We on the Same Page? Knowledge Boundaries and Transactive Memory System Development in Cross-Functional Teams," *Communication Research* 42 (2015), 319–44.

Lamine, Claire. "Sustainability and Resilience in Agrifood Systems: Reconnecting Agriculture, Food and the Environment." *Sociologia Ruralis* 55 (2015): 41–61.

Larsen, Kristian, and Jason Gilliland. "A Farmers' Market in a Food Desert: Evaluating Impacts on the Price and Availability of Healthy Food." *Health & Place* 15 (2009): 1158–62.

LeGreco, Marianne. "Building Vibrant Food Systems." *TEDxGreensboro*, video, June 18, 2014. https://www.youtube.com/watch?v=MOOk5YD3IcA&t=249s.

———. "Food Security in the Piedmont Triad." *Tiki-Toki*, 2017. https://www.tiki-toki.com/timeline/entry/842615/Food-Security-in-the-Piedmont-Triad/.

———. "How Deep Is Our 'Food Insecurity'? More Data Would Help." *Greensboro News & Record*, May 29, 2016. https://www.greensboro.com/opinion/columns/marianne-legreco-how-deep-is-our-food-insecurity-more-data/article_9c966354-52f1-586b-87bb-bfbe77c26c53.html.

———. "Working with Policy: Restructuring Healthy Eating Practices and the Circuit of Policy Communication." *Journal of Applied Communication Research* 40 (2012): 44–64.

LeGreco, Marianne, and Niesha Douglas. "Everybody Eats: Carrying and Disrupting Narratives of Food (In) Security." *Management Communication Quarterly* 31 (2017): 307–13.

LeGreco, Marianne, Michelle Ferrier, and Dawn Leonard. "Further Down the Virtual Vines: Managing Community-Based Work in Virtual Public Spaces." In *Management and Participation in the Public Sphere*, edited by Mika Merviö, 147–69. Hershey, PA: IGI Global, 2015.

LeGreco, Marianne, and Dawn Leonard. "Building Sustainable Community-Based Food Programs: Cautionary Tales from the Garden." *Environmental Communication: A Journal of Nature and Culture* 5, no. 3 (2011): 356–62.

LeGreco, Marianne, and Sarah J. Tracy. "Discourse Tracing as Qualitative Practice." *Qualitative Inquiry* 15 (2009): 1516–43.

Leonardi, Paul M. "Social Media, Knowledge Sharing, and Innovation: Toward a Theory of Communication Visibility." *Information Systems Research* 25 (2014): 796–816.

Leone, Lucia A., Lindsey Haynes-Maslow, and Alice S. Ammerman. "Veggie Van Pilot Study: Impact of a Mobile Produce Market for Underserved Communities on Fruit and Vegetable Access and Intake." *Journal of Hunger & Environmental Nutrition* 12 (2017): 89–100. DOI: 10.1080/19320248.2016.1175399.

Levkoe, Charles Z. "Learning Democracy through Food Justice Movements." *Agriculture and Human Values* 23 (2006): 89–98.

Lozano-Reich, Nina M., and Dana L. Cloud, "The Uncivil Tongue: Invitational Rhetoric and the Problem of Inequality." *Western Journal of Communication* 73 (2009), 220–26.

McCullum, Christine, Ellen Desjardins, Vivica Kraak, Patricia Ladipo, and Helen Costello. "Evidence-Based Strategies to Build Community Food Security." *Journal of the American Dietetic Association* 105 (2005): 278–83.

McDermott, Virginia M., John G. Oetzel, and Kalvin White. "Ethical Paradoxes in Community-Based Participatory Research." In *Emerging Perspectives in Health Communication: Meaning, Culture, and Power,* edited by Mohan J. Dutta and Heather Zoller, 182–202. New York: Routledge, 2008.

McPhee, Robert D. "Agency and the Four Flows." *Management Communication Quarterly* 29 (2015): 487–92.

National Resource Defense Council. "Food Waste." 2020. https://www.nrdc.org /issues/food-waste.

Nestle, Marion. *Food Politics: How the Food Industry Influences Nutrition and Health, Revised and Expanded Edition.* Berkeley: University of California Press, 2007.

O'Hair, H. Dan, Katherine M. Kelley, and Kathy L. Williams. "Managing Community Risks through a Community-Communication Infrastructure Approach." In *Communication and Organizational Knowledge,* edited by Heather E. Canary and Robert D. McPhee, 223–43. New York: Routledge, 2010.

Okamoto, Kristen E. "'It's Like Moving the Titanic': Community Organizing to Address Food (In)Security." *Health Communication* 32, no. 8 (2017): 1047–50.

Penniman, Leah. *Farming While Black: Soul Fire Farm's Practical Guide to Liberation on the Land.* White River Junction, VT: Chelsea Green Publishing, 2018.

Pine, Adam Marc, and Rebecca de Souza. "Including the Voices of Communities in Food Insecurity Research: An Empowerment-Based Agenda for Food

Scholarship." *Journal of Agriculture, Food Systems, and Community Development* 3, no. 4 (2013): 71–79.

Pollan, Michael. *Cooked: A Natural History of Transformation.* London: Penguin, 2014.

———. "The Food Movement, Rising." *New York Review of Books*, June 2010. http://www.nybooks.com/articles/2010/06/10/food-movement-rising/.

Riley, Kathleen, and Amy Paugh. *Food and Language: Discourses and Foodways across Cultures.* New York: Routledge, 2018.

Roberto, Michael Joseph. "Crisis, Recovery, and the Transitional Economy: The Struggle for Cooperative Ownership in Greensboro, North Carolina." *Monthly Review*, May 1, 2014. https://monthlyreview.org/2014/05/01/crisis-recovery-transitional-economy/.

Rojas, Hernando, and Eulalia Puig-i-Abril. "Mobilizers Mobilized: Information, Expression, Mobilization and Participation in the Digital Age." *Journal of Computer-Mediated Communication* 14 (2009): 902–27.

Ryan, Charlotte, Kevin M. Carragee, and Cassie Schwerner. "Media, Movements, and the Quest for Social Justice." *Journal of Applied Communication Research* 26 (1998): 165–81.

Salatin, Joel. *Everything I Want to Do Is Illegal: War Stories from the Local Food Front.* Swoope, VA: Polyface Incorporated, 2007.

Sandy, Marie, and Barbara A. Holland. "Different Worlds and Common Ground: Community Partner Perspectives on Campus-Community Partnerships." *Michigan Journal of Community Service Learning* 13 (2006): 30–43.

Sbicca, Joshua. "Growing Food Justice by Planting an Anti-Oppression Foundation: Opportunities and Obstacles for a Budding Social Movement." *Agriculture and Human Values* 29 (2012): 455–66.

Schraedley, Megan K., Hamilton Bean, Sarah E. Dempsey, Mohan J. Dutta, Kathleen P. Hunt, Sonia R. Ivancic, Marianne LeGreco, Kristen Okamoto, and Tim Sellnow. "Food (In)Security Communication: Addressing Current Challenges and Future Possibilities." *Journal of Applied Communication Research* (2020). https://doi.org/10.1080/00909882.2020.1735648.

Sills, Stephen. "Visualizing Data Leads to Better Local Decisions." *TEDx-Greensboro*, video, June 5, 2018. https://www.youtube.com/watch?v=oaBrAOlEyRc.

Spurlock, Cindy M. "Performing and Sustaining (Agri) Culture and Place: The Cultivation of Environmental Subjectivity on the Piedmont Farm Tour." *Text and Performance Quarterly* 29 (2009): 5–21.

Stohl, Cynthia, and George Cheney. "Participatory Processes/Paradoxical Practices: Communication and the Dilemmas of Organizational Democracy." *Management Communication Quarterly* 14 (2010): 349–407.

Taylor, James, and Elizabeth J. Van Every. *The Emergent Organization: Communication as Its Site and Surface.* Mahwah, NJ: Erlbaum, 2000.

Tracy, Karen, and Aaron Dimock. "Meetings: Discursive Sites for Building and Fragmenting Community." *Annals of the International Communication Association* 28 (2004): 127–65.

Via Campesina. "Via Campesina Declaration for Food Sovereignty of November 1996." World Food Summit, Rome Italy, November 13–17, 1996.

Wang, Caroline, and Mary Ann Burris. "Photovoice: Concept, Methodology, and Use for Participatory Needs Assessment." *Health Education & Behavior* 24 (1997): 369–87.

Weick, Karl. *The Social Psychology of Organizing.* Reading, MA: Addison-Wesley, 1979.

Weick, Karl E., Kathleen M. Sutcliffe, and David Obstfeld. "Organizing and the Process of Sensemaking." *Organization Science* 16 (2005): 409–21.

Wekerle, Gerda R. "Food Justice Movements: Policy, Planning, and Networks." *Journal of Planning Education and Research* 23 (2004): 378–86.

Whitfield, Stephen, Tim G. Benton, Martin Dallimer, Les G. Firbank, Guy M. Poppy, Susannah M. Sallu, and Lindsay C. Stringer. "Sustainability Spaces for Complex Agri-Food Systems." *Food Security* 7 (2015): 1291–97.

Yakini, Malik. "Food Justice: Challenges and Opportunities." YouTube, video, 2017. https://www.youtube.com/watch?v=duVs0uaPHPk.

———. "Keynote: Come to the Table Conference." YouTube, video, 2013. https://www.youtube.com/watch?v=m59OgburT3Y.

———. "Malik Yakini of Detroit Black Community Food Security Network Talks of the Challenges the Population of Detroit Faces." YouTube, video, January 16, 2014. https://www.youtube.com/watch?time_continue=4&v=f2pcCKGzXLQ&feature=emb_logo.

———. "Working in Community as Partners, Not Missionaries." *Johns Hopkins Center for a Livable Future,* YouTube, video, May 3, 2013. https://www.youtube.com/watch?v=qO9_dgcxdj4.

Yoon, Eddi. "The Grocery Industry Confronts a New Problem: Only 10% of Americans Love Cooking," *Harvard Business Review,* September 22, 2017. https://hbr.org/2017/09/the-grocery-industry-confronts-a-new-problem-only-10-of-americans-love-cooking.

Zoller, Heather. M. "Health Activism Targeting Corporations: A Critical Health Communication Perspective." *Health Communication* 32 (2017): 219–29.

Index

access to food: COVID-19 pandemic, effects of, 250; Food Access Research Atlas, 36*tab*, 39*tab*; food as a systems issue, 7–9, 8*fig*, 27; Food for Thought dialogues, 32–33; food trucks and local policies, 85, 89, 92, 93, 94, 95; Greensboro Fresh Food Access Plan, 41, 139, 172, 175; Guilford Food Council, goals of, 202, 207, 208*tab*, 209, 211, 213, 215, 226; intersectional narratives and, 259–63; intersections of access and poverty, 21, 252–54; Kitchen Connects GSO, 175; language of food insecurity, 9–17, 12*fig*, 14–15*fig*, 33, 34, 258; Mobile Oasis Farmers Market, goals of, 129–30, 131, 135, 141, 142, 143, 145–47; as public health issue, 60–64, 61*tab*, 62*map*, 63*tab*, 74; Warnersville Community Food Task Force, goals of, 57–58, 59, 66–67, 69, 74; Warnersville Community Garden, goals of, 108–9, 116, 120, 121–22. *See also* food (in)security

activists: in Warnersville, history of, 64–66. *See also* food advocates and activists

advocates and advocacy. *See* food advocates and activists

agnostic approach to dialogue, 238

agricultural system: Center for Environmental Farming Systems (CEFS), 203; community garden recommendations and resources, 124–26; engaging communities around, 23–24; food system, overview of, 6, 8*fig*; food waste, problem of, 6, 8*fig*, 270–71; in North Carolina, overview of, 107; sharecropping and slavery, history of, 110; state departments of agriculture, 126, 173, 192–93; urban agriculture, history of, 4. *See also* urban farms (agriculture); US Department of Agriculture (USDA)

Alamance County food council, 207

Allen, Will, 4

American Community Gardening Association, 126

A Place at the Table, 31

Appiah, Osei, 159, 169

Archie, Beth, 44*tab*

assistance programs, overview of, 16–17

Bangkok Café, 153–54, 160, 160*fig*

Barnhill, Phil, 46*tab*

Barthes, Roland, 21

BBQ Nation Indian Grill, 162–63, 163*fig*

Bean, Hamilton, 257

About the Authors and Contributors

DR. NIESHA DOUGLAS is an educator and author. Dr. Douglas has over fifteen years of experience in higher education and over six years of experience in community development. Dr. Douglas is a community activist who believes in giving back to the community that helped her grow and develop into a professional and leader. She has served on several committees regarding food insecurity/hunger and was chosen to lead a discussion on Community Activism in Adult Education at the 2016 Adult Education Research Conference in Charlotte, North Carolina, on the topic. She has a doctorate degree from UNC-Charlotte in Adult and Higher Education. Her passion is teaching and speaking to youth about personal and social development. She believes in living your best life through creativity and honesty. She is also a baker who uses food television shows as her choice of inspiration.

GWEN FRISBIE-FULTON is a writer and community activist focused on building power for working-class and poor people in North Carolina and the South. She has over twenty years of experience working in anti-poverty nonprofits, including at a large regional food bank. Her writing focuses on the intersections of gender, race, poverty, and power. She grows vegetables right up to the curb in front of her Greensboro home for her neighbors to pick but remains a horrible cook.

DR. MARIANNE LEGRECO has spent over twenty years researching, writing, and speaking about food. Since 2007, she has based her work out of the University of North Carolina at Greensboro, where she currently serves as an associate professor in the Department of Communication Studies. She earned her PhD from Arizona State University in 2007, where she took much inspiration for her work on food from her family. When she's not focused on food, Marianne also enjoys taking pictures—and she included several of her photos in *Everybody Eats*. You can usually find her hanging out with her pugs, and she's been known to make an excellent pierogi.

ALYZZA MAY is an angelic troublemaker and commoner based in Greensboro, North Carolina, by way of the former whaling capitol of the world. Alyzza is committed to expanding and rematriating the commons, for a free flow of movement of indigenous lands. They do this through public art, community organizing, relationship building, working with and learning from plants, and a belief that another world is possible. They are also a very proud Titi to some incredible twins. Alyzza is a graduate of Guilford College (BA, peace and conflict studies, sociology and anthropology, and religious studies), and the University of North Carolina at Chapel Hill (master's in city and regional planning).

DONOVAN MCKNIGHT is a writer and content producer based in Greensboro, North Carolina, where he tells stories for big brands like Verizon and Walmart. Donovan is also cofounder of Ethnosh, which uses storytelling, photography, and dining events to connect the public with the many immigrant-owned restaurants across the city.

DR. STEPHEN SILLS is a community-engaged scholar and professor in the Department of Sociology at the University of North Carolina at Greensboro. He received a BA in Spanish from UNCG in 1991, and an MA (2000) and PhD in sociology from Arizona State University (2004). In 2015, Sills founded the Center for Housing and Community Studies, which works to develop community-informed solutions to social problems, addressing housing and neighborhood issues for governments, nonprofits, foundations, and institutions of higher education. When not pushing the limits of what is possible in housing research and education, Sills is traveling in Latin America or Asia tasting street food and shopping in the open-air markets.

DR. MARK SMITH recently retired after serving for twenty-one years as the epidemiologist and head of the Health Surveillance and Analysis Unit of the Guilford County Department of Health and Human Services. He earned his MS degree in epidemiology from the Wake Forest University School of Medicine, and a PhD in sociology and MA in political science from the University of Florida. In retirement, Mark plans to shift from studying access to healthy foods to spending more time with his container garden growing Cherokee Purple tomatoes and his other favorite vegetables.

CASEY THOMAS resides in the People's Republic of Glenwood in Greensboro, North Carolina, with her wonderful husband and dog. She cares deeply about shifting money, democratic governing power, and other resources we need to live the full, beautiful lives we deserve to poor and working people, Black people and People of Color, immigrants, women, trans* and gender-nonconforming people, and all people for whom our economy and government were not made. She is a graduate of Guilford College (BA, sociology and anthropology) and the University of North Carolina at Greensboro (master's in public health).

Founded in 1893,
UNIVERSITY OF CALIFORNIA PRESS
publishes bold, progressive books and journals
on topics in the arts, humanities, social sciences,
and natural sciences—with a focus on social
justice issues—that inspire thought and action
among readers worldwide.

The UC PRESS FOUNDATION
raises funds to uphold the press's vital role
as an independent, nonprofit publisher, and
receives philanthropic support from a wide
range of individuals and institutions—and from
committed readers like you. To learn more, visit
ucpress.edu/supportus.

www.ingramcontent.com/pod-product-compliance
Lightning Source LLC
Chambersburg PA
CBHW020821270326
41928CB00006B/400